Converting the West

A Biography of Narcissa Whitman

THE OKLAHOMA WESTERN BIOGRAPHIES
RICHARD W. ETULAIN, GENERAL EDITOR

Converting the West

A BIOGRAPHY OF
NARCISSA WHITMAN

by Julie Roy Jeffrey

UNIVERSITY OF OKLAHOMA PRESS : NORMAN

For Chris, Sophia, and Michael

By Julie Roy Jeffrey

*Education for Children of the Poor: The Elementary and Secondary Education
Act of 1965* (Columbus, 1978)
Frontier Women: The Trans-Mississippi West, 1840–1880 (New York, 1979)
(with Gary B. Nash) *The American People: Creating a Nation and a Society*
(New York, 1985)
Converting the West: A Biography of Narcissa Whitman (Norman, 1991)

Maps by Alex Wallach.

Library of Congress Cataloging-in-Publication Data

Jeffrey, Julie Roy.
      Converting the West : a biography of Narcissa Whitman / by Julie
Roy Jeffrey.—1st ed.
           p.   cm.—(The Oklahoma western biographies ; v.3)
      Includes bibliographical references and index.
      ISBN 978-0-8061-2623-4 (paper)
      1. Whitman, Narcissa Prentiss, 1808–1847. 2. Cayuse Indians—
Missions.   3. Missionaries—Washington (State)—Biography.
4. Women missionaries—Washington (State)—Biography. 5. Whitman
Massacre, 1847. I. Title. II. Series.
E99.C32W474   1991
979.7'02'092—dc20
[B]   91-12326
                                                                              CIP

Converting the West: A Biography of Narcissa Whitman is Volume 3 in *The
Oklahoma Western Biographies.*

The paper in this book meets the guidelines for permanence and durability
of the Committee on Production Guidelines for Book Longevity for the
Council on Library Resources, Inc. ♾

First edition copyright © 1991 by the University of Oklahoma Press, Norman,
Publishing Division of the University. Manufactured in the U.S.A. Paperback
published 1994.

Contents

Illustrations

Maps

Series Editor's Preface

JULIE Roy Jeffrey's provocative biography of Narcissa Whitman will be cited often as a revealing life story of a notable western woman. Not only has Jeffrey re-visioned the roles Narcissa played as missionary wife on the far-western frontier; she also has cast that story in a wider interpretive web, illuminating Narcissa's multiple performances as woman, wife, and religious leader. To these accomplishments is added a previously missing ingredient: Narcissa's reactions to and treatment of the Cayuse Indians.

Readers will realize immediately how revealingly and convincingly Jeffrey situates Narcissa's life in the shifting sociocultural crosscurrents of the first half of the nineteenth century. Reared in an evangelical home, nurtured in rural and small-town New York, Narcissa initially was drawn to religious work because she longed to shape the social and moral orders of her world. Enamored of the notion of becoming a missionary, Narcissa, as Jeffrey explains, is frustrated in her dream until Marcus appears. Shortly thereafter they marry, not because they are in love but because marriage is the course by which each can hope to become a missionary. As Jeffrey makes clear, those pragmatic ties often are stretched in the demanding world of the frontier mission field.

Indeed the tensions between Narcissa's romanticized fancies and the realities of her frustrating and flawed missionary work with Indians power the second half of Jeffrey's engrossing biography. Bit by bit, Narcissa abandons her early dreams of evangelizing the "heathen savages" and turns to writing to her family and friends about the educational and domestic duties that consume her time. After her only child dies, she finds fulfillment in nurturing the orphan children of the Sager family, demonstrating how much she participates in the evangelical, domesticating culture from which she sprang. Meanwhile she—and Marcus—have largely forsaken the Indians. The Whitmans' defective understanding and unsympathetic interpretation of Indian society and culture strained their relations with the Cayuse and are the major causes of their tragic deaths in 1847.

Throughout her story of Narcissa Whitman, Julie Roy Jeffrey smoothly blends narration and interpretation. Drawing upon a rich assortment of primary and secondary materials, she reveals more tellingly than any previous biographer how Narcissa's background shaped her and foreshadowed the numerous problems she encountered in the mission field. In re-visioning her subject, Jeffrey displays again the superb capacity for synthesis and conceptualization demonstrated in *Frontier Women* (1979). Casting Narcissa against the larger backdrop of evangelical, women's, and western history, Jeffrey clearly fulfills the goal of the Oklahoma Western Biographies Series: to illuminate western history and culture through the lives of significant women and men. Scholars and general readers alike will be drawn to her provocative and revealing portrait of Narcissa Whitman.

RICHARD W. ETULAIN

University of New Mexico

Preface

IN 1851 Judge William Colvig set up camp in the beautiful Grande Ronde Valley, where plateau Indian tribes had come for hundreds of years to gather and prepare food for the winter months. When two Cayuse Indians wandered into his camp, he offered to share his own meal with them. To Colvig's amazement, the Indians removed their hats and recited grace "in excellent English" before they ate. They told Colvig that "they were members of Doctor Whitman's church at Waiilatpu and though Dr. Whitman had been dead four years, they still gave thanks at their meals and tried to practice what Dr. and Mrs. Whitman had taught them."

Colvig was impressed by the Indians' observances. Their piety was heartwarming testimony to the spiritual impact of the Whitmans, who had labored for over a decade among the Cayuse tribe. The massacre of the couple at their station at Waiilatpu, of course, made it obvious that not all the Cayuse tribe had responded as positively to the Protestant missionaries as Colvig's visitors. But there seemed little reason to question the two men's word that they had been members of the Whitman's church or to doubt that their careful recitation of grace indicated Christian commitment.

Had Colvig more sustained contact with Oregon tribes, perhaps he would have been less sanguine about the effects of the missionary effort. A tale told by one Salish-speaking Indian of western Oregon hints at the resilience of native religion and the Indians' ability to incorporate parts of the Christian message without adopting its essential meaning. The story looked back to the early days, when the Old One had expelled the people from the garden. "The people were much oppressed . . . and so much evil prevailed in the world, that the Chief sent his son Jesus to set things right. After traveling through the world as a transformer, Jesus was killed by bad people, who crucified him, and he returned to the sky. After he had returned, the Chief looked over the world, and saw that things had not

xi

changed much for the better. Jesus had only set right a very few things. He had done more talking than anything else . . . [and had] worked only for the people's spiritual benefit. . . . He taught them no arts, nor wisdom about how to do things, nor did he help to make life easier for them. . . . Now, the Chief said, 'If matters are not improved there will soon be no people.' Then he sent Coyote to earth to destroy all the monsters and evil beings, to make life easier and better for the people, and to teach them the best way to do things."

The ease with which the storyteller used biblical lore but changed its meaning highlights both the complexity of the cultural interaction between Christian missionaries in Oregon and native peoples and the limitations of the missionary enterprise. In the nineteenth century, few of those discussing the missionary endeavor focused on such problematic issues. Instead, they heroicized the noble laborers and the work of conversion. In this tradition, Narcissa Whitman and her husband became Protestant martyrs, honored not only by the college named for them but by various other memorials as well. A statue of Marcus Whitman stands at the Presbyterian Historical Society in Philadelphia, while an impressive obelisk rises over the former mission station at Waiilatpu. The importance of Narcissa's overland journey and family letters in encouraging family emigration to the Far West added further luster to her reputation.

For much of the twentieth century, however, historians have avoided studying the missionary movement, finding it a naive and embarrassing failure. The Whitmans' role in the westward movement has seemed less important with the collapse of the story that Marcus Whitman "saved" Oregon for the Americans, while historical attention has shifted to the experience of ordinary people coming to and living in the West. Why, then, look at Narcissa Whitman again? Why explore the life of one now little-known woman who, with her husband, went out to the foreign mission field in Oregon on a problematic errand?

One answer to this question has to be that, no matter what we think of the errand, Narcissa Whitman's experience as a missionary reveals something important about American life and culture. As William Hutchison has pointed out, the missionaries were the first sizable group of Americans to live among non-Western peoples. The ways in which a missionary like Narcissa Whitman thought about and responded to other cultures and the assumptions she brought to the mission field contributed to forming a distinctive American perspective on the world.

Furthermore, the missionary enterprise itself reveals the key dynamics of cultural interaction. Narcissa Whitman, like so many Americans who have wished to change the world for the better, had noble intentions. She hoped to save the Indians' souls from hell and their bodies from starvation. What neither she nor others fully comprehended was the destructive character of such a mission. Narcissa's potential converts, however, understood better than she the implications of accepting the Christian God and all that went with him. Cayuse religion and culture did change as a result of the missionaries' efforts, but Narcissa was angry at the Indians' resistance to her message and deeply frustrated by the seeming lack of progress toward her goal. Although her experience was colored by the evangelical character of the nineteenth-century missionary movement, William Hutchison suggests that similar patterns are apparent in contemporary American development efforts. Today the mission is more likely to be economic than religious, and the workers more likely to be Peace Corps Volunteers than missionaries. But the imperative to transform the other culture is the same, and so, too, frequently is the response.

If Narcissa Whitman's life reveals some of the ways in which Americans interacted with other cultures, it also illuminates important aspects of the American western experience during the nineteenth century. Often the westward movement is described from the white perspective, with the Indians appearing as an inconvenient but temporary barrier to the advance of white civilization. Narcissa Whitman's story suggests that this view is far too simple. There was, at least in some places, a brief and uneasy period of racial coexistence in the trans-Mississippi West. Furthermore, her work at Waiilatpu offers a glimpse not only of the ideological assumptions and imperatives of white people who settled in the West but also of the perspective of one Indian tribe. As historians now emphasize there are at least two stories to be told in the mid-nineteenth-century West.

Recovering the Indian point of view, however, has proved difficult. When the Whitmans arrived in Oregon Territory in late 1836, the Cayuse had already lost some of their cultural distinctiveness. They spoke Nez Percé rather than their own language and had many close cultural ties to and connections with that powerful tribe. After the Whitmans' deaths, the tribe was reduced by war with white set-

tlers, and in the 1860s the remaining Cayuse were forced onto the
Umatilla Reservation with members of the Walla Walla and Umatilla
tribes. Although Morris Swadesh transcribed some Cayuse historical
narratives in the 1930s, in comparison with the materials available for
some other western tribes, sources for Cayuse history are meager.
What ethnographic studies existed, of course, proved helpful. So
too were the historical traditions of the Nez Percé tribe, with whom
the Cayuse tribe was linked. But I have had to rely too often on
what white missionaries, visitors, or government agents reported,
although I often disagreed on the meaning they made of events. As
a non-Indian person, I have had to imagine how the Cayuse responded to events or what they meant in the conversations repeated
by the missionaries and other whites far more than I would have
liked.

Exploring the life of Narcissa Whitman also offers a perspective
on some of the constraints and opportunities middle-class women
faced during the first half of the nineteenth century. Well educated
for a girl growing up in the 1820s—she attended two academies as
well as common school—Narcissa wanted to do something important, useful, and different. She had few options to the one compelling definition of a noble vocation provided by evangelical religion
and the Second Great Awakening. Although historians have not
agreed on the meaning of the Second Great Awakening or on the
role that religion played in nineteenth-century women's lives, Narcissa seized upon the new definitions of female religious responsibilities and vocation. Her ardent hope was to spend her life among
those she called the benighted heathen. Although she probably had
in mind heathens in Hawaii, Ceylon, or India rather than American
Indians living in Oregon Territory, she realized her ambition. But as
Narcissa's experience makes clear, new opportunities could have unexpected and complex results.

Jill Conway has offered a positive view of what missionary work
meant for nineteenth-century women. She suggests that missionary
work liberated women from conventional notions of romantic sen-
sibility and encouraged unusually egalitarian marriages for the period. Jane Hunter makes a similar point about the interdependence
of missionary marriages in late-nineteenth-century China.

Narcissa's missionary experience suggests that these interpretations of both missionary work and missionary marriage may be too
benign. Narcissa arrived at Waiilatpu without any training for her

work or any real knowledge of what it would entail. She was shocked and perhaps even disgusted by "heathen" life. I suspect that her response was more typical than not. Rather than liberating, missionary work proved to be conservative, at least for Narcissa. Living in a foreign culture strengthened prejudices and preconceptions, as it so often does. Despite Narcissa's desire for a different kind of life, she was never able to free herself from the power of familiar social norms and expectations either in her missionary work or in her marriage. Narcissa's experience demonstrates the difficulty of moving into new social and marital roles, even when the possibility for change exists.

In some respects, Narcissa's life was a failed one. She failed as a missionary; not one of the Cayuse living at Waiilatpu converted during her eleven years there. And although she tried to escape from some of the limitations of domesticity, she failed to free herself from social conventions. And yet, in the end, I saw that Narcissa could not just be classified as a failure. Despite the constraints of her missionary position and the limited opportunities she had to redirect her life, she managed to carve out a satisfying existence in the last years at the mission. Her ability to do so demonstrates a resilience of spirit that is admirable and suggests that nineteenth-century women, who appear to us to have so few options, could be creative and skillful in making life bearable and even rewarding for themselves.

Some final words are in order. Although few sources exist for Narcissa's early life, enough evidence does exist, I feel, to allow an imaginative but hopefully responsible and psychologically sound reconstruction of Narcissa's early development. For her mature years, the challenge has been somewhat different. Because of a religious perspective that appears unduly harsh in the twentieth century, it has often been difficult to be sympathetic to Narcissa and her endeavor. Convinced that without a personal conversion, salvation was impossible, Narcissa, like the other missionaries, repeatedly told the Cayuse they were headed for eternal damnation. Her words made the Cayuse angry (as they often do the modern researcher). I have attempted not to blame but to understand Narcissa's psychological makeup and her cultural context and to appreciate the pervasiveness of her views in evangelical circles and the sincerity of her belief. If I have not always succeeded in avoiding a judgmental tone, my failure illustrates that my own culture and its values and my own inner needs have as powerful a hold on me as Narcissa's did on her. I hope that Narcissa Whitman emerges from this study as less heroic than the nineteenth century believed her to be but as more human and understandable.

During the years of working on this biography of Narcissa Whitman, I accumulated many debts, and now it is time to thank those who so generously helped me as I explored nineteenth-century evangelicalism and the world of the missionaries of the American Board of Commissioners for Foreign Missions. Leonard Sweet, Christopher Miller, Michael Gidley, Bruce Forbes, and Kathleen Jacklin provided me with leads, advice, and useful materials. A former student, Marian Anderson, did genealogical research on the Prentiss and Whitman families and turned up other information that proved invaluable. Mary Beth Norton, Judith Innes, and my father, James C. Roy, housed and entertained me during research trips, while Goucher College librarians Yvonne Lev and Thomasin Lamay procured research materials for me at home. My colleague Kent Lancaster shared his manuscript on, and knowledge of, rituals of death and dying.

Tom Edwards was particularly helpful throughout the entire period when I was working on this book. As one of the coordinators of the 1986 Sesquicentennial Conference on Missionary Influences on Northwest History, he made my stay in Walla Walla comfortable and valuable. He also read a draft of the manuscript and had many useful suggestions for revision. Lawrence Dodd, archivist of the Northwest and Whitman College Archives at Whitman College's Penrose Library, made those collections available to me between conference sessions. Judith Austin, who included an early overview of this work in the special 1987 issue of *Idaho Yesterdays,* was also supportive.

Friends, colleagues, and family read the manuscript at various stages of its development, and I can only begin to suggest my appreciation for their time and their frank and insightful comments. The manuscript improved greatly as a result of their help. My colleague Jean Baker shared her understanding of biography with me, as did my friend Peter Frederick. Carol Stearns's comments made the last revision meaningful, and my brother, Jim Roy, and my husband, Chris, neither of them academic historians, offered acute and provocative criticisms. My editor, Dick Etulain, who suggested Narcissa to me as a possible subject, was patient and encouraging.

In a variety of ways, Goucher College supported this work. Dean

Gerald Duff understood my compulsion with this little-known missionary woman. Toward the end of the project I was awarded the Elizabeth Todd Chair, and I found my work greatly facilitated by the generosity of the donor.

Special thanks go to my husband, Chris, who besides reading the manuscript, accompanied me on an extensive research trip in the Northwest and made it far more enjoyable than it otherwise would have been. He also accepted the presence of Narcissa as a near family member—as did my children, Sophia and Michael. Michael's departure for the Peace Corps and his experiences there helped me understand many of the dynamics of working in another culture and the emotional realities of being the mother of a modern-day missionary. Because these three have been so central to this book, I am dedicating it to them.

JULIE ROY JEFFREY

Baltimore, Maryland

Converting the West

A Biography of Narcissa Whitman

CHAPTER I

Her Mother's Own Soul

THE winters in eastern Washington State are often mild and short. But in late 1836 there was a surprisingly heavy snowfall. As the newly arrived missionaries settled into the adobe mission house, they looked out onto a shining expanse of white that rose up to meet the vast sky. Although her surroundings could hardly have been more different from the pine- and hemlock-covered hills and the farming valleys of upstate New York, Narcissa Prentiss Whitman found the spare, dramatic landscape of the Walla Walla valley appealing. Not far from the house, which stood on a "beautiful level," was the winding Walla Walla River, "barely skirted with timber." Within walking distance were low hills, then "as far as the eye can reach plains & mountains appear."

If the exterior seemed boundless, inside, the new mission house was comfortingly cozy. Though the furniture was simple and sparse, Narcissa had glass in her windows and a stove to heat her room. As she contemplated her surroundings, Narcissa's thoughts turned to the homes in which she had grown up. The first had been a rude log cabin where she had been born almost twenty-nine years before. Searching her earliest memories and remembering her parents' tales of pioneering, she concluded that she might well be starting out more comfortably than had her parents, Stephen and Clarissa Prentiss, when they settled in the township of Prattsburg, New York, in 1805.

Like so many other ambitious New Englanders, Narcissa's father had migrated to New York's western frontier seeking his fortune. Her grandfather, a chairmaker, had also been restless and had moved his family from Massachusetts to Walpole, New Hampshire, when Stephen was a boy. As Stephen reached early manhood, he decided that prospects in New Hampshire were bleak and determined to set out for the West. Possibly some of his relatives accompanied him or had already gone ahead to Onondaga County in New York State.

3

His sister, Mary Fay, and her husband, Levi, would follow him to the frontier a few years later.

Like other hopeful emigrants, Stephen probably traveled west through Albany, followed the Mohawk River to Utica or Rome, and then pushed on to Onondaga. There he found flourishing villages and farms and land that was costly for a young man making his start in the world. Stephen lingered long enough in the county to marry Clarissa Ward in 1803, but neither his marriage nor the birth the next year of the Prentisses' first child, Stephen, curbed his determination to find a situation that would offer him opportunities to do well in the world.

For someone like Stephen, who was looking around to locate, Steuben County, which lay to the southwest of Onondaga, merited consideration. "Ads, posted at all places of public resort," assured potential settlers that "the soil was fertile; the forests abounded with game, the lakes with fish; the climate was delightful and healthy." Other promotional materials highlighted the possibilities for "easy communications with different markets" and encouraged the ambitious, "those who wish their estates in a few years to increase in extent and value," to consider settling on the Steuben frontier. There was also talk that Marylander "Captain Pratt had contracted for a township lying west of . . . [Crooked] lake, and [was] offering great inducements for settlers to locate therein."

Leaving Clarissa and his infant son in Onondaga, Stephen set off to explore township number 6, which Captain Joel Pratt was promoting as an agent for the Poultney Estate, the township's owner. At a time when links to a market were critical for growth, the captain believed that Prattsburg's situation was promising. Crops raised in the township could be transported to the county seat of Bath, a half day's ride away, and from there floated down the Chemung and Susquehanna rivers to Baltimore. Pratt had successfully tested the route in 1801, when he sent his wheat crop to Baltimore and sold it for eight hundred dollars.

Pratt was now engaged in surveying the thickly wooded valley lying between the Canisteo and Cohocton rivers and in selling lots. Few settlers had to pay the full purchase price of $2.50 or more an acre outright. Eager to make the Prattsburg of his dreams a reality, the captain allowed settlers to acquire property "on contract" and to pay for it in installments. In addition to this substantial financial inducement, Pratt offered attractions for respectable and ambitious

The Prattsburg cemetery offers views of the gently rolling New York coun-
tryside. Photograph by Julie Roy Jeffrey.

settlers: land set aside for the clergy, a public square, and the beginnings of a road to Bath, fourteen miles away.

When Stephen visited Prattsburg, he was pleased by its prospects.
He staked out eighty-eight wooded acres in the western part of the
township and returned to Onondaga to retrieve Clarissa and baby
Stephen. Sometime in 1805, probably during the winter months and
by ox sled, Stephen returned to take up his claim. That year a second
son was born and named Harvey Pratt, honoring the township's pa-
tron and his father's faith in Pratt's vision of the future.

Like his West Hill neighbors Warham Parsons and Aaron Cook,
Stephen labored hard in those early years. He cleared his property of
white pine and oak, raised a log house and outbuildings, planted and
harvested crops, and built fences to keep the livestock out of his
fields. Typical frontier calamities punctuated the natural rhythms of
life and work. Charles Andrew's house burned down when a stick in
the chimney caught fire; a bear killed three sheep; Robert Porter's
mill dam broke. The excitement of community events like the November bear hunt, which involved twenty-one village men and ended

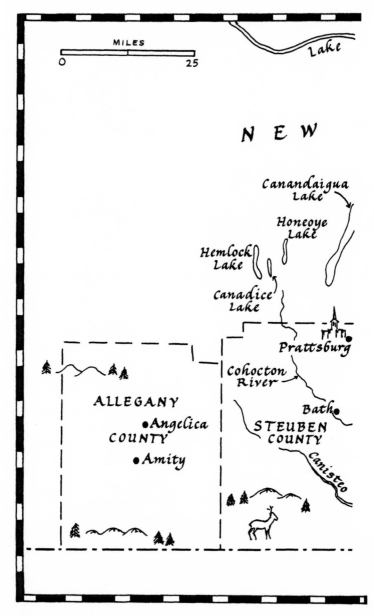

New York State during Narcissa's youth.

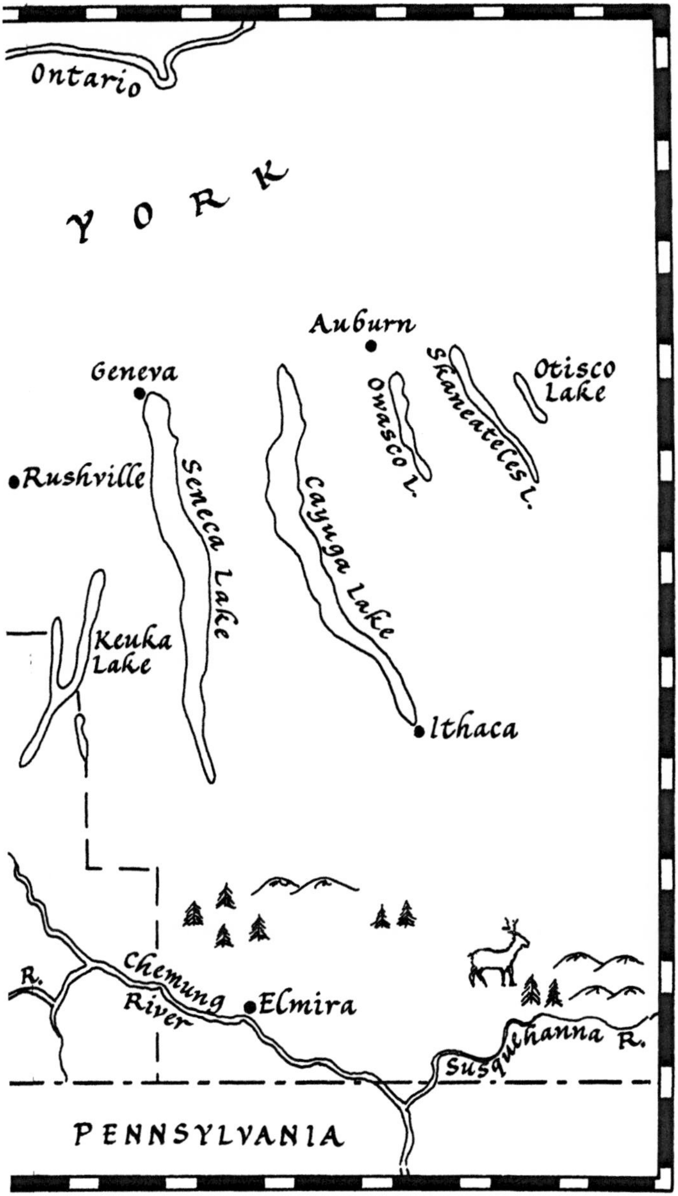
Ontario
YORK
Auburn
Geneva
Otisco Lake
Skaneateles L.
Owasco L.
Rushville
Seneca Lake
Cayuga Lake
Keuka Lake
Ithaca
Chemung River
R.
Elmira
Susquehanna R.
PENNSYLVANIA

triumphantly with the killing of a bear, alleviated the monotony of constant toil. Always there were indications of nature's power: the June 1806 eclipse, when "the stars appeared plain," or the "uncommon deep snow" that fell on April 1, 1807.

In the simple log cabin the couple's first daughter, their third child, was born on March 14, 1808, three days after Clarissa's own birthday. The timing of the birth so close to her mother's, the fact of her sex, and the choice of the exotic name "Narcissa"—so different from the rest of the children, who were named mostly after relatives and friends—hint that the first daughter was a special child.

By the time Narcissa was born, Prattsburg was already leaving its frontier beginnings behind. In 1806 Aaron Bull had opened a log hotel and tavern on the green. Nearby, merchants Joel and Ira Pratt were selling necessities, like salt, as well as luxuries, like glass and iron. Robert Porter's new gristmill allowed settlers to have their grain ground locally rather than in Naples, eleven miles away.

As the community made material progress, residents did not neglect its spiritual needs. In 1807 settlers discussed raising a log meetinghouse. With an eye to both God's glory and no doubt his own profits if the town prospered, Captain Pratt pronounced "a malediction upon them for dwelling in ceiled houses, while the Lord's heritage was left in waste." His strenuous arguments for a finished framed building rather than the frontier structure being planned carried the day. While the unpainted 22' by 50' church on the southeast corner of the square was no "feast to the eyes," it signified the determination to re-create civilized society as quickly as possible.

The next year, Prattsburg acquired a post office and reliable contact with the outside world. Once a week postriders between Geneva and Bath stopped to pick up and deliver mail. That same year, the town held its first town meeting. In 1812, when Narcissa was four, the town erected a small schoolhouse near the church and the clear cool spring.

Prattsburg was quickly becoming a rural village with some claims to regional importance. Linked by roads to centers like Bath and Geneva, it provided services for farmers from miles around and served as a place for trade and the exchange of information. Calvin Buell, the community's second settler, remembered the days when there were no roads in the township but only blazed trees to guide emigrants through the dense forest. He looked at the church, the school, the store, and the public house and decided that his carefree

days of fishing and hunting were over. It was time to leave his Prattsburg and his shanty behind and to head out to the new frontier
in Ohio.

Unlike Calvin Buell, Stephen had come to Prattsburg not to hunt
and fish but to take advantage of the varied opportunities a new
community might offer. He soon capitalized on the needs of Prattsburg's residents. In 1807 he erected a distillery with William Curtiss.
Eventually Stephen would also own and operate two other basic
frontier enterprises: a gristmill and a sawmill. The carpentry skills he
learned from his father were also in demand as townspeople made
improvements on their property. Stephen also had much of the frontier speculator about him and, in the years following Narcissa's birth,
steadily acquired land and mortgages.

In keeping with his aspirations, Stephen moved his family out of
the log cabin when Narcissa was still a child to a wood framed house
on land purchased in 1811 from Robert Porter. Half a mile from the
village center, the new house was certainly not so grand as Captain
Pratt's or Judge Porter's house, which townspeople called the "lily of
the valley." From the outside the Prentiss home, which still stands in
Prattsburg, appears to be a modest story-and-a-half building. But
Stephen raised the roof to allow full use of the second floor, so there
is more room inside than one might guess. Town residents considered it "a good frame house."

Although it was neither large nor gracious by today's standards,
the house was substantial and provided space and the possibility for
genteel life. It was in this middle-class house that Narcissa spent
most of her childhood and young adulthood. Its daily rhythms of
work and leisure, its arrangements and expectations, shaped her notions of proper family life and the material circumstances that supported it.

To the left of the entryway was a parlor lighted by several large
windows and heated by a fireplace. The room contained a settee and
probably the family's best pieces of furniture. Here the Prentisses sat
to read, talk, or rest from the heat of the summer sun or to hold
family prayers. Here they entertained visitors. A small room to the
rear of the parlor was perhaps a bedroom or a "closet" to which
Clarissa could retreat for private talks with her children or for prayer.
Across the entryway was another sunny front room that initially
must have been used only during warm weather, because it had no
fireplace. Running along the back of the house, in typical New

The Prentiss house in Prattsburg as it appears today. Photograph by Julie
Roy Jeffrey.

England fashion, were the kitchen and buttery. This arrangement
separated work areas from rooms where the family might relax or
entertain visitors. Up thirteen steep steps were several unheated bed-
rooms. The second floor was not large enough for each child to have
his or her own room, but the separate bedchambers offered some
privacy for family members. The privy, barn, pigpen, and other back
buildings also stood on the property along with Stephen's mill and
the millrace.

The house marked but one stage in Stephen's rise to prosperity
and financial security. By Narcissa's teenage years, Stephen had
achieved the middle-class status to which he aspired. The 1825 state
census showed that he possessed sixty-seven acres of improved land
in addition to his mills. While not so important or so rich as the
township's two dozen most substantial families, who could afford to
donate gifts to the town or a communion set to the church, Stephen
had more extensive land-holdings than over 80 percent of his fellow
citizens. He could provide his family with various comforts and advantages—a settee in the parlor, books, and an academy education

for Narcissa. Perhaps just as important, Stephen's position gave his family a certain status. Narcissa grew up knowing she belonged to the better part of Prattsburg society.

The Prentiss home was a symbol not only of how Stephen prospered but of how rapidly the community was moving away from its pioneer beginnings. By the 1820s over three hundred families, more than twenty-seven hundred people, were living in the township of Prattsburg. The valley was filled with framed houses, orchards, and gardens; much of the land had been cleared and improved. Five gristmills, eleven sawmills, two fulling mills, one carding mill, four distilleries, and four asheries testified to the thriving rural economy. Tanners, doctors, a blacksmith or two, carpenters, a cabinetmaker, over two dozen merchants, and several manufactories provided for the townspeople's material desires, while Presbyterian, Methodist, and Baptist clergy ministered to their spiritual needs. Although Narcissa no doubt had some memories of early Prattsburg, she was more used to the ways of a bustling township than to those of a primitive frontier community.

Known as a good citizen who "always favored public improvements," Stephen won not only economic success but also the townspeople's respect. He held various local offices and was addressed deferentially as "Esquire" or "Judge" Prentiss. Despite a reticence considered remarkable "for a man of his intelligence and standing," people valued his opinion and gravitated to his house when there was a dispute. His appearance—"quite tall, finely proportioned, [and] a little inclined to corpulency"—contributed to the dignified and deliberate impression he made. So too, did his demeanor. As a neighbor observed, "It was a rare thing for him to indulge in laughter."

If there was little humor in Stephen, he was occasionally a harsh advocate for middle-class standards of justice. At least one Prattsburg resident remembered how Stephen enjoyed the public whipping of a man convicted of a misdemeanor. "Esquire Prentiss counted the blows with a full strong voice. . . . After 30 blows had been administered, to each succeeding blow Prentiss would cry out [to the constable], as he counted, 'Tuck it on Hull.'" Another disapproved of this zeal and thought it a flagrant injustice when Stephen both tried a man and pronounced judgment—again a whipping of forty lashes.

Preoccupied with business and community affairs, Stephen seems to have left the supervision and instruction of his growing family largely to his wife. It was a responsiblity that she embraced. Although Clarissa had much more domestic work than urban middle-class women, she responded to new gender expectations that encouraged middle-class women to consider child rearing as a central focus for their lives.

An imposing person in her own right, Clarissa was "quite tall and fleshy and queenly in her deportment." Marked by an inner strength, she too, as befitted her middle-class position in the community, was solemn, "remarkably sedate, never excited, always master of the occasion." Like her husband, she found little humorous in life. Although the family found amusement in one another's misfortunes (sitting in a bed of fleas, for example) and joked about those who were different from themselves, a friend recalled, "I do not remember ever seeing her laugh."

Clarissa's serious attitude toward life and her sense of the importance of child rearing stemmed not only from new cultural norms but also from her firm religious convictions. Although she had been baptized as a child, she had not experienced conversion when she moved to Prattsburg in 1805. The new community did not yet have an established church, but the Prattsburg Religious Society offered Clarissa the opportunity for Congregational worship. Established in 1804, the group met in Pratt's barn or in private homes and relied on visiting clergymen to minister to its needs. There would be no full-time resident minister in Prattsburg until 1809.

As Clarissa set up housekeeping in the log house and cared for her two sons, she wrestled with the fact of her sinful nature and the possibility of eternal damnation. Perhaps the hazards of childbirth alerted her to the precarious human condition. Perhaps she was encouraged by changing theological views that rejected predestination and allowed a sinner to hope for salvation. Or perhaps she heard news of how others had won forgiveness and redemption during the early years of the revivals known as the Second Great Awakening. Whatever her reasons, she joined the small group in their worship. Her West Hill neighbors the Aaron Cooks also attended the services and likewise became serious about their spiritual condition.

As Clarissa struggled with her sense of sin, she strove to reach out to a forgiving Christ, believing that "all who exercise repentance towards God, and faith in our Lord Jesus" will be "immediately pardoned and justified . . . through the merits of the Redeemer." For some hopeful Christians, the period of seeking and waiting stretched on and on. There is no evidence revealing how long Clarissa lingered in the anxious state of anticipation. But finally in a moment of remarkable intensity, she experienced the overwhelming sense of God's forgiveness. Fears about sin and damnation fell away, and Clarissa was born again in Christ. By the end of the rainy, cold summer of 1807, some time after her conversion, she was ready to make her new conviction public and to become a member of the Prattsburg Congregational Church.

The church's admission procedures heightened the significance of this step. Church officers met with Clarissa to examine her theological views. Could she describe her conversion? they asked her, aware that sometimes people enthusiastically mistook an incomplete experience for the real coming of the Holy Spirit. Once she had satisfied them about her orthodoxy and her conversion to Christ, she formally accepted the church covenant and promised to observe the Congregational membership requirements. Perhaps she made her profession of faith from one of the box pews in the newly erected church on the square. Wherever she was, her words signified her determination to begin a new life. "We do this day publicly [proclaim] the Lord Jehovah to be our God, and so far as we know our own hearts, we love him supremely. . . . We resolve to make his law the rule of our lives."

Clarissa's conversion and her admission to the church represented the beginning of a lifelong Christian commitment. At the very time that she was undergoing her own spiritual birth, she must have been realizing that she was pregnant again. As she consecrated herself to Christ, how natural to link the unborn child, her "infant seed," with his—and now her—cause. The child's birth date, so very nearly her own, would emphasize the specialness of Narcissa and the particular spiritual connections binding mother and daughter together.

Clarissa's profession of faith also testified to her independent spirit in religious matters. Between 1805 and 1808 only three married women (out of approximately sixty-six men and women who joined the church) united with the Congregational church without their husbands. Clarissa was one of them. Some Prattsburg men actively opposed their wives' religious decisions and the rejection of female submission that church membership could signify. Records of the Prattsburg church reveal, for example, that one woman's family disapproved of her affiliation and "used every endeavor to hinder" it. There is no evidence that Stephen opposed his wife's decision. But he gave few signs of following her example.

Clarissa, like so many other New York State women during the Second Great Awakening, found evangelicalism enormously appealing. The belief that because women were naturally moral and pious they were especially suited to doing the Lord's work encouraged women to seize new opportunities to influence their families and communities. In a period of social fluidity, evangelical work was a means of asserting middle-class status. It may have served that purpose for Clarissa as well. Certainly she took her responsibilities seriously to bring others to Christ. Neighbors soon recognized her "great weight of Christian character" and her "potent" influence in Prattsburg. But it was within the family that Clarissa exerted her influence most energetically.

Her husband and young children were unconverted, and unless she could move them toward the moment of repentance and conversion, they would spend eternity in hell after their deaths. Her first success was probably with her sister-in-law, Mary Fay, who professed her faith in 1812 in the Prattsburg church, now formally allied with the Presbyterian synod. Mary Fay named her child born that year after Clarissa. But Clarissa made little progress with Stephen. Feelings of discouragement, despair, and even anger at her husband must have occasionally bothered Clarissa. But in the end, Stephen responded to her efforts. In 1817, five years after his sister and ten years after his wife, Stephen joined the Prattsburg Presbyterian Church.

When Stephen became a member of the church, his age (he was then forty) and his social and economic position in the community virtually assured him of a place in the all-male governing group. Although he exerted influence as a member of various church committees and as an officer of the Steuben County Auxiliary Bible Society and enjoyed public visibility as a choir member, the family leadership in spiritual affairs remained with Clarissa.

Stephen eluded Clarissa's ministry for years, but her numerous children were under her control as her busy husband was not. Because American family size was beginning to shrink in the early decades of the nineteenth century, the large Prentiss family was somewhat old-fashioned. Between 1803 and 1820 Clarissa bore nine children, all of whom lived. Two boys preceded Narcissa. After Narcissa's birth in 1808 came Jonas Galusha in 1810, Jane Abigail in 1811, Mary Ann in 1813, Clarissa in 1815, Harriet in 1818, and finally, the baby, Edward in 1820.

As the first step toward conversion, Clarissa saw to it that each child was baptized as church regulations required. Then, like many other evangelical mothers, who saw their purpose as ordering home life to bring about salvation, she imposed a system of regular discipline. Determined to break each child's independent will and to teach obedience and virtuous behavior, Clarissa probably used the rod. Narcissa, who resorted to the rod with her adopted children many years later, was doubtless following her admired mother's example. Perhaps her discipline also owed something to her father's enthusiasm for public whipping.

As they grew up, the Prentiss children became accustomed to a variety of religious observances upon which Clarissa insisted. The Sabbath was daunting: family devotions, then, announced by ten minutes of pealing church bells, a lengthy service of preaching, prayer, and song, followed by Sunday school. After a break for lunch, a second service took place at the church, ending about three o'clock. The rest of the day was free, but it was understood that it should not be devoted to worldly or trivial pursuits. Communal worship was supplemented with prayer in the family circle and the expectation of individual prayer. While as a child Narcissa may have felt restive with pious observances, later she looked back on Prattsburg religious life and her family's routines with nostalgia and used these as standards to judge the piety of others.

As the Prentiss children matured and internalized Clarissa's standards of conduct, conditioning became more gentle if not more subtle. Narcissa was apparently quick to respond to her mother's admonitions. It was often enough that her mother simply pointed out her faults, which would bring about the needed change in behavior.

The general character of these childhood years seems clear enough, but Narcissa's own development is not. As the first daughter and special child, Narcissa was no doubt warmly cherished by her mother. The intense physical closeness of mother and nursing daughter, however, was abruptly terminated with the birth of a brother when Narcissa was two, and of a sister the following year.

As the children continued to appear, Narcissa would have been unusual had she not resented these rivals for her mother's time and
affection and feared that her mother loved her less now that there
were so many children to care for.

Over the years, Narcissa seems to have developed ways of dealing
with emotions like anger and competitiveness—which women were
not supposed to have—as well as with her natural anxiety about not
being loved. By helping her mother with the house and acting like a
mother toward the younger children, Narcissa could win Clarissa's
approval and set herself apart from her brothers and sisters. Her
eager receptiveness to her mother's religious instruction and her
willingness to accept her mother's guidance also ensured Clarissa's
attention.

Serious, perhaps stern, Clarissa was also an "enlightened" mother.
She balanced discipline with what Narcissa later described as a loving
intimacy and lively interest in each child's religious progress. Clarissa
seems to have excelled at creating moments for earnest exchanges
especially as the children grew older. While the conversations served
Clarissa's purposes, they also allowed Narcissa to have her mother to
herself. As she explained later, Narcissa experienced "sweet relief" in
"giving her [mother] . . . [her] history," in allowing her mother "to
take a peep into one of the sacred chambers of her daughter's heart."
Never did Narcissa give any indication that she enjoyed greater intimacy with any friend or relative than she had with her mother.

During these close moments of conversation, counsel, and prayer,
Clarissa pressed her oldest daughter to evaluate the progress she was
"making in the divine life." Narcissa was apparently only too happy
to oblige. As Clarissa's hopes and expectations became clearer, Narcissa grew increasingly aware of how she could please "her mother's
own soul."

There must have been times when the young girl resented not only
the crowd of children but the strict discipline and standards her
mother imposed. And there must have been times when she felt her
mother did not love her enough. But these feelings, if ever recognized, were buried deep. There was never any overt sign that Narcissa was anything but receptive to Clarissa's efforts to push her to
choose a useful, Christian life rather than a life devoted to pleasure
or material gain. Her later letters expressed only affection, appreciation, and admiration of her mother, although there was often an

undercurrent of fear running through them that she was forgotten and unloved.

As part of her effort to shape her children's values and shield them from worldly temptations, Clarissa carefully supervised the family's reading material. Narcissa recalled appreciatively how her mother had guided "my youthful mind . . . and instead of allowing it to be filled with the light and vain trash of novel reading, I was directed to that which was more substantial." Sitting by the parlor window or perhaps in the sunny room across the hall, Narcissa read the serious books her mother chose. Again, mixing intimacy with instruction, her mother had Narcissa read aloud from theological tomes, "such books as Dwight's Theology, Doddridge's Rise and Progress, Milner's Church History." More exciting were the missionary tracts and biographies that were allowed because they highlighted one model of the useful life. Years later Narcissa could remember reading about missionary heroines like Harriet Newell, a veritable saint after her early death in 1812, and the popular account of the Hawaiian convert Obookiah, who also met an untimely but pious end.

Clarissa's spiritual concerns and expectations for her children could hardly have been clearer. While her own conversion came only after her marriage, thus limiting her own field of usefulness, her children might choose larger stages for their work. One possibility was the mission field. In 1812 Clarissa and other young Prattsburg women had organized the Female Home Missionary Society in the Prentiss front parlor. Although at age four Narcissa was too young to grasp either the social class or benevolent implications of the organization, she soon learned how important her mother considered missionary work. Like her brothers and sisters, Narcissa became a member of the Youth Missionary Society.

Clarissa had created an atmosphere in the family that put great psychological pressure on the children to make appropriate choices. Whether because her daughters spent more time with her or because she urged them most strongly toward the useful life or perhaps just because as young women they had fewer options than men, Clarissa's daughters proved most responsive to her message. Of her sons, only her youngest, Edward, entered the ministry. (Stephen became an organ builder, Harvey's profession is unknown, Jonas was a merchant.) But three of the five girls made choices that revealed their mother's influence. Mary Ann married a minister. Jane cared for Edward while he pursued his ministerial studies and for years contemplated going to the mission field herself. Narcissa, perhaps most anxious to please, best fulfilled parental expectations by becoming a missionary.

Narcissa's early conversion provided further evidence of the power of Clarissa's evangelicalism and Narcissa's eagerness to respond to it. Most women who went to the mission field in the first part of the nineteenth century converted in their late teens or early twenties. But Narcissa was only eleven at the time of her conversion. Only her youngest brother, Edward, would rival her youthful commitment, although not until years later. The other seven Prentiss children were two to four years older than Narcissa when they made their profession of faith.

Narcissa's conversion also illustrated the convergence of family and community influences, for her change of heart took place in the midst of Prattsburg's first revival, in 1819. Like other commercially oriented towns and villages in central New York State, Prattsburg experienced several periods of intense religious excitement during the 1820s and 1830s. During each revival sinners came forward, repented, and made a commitment to Christ. While Narcissa would play a role in all of Prattsburg's revivals, her own conversion in 1819 made that event a milestone for her.

Not only did the revival of 1819 allow her to make her first public statement of her Christian faith, but it also began to shape her understanding of how one made a religious commitment. In an earlier period, conversion took place in the privacy of the closet. The Second Great Awakening made the event public. During revivals, sinners, moved by whatever fears or encouragement their preachers could inspire, wrestled with sin in the midst of the church community. Behaviors like weeping, shaking, or groaning revealed the sinner's inner turmoil to those who were watching. When a seeker won victory over sin, believers and the curious alike shared and celebrated the occasion.

The revival of 1819 revealed patterns that would soon become familiar to Prattsburg residents and to Narcissa. The revival lasted for several months as interest and spiritual intensity grew. Moments of high excitement like the meeting in early February brought Prattsburg residents crowding into the church. On that day, "the house of worship was filled to overflowing, and from the necessity of the case, and the powerful state of feeling existing, it became necessary to continue the meeting from day to day for several days in succession. Individuals were seen trembling on their seats, and the silent tear trickling down their cheeks, but entire stillness reigned. Nothing was heard but the voice of the speaker imparting instruction, addressing exhortation to the assembly, or lifting up the prayer to God."

During that eventful week in February, the Reverend James Hotchkin's efforts resulted in thirty conversions. Whether Narcissa was one of the thirty is not clear. But she was among the fifty-nine believers to profess their faith in early June.

This day in June was a community celebration and more. As the harvest of the Prattsburg church's first revival, the event drew "people from neighboring towns, and persons of every character and grade." Because the meetinghouse could not accommodate the expected crowd, "preparation was made to hold the meeting for that day in a neighboring grove. The day was fine, the sky clear, and no wind to rustle the leaves. God seemed to be present with his aid. The pastor preached from Isaiah liii.11. *He shall see of the travail of his soul, and shall be satisfied.*" Given its emotional power, this rite of passage remained vivid for Narcissa for years, and she traced her "particular [if intermittent] interest for the salvation of the heathen" to this event.

While no detailed description exists of this important event, a diary kept by young William Pratt only a few years after Narcissa left Prattsburg reveals the rich and compelling assortment of activities organized to increase spiritual fervor. During one week in January 1843 William attended two services on the Sabbath; a pastor's prayer meeting the next evening, followed by a discourse from the minister; both daytime and evening meetings on Tuesday; a meeting as well as a special youth prayer meeting with sermon on Wednesday; on Thursday, which was a day of fasting and prayer, another youth prayer meeting; a morning and evening meeting on Friday; and finally an early afternoon meeting on Saturday "for prayer and personal conversation"—a grand total of eleven services in six days.

While religious interest in Prattsburg was not always at such a pitch, many organized events attempted to raise religious consciousness and nourish piety. The stream of ministers, missionaries, and clergy wives from the Prattsburg Presbyterian Church testifies to the power of the organized evangelical community to encourage vocations and to supplement a mother's training.

Among the activities that contributed to Narcissa's vision of how she might live the useful life were those focusing on missionary causes. In addition to the missionary societies for mothers and for their children, the Prattsburg church held monthly meetings called concerts, devoted to praying for the missions, hearing mission news, and raising money to support them. Some young people resented all the pressure. As one Prattsburg resident recalled critically, "The boy who would not give up a promised sled or book or knife to aid in sending the Gospel to . . . Africa, or to help convert the heathen in Wisconsin, was doomed to perdition."

For Narcissa, however, the missionary cause was something she dreamed about off and on since her conversion. It was not surprising that she was attracted to what seemed a heroic life. Missionary work not only represented a noble and dramatic alternative to the predictable course of marriage and domesticity but also seemed likely to win her mother's approval. At first, however, she thought of missionary work only intermittently. When she was fifteen, however, she pledged herself "without reserve to the Missionary work." What event or insight prompted this decision on "the first Monday of Jan. 1824." is not known. Narcissa had recently spent several months as a student at Auburn Academy, and the atmosphere there may have encouraged her to consider missionary work more seriously. Perhaps as she reached her midteens, she was also yearning for some independence from her family. She later told her adopted children that reading a missionary biography had triggered her decision. But more fundamental forces were at work in her decision than reading a book.

Narcissa gave only the barest outline of her resolve to become a missionary, having determined when she applied to the American Board of Commissioners for Foreign Missions in 1835 to "say but little" about "her feelings upon the subject of missions." But language in some of her letters from the mission field hints at the roots of her own vocation. She described her mother as giving up, or sacrificing, her children to the greater cause of the Lord's work. The words made Clarissa the Lord's agent and suggested that on some level Narcissa understood the decision as her mother's rather than her own. On another level, of course, she was quite aware that each person, in the end, chooses his or her own vocation, helped by wise persistent counsel. Years later, responding to her brother Edward's indecisiveness, Narcissa acted out the forceful and directive role her mother had played. She could not "bear the idea" that her brother would live for himself, she wrote. All the Prentisses were "the children of too many prayers and consecration to the work thus to live and be contented with this world's portion and applause."

Family and community activities reinforced Narcissa's emerging commitments and also provided the focus for a lively and interesting social life. While there were other convivial gatherings for the town's young people, like singing schools, lyceum debates, occasional concerts and lectures, and sleighing parties, church and church-related events provided many opportunities for socializing. They were a way to get socially acquainted with people, as Narcissa's future husband discovered when he attended a prayer meeting at the Prentisses' house.

When Narcissa later acknowledged how fond she had been as a young woman of social activities, she was probably thinking of church-related functions. There was no reason for her to suspect the important role conviviality played in sustaining her religious commitment and her hopes for the missionary life. Nor could she have any idea of how she might feel when she practiced a religion stripped of its sociable trappings. Perhaps Clarissa suspected, for she often remarked, "I wish Narcissa would not always have so much company."

If, as she later claimed, Narcissa determined at age fifteen to become a missionary, the means for achieving her goal were far from clear. Like other pious young women who hoped to serve the missionary cause, she could not take direct steps to ensure realizing her dream. The best she could do was to ready herself for a useful life by undertaking benevolent work. In the early decades of the nineteenth century, voluntary associations flourished and offered women, especially those of the middle class, many new opportunities for influence and involvement outside of the home. The 1817 Presbyterian General Assembly had approved women's benevolent activities, finding "it . . . among the distinguished glories of the nineteenth century that PIOUS FEMALES are more extensively associated, and the more actively useful, in promoting evangelical and benevolent objects, than in any former period of the world." Despite the town's modest size, several female organizations, including the Female Home Missionary Society, the Female Mite Society, the Prattsburg Laboring Society, and the Sunday School Association, flourished in Prattsburg.

In her mid teens, Narcissa belonged to the Female Mite Society. The organization was typical of conservative benevolent societies.

Members visited Prattsburg's less fortunate residents to determine their material and spiritual needs. In 1826 Narcissa reported finding five families without Bibles, but the problem of spiritual deprivation was far more serious than her visits revealed. The Steuben County Auxiliary Bible Society, of which her father was an officer, discovered eighty Prattsburg families (about a quarter of the total) "destitute of an entire copy of the Bible."

Narcissa's visiting exposed her to families who enjoyed neither her family's religious privileges nor their domestic comfort. While Prattsburg had all the marks of a prosperous community, the 1825 state census listed five paupers in the township. Fully 18 percent of the township's families held no improved land. Many of these must have hired themselves out to Prattsburg landowners, and at least some must have had a hard time in making ends meet. Widows like Dorcas Judson, who lived just north of the Prentisses and who made her living knitting for the Porter family, lived close to poverty. Her only contribution to Reverend Hotchkin's upkeep was a pair of initialed mittens that she had knitted for him.

The Sabbath School Association, of which Stephen Prentiss was one of the founders and superintendents, was established in 1826. Teaching Sabbath school allowed Narcissa to serve as her students' spiritual guide and instructor. Sunday school teachers frequently recruited their own students, helped them to learn essential doctrines, explained Bible passages, and taught them to sing hymns. Narcissa seems to have had some success with her students. In later years, at least one "lady in Prattsburg . . . held Narcissa in loving remembrance as her first Sunday school teacher."

During these years as Narcissa was experimenting with benevolent work, the great revivalist Charles Finney was beginning his most successful period of preaching in New York State. Although Prattsburg Presbyterian Church was still guided by its "educated . . . dignified . . . [and] orthodox" minister, Reverend Hotchkin inspired the community once again to confront the issues of salvation and damnation. The highly emotional experiences of seven years earlier were repeated.

At seventeen, Narcissa was old enough to work behind the scenes with those hovering on the brink of conversion. She was in a serious frame of mind about religious matters, having only recently consecrated herself to missionary work. And among those who were grappling with guilt, repentance, and hopeful belief were her favorite sister, Jane, and her brother Jonas. She may have begun to recognize that, like her mother, she too had skills in the intimate work that assisting a conversion involved. And while, in the end, the Holy Spirit deserved the credit for any sinner's change of heart, she soon learned that those who dealt faithfully with a sinner felt elation and a share in the victory.

The Prattsburg revival of 1824–25 provided drama and created a community of feeling. It also reinforced the identification of a certain set of behaviors—trembling, weeping, and moaning—with the process of conversion. Someone like Narcissa, who had never traveled outside of her state, whose reading and knowledge about the world had been carefully controlled, could hardly have recognized that these behaviors grew out of an American evangelical culture and might well be absent in another religious setting.

Revivalism and other evangelical activities reinforced what Narcissa had learned from her mother—that it was important to judge others, to draw distinctions between what was good and what was bad. While Clarissa had counseled charity and temperate speech at home, Narcissa developed a critical tongue—and for good reason. True believers were in the minority in Prattsburg. As was true in other New York communities, the combined membership of the Prattsburg Presbyterian, Methodist, and Baptist churches probably never made up more than a quarter of the town's population. Confronted with sinfulness and heresy—even the claim that salvation was open to all—the faithful could not afford to believe that quiet tolerance was a virtue.

Even within the fellowship of the church, where strict standards of conduct were supposedly the norm, there were shocking instances of worldliness, sin, and lapses of belief. The session of the Prattsburg Presbyterian Church investigated many such cases. Lucy Phelps had committed fornication but proved reluctant to acknowledge "the heinousness of her crime." Fights in the Niles family suggested that no one remembered the rules of Christian conduct. Mary Hubbard was guilty of stealing, Anne Clark drank during bouts of "hysteria," while Willis Fay spent Sabbaths imbibing at the tavern. Brother Higby broke down the church door. Only if church members observed and chastised one another was there any hope of making the rest of the community aware of how to live the Christian life.

Stephen's involvement in church disciplinary proceedings and his membership in a committee charged with investigating reports of evildoing among the congregation further legitimized for Narcissa the importance of looking after the moral and religious state of others. Watchful piety and the clear enunciation of the differences between the way of salvation and the ways of the world were part of every Christian's obligations.

While Prattsburg seemed to offer plenty of examples of reprehensible behavior, its homogeneous population hardly prepared Narcissa for understanding or appreciating cultural and racial differences. Most Prattsburg residents came from New England, New York, and the mid-Atlantic states. In 1825 the census taker could find only nine "aliens" (probably Irish) and twenty-one "persons of color" in a population of over twenty-seven hundred. Among the town's enumerated misfits were five "idiots"—four male and one female. Only one of these was so retarded as to be unable to work.

Narcissa did learn something of the world, of course. Outsiders came to town when the Presbytery of Bath met in Prattsburg in 1821, 1827, and 1833. Her own father went as far as Philadelphia to represent the local church while she visited relatives in Onondaga. Some of the books she read had maps and illustrations of other places. One contained a picture of an Indian portage, and the image stuck in her mind for years. And, of course, missionary literature provided sketches of life in foreign lands. Still, Narcissa encountered nothing to prepare her for understanding cultural diversity, nothing that might give her critical distance from familiar norms, values, and the way of life to which she was accustomed.

Narcissa did receive a good education, but, as was to be expected in the nineteenth century, not one that encouraged cultural relativism. She started her formal schooling in the town's common school. When she was in her teens, Prattsburg residents began thinking about the educational and economic advantages an academy would bring to Prattsburg. Narcissa's father, Stephen, and others pledged funds. Robert Porter gave land on the north side of the square for the school. By 1824 Franklin Academy, a handsome two-story building with a cupola and bell, recitation rooms, a library, and a laboratory, was ready for students. The academy offered both practical and classical courses to boys and young men who had completed grammar school.

While Narcissa could not attend Franklin Academy, she had already had a taste of an academy education. In another demonstration of their interest in their oldest daughter and perhaps in sympathy with her dreams of a life outside of the confines of Prattsburg, the Prentisses had sent Narcissa to Auburn Academy for six months when she was fifteen. The town of Auburn was also the home of the Auburn Theological Seminary, an institution known to, and financially supported by, the Prattsburg Presbyterian community. The seminary faculty, Auburn's Presbyterian minister, and doubtless the academy faculty were revival enthusiasts. Not long after Narcissa's departure, Charles Finney led a successful revival in Auburn that may have converted as many as five hundred people. The months Narcissa spent at the academy not only exposed her to more advanced work than she had had in the town school but the teachers and the school's values also must have reinforced her evangelical perspective on the world. For many young women hoping to enter missionary work, the academy experience was critical not only in fostering and encouraging their vocation but also in providing them with suitable credentials. It was probably no coincidence that Narcissa resolved firmly to become a missionary after her period at Auburn.

In 1827, when Narcissa was nineteen, Franklin Academy opened a female department. Narcissa attended the academy the following year and again in 1831. While she had less than three years of academy education, her intermittent studies at Auburn and Franklin were not unusual for women hoping to become missionaries. They prepared her for teaching, one of the primary components of female missionary work.

Like Auburn Academy, Franklin Academy had close ties to the evangelical community. Teachers at the academy encouraged their students to take religion seriously. One of them, Cornelia Pratt, followed her former students' spiritual progress even after she left Prattsburg. Hearing news of a revival in 1830, she wrote to her aunt, saying, "I am anxious to know whether any of my beloved pupils . . . are sharers in the gracious work. . . . No intelligence from Prattsburg could gratify me so much as to hear that those there in whom I feel a lively interest had consecrated themselves to the service of the Prince of Peace." In such an atmosphere, Narcissa continued to nourish her particular understanding of her own service to Christ.

A thorough education in housewifery supplemented the formal training Narcissa received at school. While the family occasionally had a domestic servant as Narcissa was growing up, there was much to do at home. As the babies came, Clarissa must have relied increasingly on her eldest daughter to help her with child care and household duties. The shared responsibilities reinforced Narcissa's identification with her mother. The maternal tone Narcissa adopted in her letters to her younger sisters and brother Edward suggests how well she acted as her mother's assistant with the little ones and how much she relished that important role.

While Narcissa mothered her younger sisters and young Edward, she was far less intimate with her two older brothers and Jonas Galusha, two years her junior. They were probably often out of the house helping their father. Her own influence over them was limited. To Stephen and Harvey she was the little sister. In later life, she would show only a minimal interest in learning the news of these brothers, while devouring every scrap of information about the others.

Like most girls of her time and class, Narcissa acquired all the necessary domestic skills. She learned how to cook, bake, make soap and candles, and wash and iron clothes. The 1825 census revealed that the Prentiss household produced forty yards of fulled cloth and fifty yards of woolen cloth in the previous year, so Narcissa was carding, spinning, knitting, and sewing too. While primary responsibility for the household's ten cows, two horses, thirty-four sheep, and eighteen hogs probably rested upon her older brothers' shoulders, Narcissa helped with the garden and the dairy work. Under Clarissa's guidance Narcissa became a competent and capable household manager with high standards.

Clarissa not only taught her daughter household skills but inculcated in the growing girl some definite notions about a woman's role in the home that went beyond "first rate" housekeeping. American women were increasingly being urged to make their homes into gracious retreats for their families. Even in a rural village like Prattsburg, matrons responded to some of the emerging norms of middle-class gentility. The Prentiss house certainly did not provide a great deal of individual privacy for the eleven family members who lived there along with assorted servants or helpers. But Clarissa's frustration with having men in her kitchen when she was working highlighted the importance to her of that ideal and her wish to do things nicely. Narcissa adopted her mother's views as well as her interest in manners, taste, and "polish." Later, others would comment on Narcissa's cultivation and interest in "*civilized* life" and "*refined* society."

While the outlines of Prentiss family life can be recovered, it is more difficult to ascertain the emotional dynamics that operated. Admiring reminiscences of family friends given after Narcissa's death and nostalgic letters written by Narcissa recollecting life in Prattsburg provide only a few insights. But in the late 1820s a series of incidents, provoked by the emergence of the temperance issue in Prattsburg and changes in the Prentiss household, revealed some of the intricacies of family relationships.

Temperance was new to Prattsburg. While drunkenness had long represented a clear violation of church norms, drinking in moderation had not. By the mid-1820s, however, toleration of any liquor was evaporating in evangelical circles. The influential Presbyterian pastor Lyman Beecher delivered a set of sermons denouncing drink. In 1826 he called upon the faithful to banish "ardent spirits from the list of lawful articles of commerce, by a correct and efficient public sentiment."

That same year, the Franklin Academy principal read Lyman Beecher's temperance sermons on several successive Sunday evenings. Stephen apparently attended one of these meetings and, as the owner of a distillery, left angrily, "feeling that he had been personally abused and insulted." Other church members disliked the idea of a ban on alcohol, but Reverend Hotchkin became an enthusiastic proponent. The minister's conversion to the antiliquor position increased Stephen's resentfulness. While there is no evidence of where Clarissa or her daughters stood on the temperance issue, Narcissa was later an advocate of complete abstinence.

During 1826 and 1827 there were also significant changes in the composition of the Prentiss family. Both older boys married. The sexual balance of the family shifted dramatically, with the females of the household outnumbering the males by two to one.

Seventeen-year-old Jonas, only recently converted, was the first to reject his mother's values and her domination of family life. He refused to attend the celebration of the Lord's Supper and behaved in public in a scandalous manner. The most damning incident occurred one spring evening after a concert at the village square. At the "unreasonable hour" of ten or eleven, Jonas and a friend had wandered through the village, approaching first one house, then another, "under circumstances manifesting that their design was to have unlawful intercourse with females." Perhaps their boldness owed something to the demon of drink, although the church session records make no mention of liquor.

The young women thus approached rejected the "improper" familiarities. But the news of the incident soon reached the ears of the Presbyterian session members, who undertook to investigate Jonas's conduct in June 1827. Jonas presented only the lamest of excuses for his behavior. Blaming his friend for soliciting the girls, Jonas claimed that he was only guilty of holding the horse. Reports of profanity further weakened his pretense of innocence. Ralph Hopkins told session members that when he had asked Jonas about the incident, Jonas had uttered several profanities. Deacon Loomis claimed that Jonas had said that he "did not care a *damn* for the church." To make his contempt for the church entirely clear, Jonas failed to turn up for his church trial. An embarrassed but strangely subdued Stephen explained to the group that "no circumstances [had] prevented Jonas from attending. He was not disposed to come." In March 1828, after eight months of investigation and deliberation about the "heinous" misdoings, Jonas was publically excommunicated during a Sunday service. Most likely all of his family were sitting in their pew to hear the sentence.

Church members and village residents must have had plenty to say about the incident, and more gossip about the Prentisses was yet to come. Stephen, too, was becoming disaffected. The first hint came in October 1827, when he was not reelected as an officer in the Steuben County Auxiliary Bible Society. A more obvious indication followed. He began to go to the Methodist meetinghouse on West Hill rather than attending the Presbyterian Sabbath service with his family.

As any good Presbyterian knew, Stephen's action clearly violated church norms. While Presbyterians acknowledged that other Protestant denominations possessed partial truth, they considered all seriously flawed. In 1825 the church had specifically identified the "great and dangerous errors" of Methodism. By venturing beyond the doors of the Presbyterian church, Stephen not only broke his covenant but ran the risk of imbibing "fatal errors" and losing his soul.

In its March 11 meeting, the session noted Stephen's absence. A few weeks later, Stephen came forward to explain that "he was best edified in attending with the Methodists." Almost casually he remarked that it was a small matter to miss Presbyterian worship if he liked the Methodist service better. He also expressed his dissatisfaction "with the administration in . . . [church], particularly with respect to discipline." Not long after this appearance, Stephen formally became a Methodist.

The actions and statements of both father and son seemed to be directed not only at church mores and church discipline but at targets at home. Clarissa's zeal and her system of discipline, so much valued by Narcissa at least, were also under attack. With the departure of the two oldest boys, Stephen and his son must have felt like a beleaguered minority in the female household. They now were asserting their independence of the female world.

Some evangelical churches encouraged their congregations to stop speaking to members who transferred their allegiance to another denomination. While it is unlikely that matters took this turn in the Prentiss household, the atmosphere could only have been strained as Clarissa and her younger children continued to attend the Presbyterian church and to observe the proprieties.

When the new minister, George Rudd, replaced Hotchkin and Stephen heard news of his own father's death in New Hampshire, he reconsidered his decision. In January 1831 Stephen requested readmission, "with an acknowledgement of his faulty withdrawing from this church and his cordial assent to . . . [the] articles of Faith." In May, Jonas followed his father's example, confessed his faults, and was also restored.

A few years later, Narcissa's oldest brother, Stephen, acted out in an even more obvious manner his rejection of female norms and evangelical values. While the circumstances of the younger Prentiss's family life are unknown, Stephen abandoned his pregnant wife and young children and set off for parts unknown. His own son would run away from the elder Prentisses at the age of sixteen.

Narcissa never referred to any of these events. Perhaps she had already adopted the habit of suppressing the mention of unpleasant and shameful events. Surely the pious young woman who identified so closely with her mother must have been unhappy with the gossip and embarrassed, perhaps angered, by the behavior of her brothers and father. But one can only guess at her feelings. So used was she to sharing intimacies with her mother, that she must have told Clarissa how she felt.

At the time of these family crises, Narcissa was in her early twenties. Of medium height, with a sandy complexion and lively eyes that occasionally troubled her, she had the kind of looks that people disagreed about. Some thought her "not a beauty," with "plain" features, but others found her manner attractive, especially when she was talking or singing. Her behavior was a tribute to her mother's

careful child-rearing techniques. Like Clarissa and perhaps in imita-
tion of her, she gave an impression of "deliberative good sense." "She
was never given to light and trifling conversation, her thoughts were
burdened with sound and religious topics."

It was a time when many of Narcissa's contemporaries, such as
Rebecca Hull, were fulfilling the usual expectations by marrying.
Her oldest brother, Stephen, had wed Jane Holbrook, who was only
three years older than Narcissa; Harvey was married, while Mary
Ann, five years younger than Narcissa, was also planning marriage.
Marriage and domestic life in Prattsburg, of course, would mean
the end of her dreams. But unless she was willing to pursue a missionary post so zealously that she could overcome the reluctance of
the ABCFM to send out single women, she needed a missionary
husband.

But her fervor for the mission field did not mean that any missionary candidate would do as a marriage partner. Henry Spalding, one
of the students at Franklin Academy in 1825, 1827, and 1828–31, was
well known for his burning desire to enter the mission field. He
proposed to Narcissa and was rejected. Apparently his missionary
zeal could not overcome the fact of his illegitimate birth, inferior
social position, and lack of polish and grace. The middle-class values
that Narcissa had learned at home were stronger than her commitment to duty and service. Narcissa was not the only hopeful missionary to turn down a proposal, of course. Laura Judd, who went to
the ABCFM's Hawaiian mission, also turned down her first offer.
But a refusal left the future frustratingly vague. Narcissa continued
to await the "leadings of Providence," while Spalding sought out a
"young lady with missionary interests" elsewhere.

Since there was no direct path young women who hoped to become missionaries could follow, Narcissa spent some of her time
teaching in district schools in Prattsburg and in Butler, seventy-five
miles away. Teaching was a major component of female missionary
work and an acceptable way for single women to earn money and
live away from their families. Despite her close identification with
her mother, Narcissa probably felt the usual desires for some independence. And as she knew from her own schooling, teaching also
offered opportunities to influence young people toward a Christian
commitment.

Narcissa enjoyed teaching and was good with children. She had
had plenty of practice with all her younger brothers and sisters. Later

her former pupils could "distinctly remember her simple stories that never failed to arrest the ears of children and the well adapted songs interspersed to remove the tedium of the school-room." Narcissa's advanced training also allowed her to instruct older students. One recalled that Narcissa was "sufficient to teach in any academy instead of a common school. . . . She had a class in natural philosophy [science] and wanted to start one in chemistry also, but that was more than we could venture to try until we had graduated in philosophy. She taught the best school of any teacher in our district."

While Narcissa was waiting for someone else to provide her life with its central focus, changing revival techniques provided her with new opportunities to use her talents in the service of evangelical religion. The Reverend George Rudd replaced the correct, somewhat old-fashioned Hotchkin. Rudd was vigorous and energetic with "forcible gestures, animated and impressive countenance, and . . . solemn appearance." Influenced by the most up-to-date approaches to revival work that Charles Finney was using so effectively, the new minister introduced Prattsburg to some of the so-called new measures.

Finney understood the importance of emotion during the conversion process. "Where mankind are so reluctant to obey God, they will not until they are excited." Like Finney, Rudd labored to create an atmosphere during a revival that would touch even the hardest of hearts. He was a compelling preacher who could make the unconverted squirm when he dwelt on the fires of hell or the wickedness of the unregenerate heart. To a far greater extent than Hotchkin, Rudd utilized the talents of his congregation during the service. Men and even women learned how to make spontaneous prayers. Under Rudd's leadership, Narcissa became used to praying in public and considered the practice a sign of "high-toned piety."

Rudd also relied on music to stir up the emotions of the congregation. As a member of the choir and as an occasional soloist, Narcissa learned to use her voice to move her listeners. One newcomer to Prattsburg recalled the impact music had had on his unconvinced heart. "This hymn when sung with pathos as it usually was; never fails to melt the audience. I remember distinctly hearing it before I was particularly interested in religion, and was so impressed, I really desired to be a Christian."

Other new measures encouraged by Rudd included use of the "anxious seat" during public services. As guilty sinners came forward to sit before the congregation, those in the pews took "heavenly pleasure in mingling . . . prayers and tears together" on the sinner's behalf. "Those on the anxious seat," wrote one observer, "could hardly avoid being affected by the tide of emotions. Tears and moans were heard all around."

Rudd held stirring public services but relied upon his parishioners to hurry the work of conversion along behind the scenes. Prayer meetings were particularly effective in promoting explorations of the soul in an intimate and supportive atmosphere. Narcissa's "voice was an important factor" in these private settings. In the summer of 1832 the entire Prentiss family was instrumental in keeping a series of sunrise prayer meetings going. "No one devoted more time in personal efforts to win souls to Christ than Narcissa." Many traced "their first serious impressions to her charming singing and tender appeals to yield to the overtones of mercy." The emotional strategies that Narcissa used so effectively within an evangelical culture were among her major qualifications for missionary work.

Rudd also called on outside evangelists to stoke the fires of revivalism. In 1832 preachers Boyle and Higby held a four-day protracted meeting, which was a community event. Teams went out from the village to bring in families to the meetinghouse in time for the morning sermon at 10:30. After a break for lunch, there was "prayer and laboring with the anxious." A second sermon followed at 1:30. Families then returned home to rest and ready themselves for the evening service.

Boyle and Higby utilized Narcissa's talents in ways that moved the congregation and brought her admiration and praise. One evening Higby gave a sermon on the last judgment. "By a previous arrangement Miss Narcissa, with two or three leading singers, took their seats near the pulpit and the moment the speaker closed his sermon they struck in and sang the old judgment hymn. . . . Christians were melted to tears, and hardened sinners bowed their heads and wept bitterly."

The Prentisses sustained such efforts in other ways as well. They entertained both the evangelists, and more important, they "had prayer meetings in their house every evening after service." For weeks after the protracted revival had ended, the family continued with the work by holding prayer meetings at their home.

One of Rudd's special interests was the missionary movement. He

must have fed Narcissa's hopes with his frequent reminders of the
need for missionaries and his accounts of news from the mission
field. Each month he held a special concert of prayer "for those who
had gone out to tell the glad story to the benighted." Those who
attended prayed aloud, "Lord, open the door to China," or "Prepare
the way for the gospel to enter Africa."

But Narcissa was far from any mission field in the early 1830s. She
could act forcefully enough in certain defined areas—her evangelical
work showed that—but was not used to shaping life into a pattern
she had chosen. As the eldest, "loving, dutiful daughter," Narcissa
was intermittently keeping house for her mother. Her relationship
with her mother continued to be a close one in which Narcissa felt
comfortable in pouring out all her "feelings, both sad & rejoycing,"
when her "heart was full."

While others remarked on how "cheerfully [Narcissa] assumed the
cares and burdens of the family," there were signs of "nervous affections." The phrase was imprecise and could easily mean Narcissa experienced any number of different aches and pains. As one physician
explained in 1827, the female nervous system was considered "far
more sensitive and susceptible than the male, and extremely liable to
those distressing affections which for want of some better term, have
been denominated nervous, and which consist chiefly in painful affections of the head, heart, side, and indeed of every part of the
system." What was at the root of these nervous illnesses that afflicted
so many women in the nineteenth century has been much debated.
Some have argued that cases of female nervousness stemmed from
the internalization of anger that could not be openly expressed,
while others have regarded them as evidence of "the human body at
war with 'civilized' Victorian society." There is no way of knowing
what was at the root of Narcissa's physical problems, but they do
point to some inner unease.

Certainly, Narcissa was restless. In 1834 she and Jane went to Bath,
probably boarding with the Rumsey family. The sisters ran an infant
school in which Narcissa took "great delight."

Stephen and Clarissa were now in their late fifties; several of their
children had already left home, although Edward, their youngest,
was only fourteen. At this juncture, they decided to relocate to the
west in Allegany County. Allegany was less developed than Steuben
County, and Stephen may have decided that his carpentry skills

would be more in demand there. He started disposing of his Prattsburg properties, and in June 1834 the family settled in the small village of Amity, where he was engaged in building several houses.

While Amity, surrounded "by a dense forest of pines," must have
seemed primitive after Prattsburg, Narcissa threw herself into the
work of the newly organized church and the Sunday school. Early
in the next year, the family moved a few miles to Angelica, where
Jonas had opened a dry-goods store. Again Narcissa busied herself
with church affairs. As her sister Harriet recalled, "Narcissa was very
active in Sunday school and in prayer meetings . . . and it was owing
to her efforts that they were established." "She was the life of the
ladies' prayer meetings." She also interested herself in the new and
more radical causes of moral reform and antislavery, two avenues
through which strong female feelings could be safely channeled.

Narcissa's period of waiting was coming to an end. By most evangelical standards, she was well prepared to embark on the useful life.
She was talented, pious, dutiful, and well educated. Her work for
the church encouraged her to believe that she could touch the hearts
and souls of the uncoverted. She knew she was well suited to run
a school. Family, church, and community judged missionary work
as a noble calling and necessary. While that work was demanding
and could be fatal (Harriet Newell died at nineteen when she had
only just arrived on the mission field), there seemed little reason for
her to doubt the validity of her vocation, so carefully nourished by
her mother, or the talents and commitment that she might bring to
that work.

CHAPTER 2

When Will the Work Be Done?
How? By Whom?

"THE church in this country must not only sustain herself, and purify the nation, but she must stretch out her arms, and make the whole world feel the strong embrace of her benevolence," the Reverend J. H. Price emphatically told his Philadelphia congregation in 1828. Narcissa was not in Philadelphia to hear Price's sermon on the importance of missionary work, but she had often heard similar exhortations that "the gospel must be preached to every creature" as she sat in the family box pew in the Prattsburg Presbyterian Church. The burning conviction of the necessity of Protestant missionary work drew its strength from the belief that every human being might be saved and its urgency from the knowledge that millions around the world had never heard of Christ and were doomed to eternal suffering unless someone brought the good news to them.

American missionary activity was not new, although the worldwide focus and sense of urgency apparent in Price's sermon developed only during the early decades of the nineteenth century. In 1810 concern with the fearful fate awaiting pagans around the globe prompted the formation of the American Board of Commissioners for Foreign Missions. This interdenominational organization that directed both Presbyterian and Congregational foreign missionary activities became the most important American missionary organization during the first half of the nineteenth century. It sent out 1,250 missionaries at a cost of more than $8 million in its first forty years. The board's stated goal was religious, but its effort represented the first major attempt to bring American culture and values to other parts of the world.

Although "aboriginal tribes of the North American Wilderness" were considered part of the foreign mission effort, the discouraging early history of missionary work among American Indians persuaded board members "that for the Pagans on this continent little can immediately be done." Instead, early attention focused on Asia

and its multitudes. In 1819 the board broadened its effort and established stations in Palestine (to convert both the Jews and Muslims)
and on the Hawaiian Islands. Eventually, the board changed its mind
about the Indians and sent missionaries to the southern "civilized"
tribes. When, in 1819, the board obtained access to a congressional
educational fund to support the endeavor, Indian missions became
an important part of the ABCFM work worldwide. By the time of
the Civil War, 10 percent of all American Board missionaries had
been sent to the American Indians, a percentage equaling that of
missionaries assigned to Africa and surpassing those laboring in East
Asia. The attempt to Christianize the Native American tribes, therefore, represented a significant test of the effectiveness of American
efforts to export culture.

As the ABCFM's understanding of its calling broadened, the organization stimulated popular interest in and financial support for
the missionary cause among the laity. The board hired agents to collect funds for missionary initiatives and promoted the organization
of hundreds of auxiliaries and missionary associations. Its monthly
newspaper, the *Missionary Herald,* kept readers informed of the work
of the board's missionaries and encouraged continuing assistance for
their efforts.

The ABCFM quickly recognized how important laywomen were
to the success of its endeavor. At first, women had been encouraged
merely to pray for the success of the missions. But before long they
were also organizing societies to raise funds. Eventually, women like
Narcissa's mother, Clarissa, played active roles in female missionary
societies and set up missionary groups for their children. Through
these activities, they kept in touch with the progress of the missionary efforts around the world, lent their material support to them,
introduced their children to the importance of the work, and encouraged them to consider a missionary calling.

In the beginning years of missionary activities, the ABCFM saw
the need only for married women in the missionary field. Accepting
the definition of woman's nature as different from and purer than
man's, the board believed that missionary wives could do "incalcu-
lable good." Not only could they teach the heathen to read and
write, but they could also demonstrate the merits of Christian family
life to those who were unacquainted with "domestic virtue and domestic happiness." Familial "duties cannot be *exemplified before the
heathen* unless by missionaries, who are married to well educated and

pious females who have formed all their habits and modes of thinking in a Christian country." Later, other rationales appeared. Male
missionaries would be more contented and productive if married.
And they would be safer, for "no symbol of peace is so significant or
so well understood and appreciated by savages, as the presence of
wives and children."

Although the board accepted the need to recruit married women,
sometimes designating them as "assistant missionaries," members
were hesitant to send unmarried women to foreign missions. Single
women could, of course, teach, but they could not carry out the
other family and domestic duties the board saw as so important. Furthermore, pagan surroundings posed special problems for women
who had no husbands to protect their virtue. Wives, then, made up
most of the early female missionary contingent to foreign stations.

Only gradually did the board recognize the value of having female
workers who were free of family cares at ABCFM mission sites. Cyn-
thia Farrar became the first single woman to be commissioned as an
assistant missionary by the ABCFM when she set out for India in
1827. By 1860 a total of 30 unmarried women had joined the board's
overseas missions. Far less reluctant to place single women in missions working with Native American tribes, however, by 1860 the
board had commissioned 108 to work in the South and West, usually
as teachers. Still, for a young woman like Narcissa, who longed to
work among the heathen, a suitable missionary marriage represented
the best and most reliable way to secure an appointment.

In any case, by the time Narcissa had completed her studies at
Franklin Academy, the ABCFM's initiative with the southern tribes
was floundering. Although board publications presented a favorable
picture of its work in the South, the reality was sobering enough to
make it unlikely that the board would appoint single women like
Narcissa to any of its seventeen stations there. The cost of supporting the enterprise was high, and the number of conversions low,
especially when contrasted to the dollars spent. In 1830 only 167
Cherokee could be counted as Christians; of these, only about 20
were students from the mission school.

Andrew Jackson's policy of Indian removal halted the ABCFM
southern initiatives and encouraged the board to shift its attention
to the Indians of the trans-Mississippi West. Whereas Narcissa may
well have originally pictured herself laboring in Asia or Africa, new
political and religious realities made her one of the first to participate

in the ABCFM's effort to convert Native Americans in the trans-
Mississippi West.

Although most of the western half of the continent lay beyond the
boundaries of the United States, interest in and exploration of these
foreign territories was already well established by the 1830s. Few ordinary Americans were thinking about moving to the Far West, but
trappers and mountain men, such as Jedediah Smith, were discovering the routes and mountain passes that would make travel possible.
Much of the information about the West appeared in government
reports, pamphlets, and newspapers and captured the attention of a
large reading audience.

American fur companies, operating out of St. Louis, had already
demonstrated the profits to be found in the Rocky Mountain region
during the 1820s. Each summer a caravan left St. Louis loaded down
with goods, liquor, and ammunition. At midsummer the traders
met with Indians and mountain men at the site chosen for that
year's gathering, or "rendezvous." The commercial exchange—trade
goods for beaver pelts—was a wild occasion, accompanied by eating,
drinking, and general carousing.

Although American profits from the fur trade were substantial, the
American companies were competing with the British Hudson's Bay
Company for control of the western trade. The Hudson's Bay Company dominated the fur trade in Oregon Territory, which was legally
under joint American and British occupation. The company not only
operated trading posts or forts there but also carried on agricultural,
lumbering, and fishing operations.

While the ABCFM's concern with western tribes was a predictable
response to the end of its southern initiative and growing American
interest in the West, the board's concern with these tribes was not
entirely the result of expediency. When the board sent missionaries
to the Hawaiian Islands in 1819, some believed that the mission had
as a "leading object . . . the christianization of the western heathen
of this continent." In 1827, the year that Great Britain and the United
States agreed to extend their joint occupation of Oregon, the board
tentatively moved toward a commitment by instructing the Hawaiian mission to investigate the possibility of establishing an Oregon
station. J. S. Green explored the Oregon coast two years later and
reported that white traders had so corrupted the coastal tribes that
they were poor targets for missionary endeavors. But he suggested
that those living in the region of the Columbia and Umpqua rivers

(neither of which he visited) might be better candidates for Christianity. By 1832 the board had tentatively decided on a mission.

Before the board came to any final decision, a sensational call to action came from another quarter. The March 1833 edition of the Methodist newspaper the *Christian Advocate and Journal and Zion's Herald* described a remarkable meeting in St. Louis between William Walker, part Wyandot Indian and a Methodist, and three Flathead Indian chiefs. Walker, the source for the account, alleged that Flatheads had learned from a white visitor that their "mode of worshipping . . . [was] wrong and displeasing to the Great Spirit." "It is time we had laid it aside," the Indians had supposedly reasoned; "we must know something of this." Their visit to St. Louis was the result. The chiefs, Walker claimed, were seeking the white man's religion and its sacred book.

The story, with its accompanying illustration of a pathethic misshapen flatheaded Indian, was stirring enough. A covering letter by the distinguished Methodist G. P. Disosway made sure that *Advocate* readers did not miss the significance of the incident. "How deeply touching is the circumstance of the four natives traveling on foot 3,000 miles through thick forests and extensive prairies, sincere searchers after truth! . . . The story has scarcely a parallel in history. . . . Let the Church awake from her slumbers and go forth to the salvation of these wandering sons of our native forests."

Although it is unlikely that the meeting Walker described occurred, he had probably heard stories of the visit of four Nez Percé Indians to St. Louis two years earlier. Accompanying American fur traders returning from the annual rendezvous, the Indians apparently had been seeking greater knowledge of the Christian god. If none of Walker's details were right, the general picture of some Indian interest in Christianity seemed to be.

In any case, the truth or falsity of the story did not matter. Pious Christians heard the tale from their pulpits and read about it in the *Advocate* or one of the other papers that reprinted the original article. Evidently the western tribes were eagerly seeking the truth. The time had come for action. Three weeks after the original article, the *Advocate* issued the challenge. "Hear! Hear! Who will respond to the call from beyond the Rocky Mountains? . . . All we want is men. Who will go? Who?"

One of those stirred by the *Advocate's* challenge was Congregational minister Samuel Parker. Parker had served as a home missionary on the New York frontier early in the century and had then ministered to churches in Massachusetts and New York. Now the plight of the western Indians moved him to write the board in April 1833 to accuse its members of moving too slowly on western missions. "The heathen themselves are chiding Christians for their negligence in not obeying the commandment 'go ye into all of the world, and preach the gospel to every creature,'" Parker claimed. He advocated a mission outpost in Oregon, and although he was over fifty and had a wife and three children, he offered to go the Far West himself.

His appeal to the ABCFM met with some skepticism. Although the ABCFM's method of selecting missionaries today seems amazingly casual, the board was operating in a society where professional credentials were looser and often earned more informally than is true in the late twentieth century. What the board was most interested in discovering was the candidate's character, piety, and commitment. Letters from the candidate and testimonials from local ministers who knew the candidate were deemed "proper evidence" of these. In a leap of faith, board members presumed "that whom the Lord calls to this work will be endowed with the requisite physical, mental, and spiritual abilities."

Although Parker's character, piety, and commitment were not questioned, his application was problematic. The board was not enthusiastic about sending a family man in his fifties on an exploring trip. Furthermore, the Methodists were already mounting a mission and considered the Oregon field "claimed."

The board's refusal did not deter Parker, who was unwilling to give up his dreams of missionary glory. Realizing that direct appeals would be fruitless, he decided to try to force the board's hand. He urged the congregation of Ithaca's First Presbyterian Church "to increase their efforts for the extension of the Redeemer's Kingdom," first by raising money to support missionaries in the field and then by recommending specific missionary appointments to the ABCFM. The community responded enthusiastically and collected a substantial sum for Parker and his cause. After a "considerable delay," Parker's strategy paid off. In 1834 the ABCFM approved Parker for an exploring mission to "ascertain the condition and character of those remote tribes" beyond the Rockies. He was to travel the first leg of the journey with two other ABCFM missionaries assigned to the trans-Mississippi West. Pealing church bells announced the missionaries' early morning departure from the town. The church was packed with well-wishers, who sent the men off with prayers, benediction, and song.

Knowing little about travel to the West, the three missionaries did not leave for the frontier until May. When they arrived in St. Louis, they discovered that the American Fur Company, with whom they planned to travel, had left for its annual rendezvous a month earlier. Realizing that it was "too late to go with any safety to the Oregon Territory that year," Parker returned to the East. In the late fall of 1834 he began raising money and helpers in western New York.

Traveling by horse and wagon over bad roads, Parker visited small towns where missionary support was strongest. Many in Parker's audiences were already knowledgeable about the ABCFM's missionary activities. In a town like Prattsburg, Presbyterians were holding their monthly concerts. Contributions listed in the *Missionary Herald* suggested the extent of Prattsburg's financial support and interest. In 1831 the church collected eighty-two dollars for the ABCFM; the next year, more than one hundred dollars. In 1832 the Prattsburg Female Missionary Society also raised ten dollars for a fire-damaged mission in Ceylon—in which country several children in mission schools were supported by the well-to-do Bridges family.

When Parker drove his wagon into town, he applied to the local Congregationalist or Presbyterian minister for permission to hold mission meetings. If interest was high, he was able to sustain the meetings for as long as three or four days. His audiences learned of the context for the new endeavor in Parker's sketch of the worldwide mission effort, while his description of the work of early American missionary heroes reminded them of their obligation to the native Americans. Only then did Parker turn to the spiritual needs of the Indians living beyond the Rocky Mountains and appeal both for funds and volunteers. In a letter written to his family in early December 1834, Parker reported he had raised small sums for the ABCFM, and about eighteen people seemed interested in volunteering for the missionary life (about half of these eventually went). Some who came forward were women.

In late November Parker arrived in the village of Amity. The Presbyterians had organized only two years earlier and so far had no church building, so the missionary meetings were held in the log schoolhouse. Naturally, Narcissa came to one of the meetings and heard his plea for volunteers. Like many nineteenth-century women, even those who harbored dreams of doing something out of the ordinary, Narcissa had found it possible to shape her own future only up to a certain point. She had acquired an academy education, taught school, and done benevolent work. Now she was waiting for a person or event that could move her life forward in the desired direction. She described herself as awaiting the leadings of Providence, and providentially enough Parker came to her. His talk may well have offered her the first real opportunity to act decisively. After the meeting she told him that she wished to volunteer for missionary work.

As Narcissa sat on the schoolroom bench listening to Parker, his words only reinforced well-formulated ideas about missionary work and her conviction that she was well qualified to do it. Over the years, she had attended numerous missionary meetings, heard countless sermons and talks on the mission movement, and discussed the missions at home. Her mother was a staunch advocate of the value of the work. Like many other pious young people, she had also fed her "increasing desire for information" about "the salvation of the heathen" by devouring books, periodicals, and newspapers that purportedly revealed the realities of missionary life. She was particularly fond of the ABCFM's paper, the *Missionary Herald,* and greeted its arrival "with peculiar feelings."

What had Narcissa learned from her reading about the life of a missionary? At one level, the *Missionary Herald* suggested that missionary work was colorful and adventurous. Male missionaries from all over the world reported back to the ABCFM, and the *Missionary Herald* published excerpts from the correspondence and journals the board received. Each month, Narcissa could follow the fortunes of missionaries in Jerusalem or Buenos Aires, Cuba or Ceylon. Part religious progress reports and part travelogues, the excerpts often described amazing heathen customs, fantastic landscapes, and thriving missionary schools. General articles heightened the impression that the missionary work was varied and rigorous, with room for boundless enterprise. Especially for a young woman like Narcissa who had been prevented from reading "trashy" novels, the newspaper must have provided a picture of a wonderfully exciting and exotic life that contrasted sharply with the daily female routines of Prattsburg or Amity.

No reader of the *Missionary Herald,* and certainly not Clarissa's daughter, could be blind to the pressing necessity for volunteers and the importance of the noble work. "A generation of heathens lives no longer than a generation of Christians," the paper pointed out in April 1832. "Time is hurrying both on the bosom of its mighty tide into eternity." The numbers of those heading for the everlasting torments of hell were daunting. "SIX HUNDRED MILLIONS OF HEATHENS . . . miserable, and perishing in sin . . . [require] *immediate* help." And while the paper made clear that the task of converting millions was formidable, the optimistic tone of the newspaper suggested that it was not impossible.

Faith in God's plan and the need for both funds and volunteers encouraged the paper's editors to present an optimistic picture of missionary efforts. By including information about missionary work supported by other Protestant denominations, the editors made their missionary movement appear more impressive, in terms of both workers and converts, than it actually was.

The *Missionary Herald*'s editors arranged mission reports and dramatic little vignettes to support the idea that "the *grand object* . . . the CONVERSION OF THE WORLD" was feasible. The account of one young woman's work at a Choctaw mission school, for example, focused not on the small number of converts but on the "interesting" scene of one of her students reading the crucifixion story to the others. Another article encouraged readers to view the number of students in Mrs. Wilson's school in India and the girls' proficiency in needlework as some kind of missionary victory. Although the paper did report low conversion statistics, editors suggested in 1831 that the figures themselves could not be intepreted as a sign of failure, for they might actually be the firstfruits of a great harvest.

In the 1830s, when Narcissa was probably reading the *Missionary Herald* quite regularly, she learned much to encourage her about the progress of American Indian missions. In 1831 she must have been pleased to discover that many Arkansas Cherokees attended Sabbath services and that Choctaw women supported female prayer meetings in small numbers but spent many a "long afternoon in singing and prayer." The next year, she could read about a Miss Sawyer, an instructor at the Cherokee station at New Echota, who emphasized the need to instill moral principles and habits of industry and who confessed that she "sometimes" had recourse to the rod. That ambiguous item was balanced, however, by the report of the Arkansas Cherokees' spiritually interesting school and conversions in that mission.

In 1833, even before the news of the Flatheads' search for the white man's religion appeared in the *Christian Advocate,* the *Missionary Herald* was highlighting the importance of work with western Indians and suggesting that they were ripe for Christianity. "Very many, if not all the leading superstitions of the world, are comparatively in their dotage," the paper proclaimed in the January issue. "Not one of them stands forth in the giant strength of their youth. . . . Our western Indians, for instance, have scarcely of their ancient superstitions to oppose the gospel." In March the paper expressed the desire to enlarge the Indian missionary field and, at the end of the year, raised the possibility of establishing stations among tribes living between the Rocky Mountains and the Pacific. "Probably no heathen nations entertain less definite prejudice against the Gospel, or the arts of civilized life." Early in 1835 readers learned that there were more churches and converts among the American Indians than elsewhere in the world. These articles must have piqued Narcissa's interest in American Indian mission work before she heard the tale of the Flathead chiefs' visit to St. Louis and Parker's talk in Amity.

The *Missionary Herald* also shaped Narcissa's understanding of the nature of female missionary work and its qualifications. There was no denying the exotic setting of missionary work and the importance of becoming fluent in a foreign tongue, but many tasks resembled those that pious young women already performed at home. Rather than taking on culturally unfamiliar duties, women could slip into familiar roles. Articles described women teaching young children and leading prayer meetings for native women. Even visiting native women in their houses in India or Burma was a variation of the pattern of informal sociability that Narcissa knew so well. One might presume that the approaches that worked in familiar settings would also work in much the same way in foreign surroundings. Although the articles often had undertones of frustration and failure, they rarely made explicit the potential difficulties facing female missionaries or the cultural discomforts awaiting them.

Articles in the *Missionary Herald* made clear that a female missionary ought to be prepared to teach but that women, unlike men, needed no other special training. Rather, a woman who wanted to be a missionary should ask herself if she had qualities such as perseverance, good sense, habitual industry, and a cheerful devotion to the cause. That she ought to be pious was obvious, for piety was central to the conception of missionary life. The emphasis on a female piety that was intense, inward looking, and even anxious, however, encouraged judging the missionary efforts in terms of the spirituality of the missionaries, deflecting attention from the difficult task of conversion itself.

Missionary literature suggested that women who became missionaries enjoyed not only the opportunity for sacrifice and heroism but also an unequaled chance for applause and admiration. Like many other pious young readers, Narcissa had found the story of Harriet Newell, one of the first missionaries to India, particularly compelling. Although Harriet had early recognized her desire to give herself to Christ, she had to wrestle with her "cold, stupid heart." When she was eighteen, Mr. Newell, a young man who was planning to become a missionary, became acquainted with her family. Within a year, Mr. Newell proposed to Harriet. She wavered, uncertain as to what God required, but finally concluded to aid Mr. Newell in his effort to promulgate the gospel to those living in the "sultry climes of India." There was no question that Harriet's decision to choose the missionary life was even more admirable than her husband's, for "the tie, which binds her to relatives and her home," was more powerful for her than it was for him. Harriet's noble commitment did not yield immediate fruits, for she died soon after reaching the mission field. But she had not failed. "She died in a glorious cause. Nor did she pray, and weep, and die in vain. Other causes may miscarry; but that will certainly triumph." Harriet Newell was to be "universally admired," for she was "a lovely saint, who has finished her course, and gone to receive an unfading crown."

Harriet Newell died at nineteen, and many other female missionaries likewise ended their lives in heathen lands far from home. The *Missionary Herald* informed its readers of women's deaths and published their obituaries. This material could have provided female readers with some degree of realism, given them some hint of what the sacrifices of missionary life entailed. Certainly death called into question various assumptions underlying missionary work. If workers perished in the field, who would teach the heathen the truth? If women died more often than men (as the number of obituaries seemed to suggest), then perhaps they should not go to foreign climes.

The *Herald's* editors cast the news of women's deaths in ways that made objective assessment difficult. The paper denied, on several occasions, that climate had anything to do with female mortality, although it acknowledged that domestic work and privation contributed to weakening women's health. But most articles diverted attention away from reality by focusing on heroic women on their deathbeds. Mrs. Stone, who perished in Mahrattas, was pictured in her last illness as fearless and serene, joyfully anticipating her departure to heaven. While obituaries often pictured pious women at home in similar terms, their stage was modest, confined mainly to family and friends. For female missionaries, the setting was heroic, as the commitment to both Christ and the heathen merited. So Mrs. Hervey, another missionary in India, enjoyed an exalted end, departing "thus triumphing in God her savior." Female missionaries achieved a sanctity through death, no matter how few their achievements on earth.

It was not suprising that the *Missionary Herald* whetted Narcissa's interest and encouraged her to see herself as a missionary. But it was a poor guide for the actual experiences that might await her. Had Narcissa a more accurate conception of missionary work, she might not have been so eager to volunteer at the end of Parker's talk. The paper contained few warnings that the most sensible, industrious, cheerful, and pious female might struggle unsuccessfully with loneliness, exhaustion, or depression or that a missionary marriage might suffer from the demands of missionary work. It did no more than hint that the possession of all the most desirable qualities might still result in failure, that natives might reject the Christian message. The frustrations of working within an alien culture were rarely adequately conveyed, although the most careful reader who was looking for signs of difficulties could find them.

Narcissa was not one of those careful readers, and Parker's call for volunteers seemed opportune. When she talked to Parker after the meeting in the Amity schoolhouse, he was impressed that she was "a daughter of Judge Prentiss of Amity" and thought she was "talented, pious, with good education." But, uncertain whether the board would send unmarried women to the proposed mission, he was not very encouraging to Narcissa or to another young woman who had also volunteered. "I think I said nothing about . . . going among the Indians, or to any particular part of the world," he wrote to the board, "but only that they would offer themselves if their services were needed. I recollect that I told them if they offered themselves, it must be to go anywhere the Board should choose." The board's secretary, David Greene, approved of Parker's discretion. The exploring trip had not even taken place, and he did not think the board had "missions among the Indians where unmarried females are valuable just now."

Parker's initial response discouraged Narcissa more than he remembered or intended. She was not used to striking out on her own, and she may well not have been ready to offer to go anywhere in the world alone. It may be that as a single woman she supposed her services were not wanted or that she felt ambivalent about really leaving home for a missionary life. Whatever the reason, Narcissa did not write to the ABCFM and offer her services. She again waited for the leadings of Providence.

If Parker had been discouraging to Narcissa, he had been very encouraging to some of the men who had come forward during his speaking tour. A few weeks before Parker had reached Amity, he had interviewed several Steuben County residents who expressed an interest in going to the western heathen. Among those "of good promise" was a doctor living in the town of Wheeler, not far from Prattsburg, where the Prentisses had lived for so many years. Although Parker did not recollect the name of the doctor, he planned to see him again. When he did, he decided that Marcus Whitman was a "choice" candidate. "His general reputation in regard to all the particulars required, and into which I have made . . . inquiry, I think place his case beyond any . . . doubt."

At thirty-two years of age, Marcus Whitman had the qualities that Parker thought important for missionary work. Of medium height, he gave the impression of physical strength and energy. He was unpolished, with "easy, *don't care* habits," but he was also earnest and quick to speak his mind, determined and energetic. Although he had been practicing medicine for thirteen years, he had been active in church affairs and had often thought of becoming a missionary. He was unmarried, perhaps the result of a troubled family life, but Parker knew that many male missionaries found themselves missionary wives before they set off for the mission field.

Although Parker gave few details of Marcus's history, the doctor's youth had not been a happy one. Marcus was the second living son of Alice and Beza Whitman, who had migrated from western Massachusetts to the New York frontier at the end of the eighteenth century. Beza died when Marcus was only seven. Unlike Narcissa, who had a secure childhood, surrounded by family, friends, and neighbors, Marcus early experienced loss and emotional and physical rejection.

Within a few months of Beza's funeral, his mother, Alice, sent
Marcus to live with his father's family in Massachusetts while she
kept her four other children with her. Why she chose to send away
her second son is not clear. Perhaps Marcus was already stubborn,
"offhand," "careless," and given to "speaking his mind before he
thought the second time." When Alice married again the following
year, she left the boy in Massachusetts. Although his father's family
did not neglect him—his uncle and grandfather gave him "constant
religous instruction and care"—the young boy must have felt his
mother's rejection keenly.

He did not see her again until he was thirteen. The homecoming
did little to reassure him of his mother's affection. A family member
recalled, "Coming in at evening, he went up to his mother and
reached out his hand, saying, 'How do you do, Mother?'—and
she drew back thinking herself no mother to him. This so grieved
him that he burst out into tears." While others described Marcus's
mother as an abrupt person who "never spent any time in sentiment,
but abounded in deeds," her lack of recognition and coldness could
only have reinforced Marcus's feelings of rejection and separation.

Certainly there was no place for Marcus in this family. In five years,
his brothers and sister had changed and adapted to the new family
structure: a stepfather, Calvin Loomis, and a new half-brother. While
Narcissa formed extremely close bonds during childhood and ado-
lescence with her family, especially with her mother, her future husband had the opposite experience in his youth.

For the next five years, Marcus attended a school in Plainfield,
Massachusetts, and boarded with a local family. The school, founded
and supervised by the town's Congregational minister, Moses Hallock, provided the classical curriculum needed for divinity school.
Like Franklin Academy, the school encouraged students to consider
a life of evangelical commitment and service. About a sixth of Hallock's students later became ministers or missionaries.

From a religious perspective, these years were formative ones for
Marcus. The head of the family with whom he boarded was a church
deacon, his schoolmaster the church's minister. Commitment to
the Congregational way gradually replaced his early Baptist training
with his father's family. He attended the church's Sunday school,
experienced conversion at the age of seventeen, and dreamed of the
ministry.

When he returned to live with his family in New York the following year, he found little sympathy for his aspirations. Neither his mother nor his stepfather belonged to the Rushville Congregational Church; indeed, his mother was "not attracted to any church." He could hardly expect her to support his half-formed plans for the ministry. Nor did his brothers approve, because they believed "his limited means would compel him to be a charity scholar" during the years of education that would be required for ordination. His family's opposition brought forth unmanly signs of his frustration, sorrow, and, doubtless, anger. His niece recalled her mother saying that "many a time she has seen the big tears on his face as he thought of his disappointment in his course of life."

For the next three years, Marcus lived at home, working in his stepfather's shoe shop and tannery. Though thwarted in his ministerial hopes, Marcus was active in the Rushville Congregational Church, with which he had united upon his return. He taught Sunday school, conducted "sunrise prayer meetings with two other young men," and perhaps interested himself in the news of one of the town's residents who had recently gone to Hawaii as a missionary.

In 1823, when he came of age, Marcus began assisting a local doctor. Marcus's sister claimed that her brothers had forced Marcus "against his will to take up the study of medicine." It is hard to see how they could have done so. Certainly Marcus must have seen how limited his options were. He had spent three years working in the tannery and shoe shop; he taught school from time to time while he was working with the local doctor. Medicine was a more congenial and respected occupation than these alternatives. After two years of apprenticeship, Marcus took a short course at the College of Physicians and Surgeons of the Western District of New York and then received his license to practice. In the next few years, he practiced in Pennsylvania, then in Canada. By 1830 he was back in Rushville.

Neither the practice of medicine nor voluntary religious activities satisfied Marcus's longings for a life of Christian service. Now twenty-eight, he put aside the practice of medicine and began reading theology in preparation for the ministry. "I had not continued long," Marcus explained, "when for want of active exercise I found my health become impaired by a pain in the left side which I attributed to an inflammation of the spleen. I immediately resorted to remedies with apparently full relief, resumed study so soon that it caused a return of the pain & again I used remedies with partial relief. Then I used exercise & continued it for a number of months when I found I was not able to study & returned to the practice of my profession."

Did the mysterious lingering pain that halted Marcus's studies stem from psychological rather than physical factors, or did it persist just because of inadequate medical treatment? Certainly, Marcus did not have a contemplative or sophisticated mind, and the study of theology was difficult. His five years of schooling at Moses Hallock's school so many years before was perhaps an insufficient preparation for what he hoped to do. Being in the midst of his family in Rush- ville could hardly have helped. Whatever the causes of his pain, the study of theology halted. Marcus returned to the practice of medi- cine and earned an additional medical degree in 1831. Despite the seeming finality of these events, old aspirations stubbornly remained. Recalling these years, Marcus remembered that his mind still "was set on the [missionary] work."

Marcus did escape from his family, however, and in 1832 he settled in the small town of Wheeler, forty miles from Rushville and seven miles from Prattsburg. His far-flung practice kept him in the saddle, but Marcus made time for church affairs. As a trustee of the newly formed Presybterian church, Marcus was one of its most active members.

By this time Marcus saw clear connections between medical and religious matters. Believing that liquor ruined not only the body but often the soul as well, and that "an army of drunkards" reeled into hell every year, he organized temperance meetings. A Prentiss family friend also recalled that Whitman was doling out spiritual as well as medical advice to his patients.

In early January 1834 Marcus was observing a day of fasting. When his thoughts turned to the familiar subject of his life's work, he ex- perienced some kind of stiffening of resolve and felt "more especially called to the work" of a missionary. The ministry was not the only route to the mission field. That spring, on a visit to Rushville, Mar- cus talked over the possibilities of becoming a medical missionary with Henry Strong, the Congregationalist minister. Strong was en- couraging and wrote to the ABCFM on Marcus's behalf. Describing Marcus as possessing a "solid judicious mind . . . more than ordinary piety and perseverance, a regular bred Physician," Strong recom- mended him as a missionary doctor. "He has thought of being a missionary for some time past," Strong wrote, wondering whether

"a station with some of our western Indians would be useful to him."
He added, "Altho I know not that he thinks of it, yet I think he
might, if thought expedient, after a time be ordained to advantage."
Strong made only a passing reference to Marcus's earlier bout of ill
health.

The board, which relied on such referrals for potential candidates
for the mission field, received the letter from Strong just at the time
that Parker was making his abortive attempt to explore missionary
possibilities in the Far West. The board's secretary asked to hear directly from Whitman, who replied with an account of his background and interest in going to "any field of usefulness . . . as Physician, Teacher or Agriculturalist." The board particularly wanted to
know if Whitman was married. In his letter, Marcus explained that
he had "no present arrangement upon that subject. Yet I think I
should wish to take a wife, if the service of the Board would admit."

Over the course of the next month, letters passed back and forth
between the board and Marcus. The ABCFM secretary told Marcus
that there was a place for a doctor at a mission in the South Pacific
and advised him to "get a good missionary wife." Questions were
raised about Marcus's health, for "good health and good constitu-
tion are very important prerequisites for missionary service." The
board secretary had doubts about Marcus's education, which he expressed to Strong.

Marcus's description of his health was not promising. In addition
to the bout of illness he had experienced when trying to prepare for
the ministry, Marcus revealed that "I have not been for any length of
time without a slight pain & for the last two or three weeks there
has been an agravation [sic] of pain & soreness so that I have used
remedies & shall have to use more still." In fact, despite his offer to
go anywhere, he feared being in "a hot climate" and refused the place
in the South Pacific. He was more sanguine, however, about a mission in a more reasonable climate.

The detailed account of Marcus's ill health prompted the board's
secretary to write a discouraging reply. Most of the world's heathens
were perishing in the warm climates that Marcus feared. Among the
Indian missions in more temperate climates, "we have no demand
for a physician at this time." The secretary concluded, "Indeed it
seems doubtful whether your health is such as to justify your going
on a mission at all."

Again, hopes soared only to be dashed. The rejection sounded final enough, but still when Parker came to Steuben County, Marcus talked to him about volunteering. His health was better; indeed he struck Parker as being in stout good health. The proposed Indian mission was in a temperate climate. Marcus spoke to Parker, who urged him to apply directly to the board with the appropriate references.

Since the board's rejection of Whitman, it had had limited success in finding candidates for the Indian mission field. The collapse of missionary activities in the South might have contributed to young men's reluctance to volunteer for work among American Indians. The board's secretary David Greene thought that the Indian field just did not seem important enough to future missionaries. "They had rather learn a language spoken by tens of millions & live among a dense and settled population . . . & think that the fruits of their labors will be felt by large nations . . . than to spend their lives in what they apprehend will be almost fruitless toil in reclaiming small tribes of sparsely settled migrators and nearly inaccessible men, who . . . [seem] devoted to extinction." The difficulties of recruiting for the Indian mission made the board sympathetic to Marcus's second application, which specifically requested an appointment with Parker on his venture "beyond the Rocky Mountains." Since he now claimed good health, the board in early 1835 commissioned Marcus to accompany Parker on the exploratory trip that spring.

The next weeks were hurried ones for Marcus. He visited Parker in Ithaca to plan their journey, wrote to the board to clarify the goals of the venture, collected fees from patients, and arranged his other business concerns. He planned to leave Wheeler by mid-February and meet up with Parker in St. Louis at the beginning of April.

During these weeks as Marcus prepared for his first missionary adventure, he was also thinking about marriage. He had delayed matrimony long past the time that most young American men married. His own family experience neither provided him with a positive picture of family life nor prepared him well for the intimacy of marriage. But his original correspondence with the board had made it clear that a good missionary wife was desirable. While he had reported that he was not averse to the idea, he had not been courting any young woman in that summer of 1834. Now that he had an assignment, it was time to seek out a possible bride.

Like most newly appointed male missionaries, Marcus apparently had no one definite in mind. Samuel Parker's son recalled that his father had acted as a matchmaker by urging Marcus to approach Narcissa Prentiss. "I told Dr. Whitman," Parker claimed, "to find, and marry her because in 1834 she had told me she had given herself to be a missionary." But there were others besides Parker who could have acted as go-betweens. George Rudd, minister of the Prattsburg church in which Narcissa had been so active before her move to Amity, wrote a letter in support of Marcus's application to the ABCFM. Another of Marcus's supporters was Wheeler's minister, J. H. Hotchkin, who had served as Prattsburg's minister until 1830. Either could have suggested that Marcus consider Narcissa Prentiss as a possible wife. Certainly they would have seconded Parker's advice. None would have thought they were doing anything unusual in encouraging two people who knew each other slightly or even not at all to marry. Friends of would-be missionaries and even the ABCFM board itself often acted as matchmakers for those who needed wives or husbands in order to take up a missionary assignment.

Probably Narcissa and Marcus were acquainted. Wheeler was only seven miles from Prattsburg, which had an older and more flourishing religious community than Wheeler. Marcus first met the Prentisses at a prayer meeting held at their house when Narcissa was away teaching school. Doubtless, Narcissa and Marcus were introduced at a similar event. Most likely the initial meeting did not seem particularly important at the time, and it may be that neither remembered it specifically.

When Marcus left home, he headed directly for Amity to visit Narcissa. Almost two months had passed since Narcissa had heard Parker, and she had done nothing to follow up on her expression of interest in missionary work. Marcus's arrival must really have seemed like the work of Providence. Over the weekend of February 21 and 22, the two quickly came to an agreement to enter into God's work together. In a period when many young middle-class men and women were choosing partners on the basis of romantic feelings tested during a frank and intimate courtship, there was no pretense about romantic love. Both saw the marriage as the means of fulfilling cherished dreams.

In the larger culture, both Marcus's pragmatic proposal and Narcissa's hasty acceptance were out of the ordinary. In missionary circles, however, Narcissa's agreement to marry someone she knew only slightly was not particularly unusual. Those who were eager to do the Lord's work, as one missionary novel made clear, did not "let fancy run away" with their better judgment, did not "fall in love." Rather, a young man headed for the mission field sought out a sound, healthy, and pious companion to share in the "great work." Any young woman who had spent her early years constantly engaged in helping at home and in doing the Lord's work in her community possessed the good sense to accept the proposal without any expectations of romantic flourishes. Other women who became ABCFM missionaries accepted proposals from men whom they knew even less well than Narcissa knew Marcus.

Although Narcissa's refusal of Henry Spalding several years earlier suggested that her interest in the mission field was not strong enough to overcome a suitor's social and personal shortcomings, Marcus also lacked some of the qualities a refined and sociable woman like Narcissa hoped for in a marriage partner. He was not polished; some would go so far as to say he lacked a "sense of *etiquette*." His appearance "among respectable people [was] rather forbidding at first." He was casual in dress and had a "peculiar" mixture of dark brown and white hair, a large mouth, sharp nose, and "deep blue eyes." But he ultimately made a good impression. He was a well-established doctor of excellent character whose "talents and acquirements [were] quite respectable." In contrast to Narcissa, he was a person to act rather than to propose. He seemed sincere and earnest. Now, almost twenty-seven, Narcissa may well have realized that Marcus might be her last chance to marry and her last chance to realize her hopes of a missionary life. With her affirmative answer, she escaped from her uncertain position as eldest unmarried daughter, sometime housekeeper and schoolteacher. Now she was a bride-to-be and, as a future missionary, the center of attention both in her family and in her church community. Her mother's response to the proposal is not known, but surely she supported and perhaps even urged Narcissa to accept.

The letter that Oliver S. Powell, Amity's Presbyterian minister, wrote to support Narcissa's application to the ABCFM highlighted the pragmatic nature of the marriage commitment and made it sound more tentative than perhaps it was. "It is probable [that] Miss Prentiss will hereafter become the companion of Doct. Marcus Whitman (should he be established missionary beyond the Rocky Mts.)."

Parker's visit had also inspired Powell and his wife to secure appointments as missionaries to the Pawnee. During that weekend,

Marcus and Narcissa discussed the possibility that she accompany the Powells to their mission in order to become "acquainted with the labours" of that life. This seemed like a good scheme, and Powell mentioned in his brief letter that Marcus hoped that Narcissa would be allowed to join them in their western mission.

Marcus did not linger in Amity. Despite the engagement with Narcissa and despite the brevity of the courtship, Marcus left the village as soon as the weekend was over. He had already made plans to visit relatives on his way to St. Louis and felt no need to change them. Becoming better acquainted perhaps did not seem necessary to either Marcus or Narcissa. The most important fact of the couple's relationship, their commitment to missionary work, was clear and outweighed more personal concerns. In any case, not for the last time, Marcus took early leave of Narcissa. He spent almost six weeks traveling by horseback to St. Louis, staying with family along the way. Parker, who traveled by stage and steamboat, made the trip from Ithaca in about two and a half weeks.

As soon as Marcus left Amity, Narcissa wrote her brief letter of application to the ABCFM. She said nothing of her arrangement with Marcus or of her specific desire to go to the Indians in the West. Her supporting letters, three from local ministers and one from an elder of the Amity church, were equally brief and asserted that Narcissa was "well qualified for usefulness in instructing the heathen in the way to Heaven." Despite his own inexperience as a foreign missionary, Parker, to whom the materials were sent first, asserted that "Narcissa's education, talents, person, disposition, conciliatory manners, and sound judgment promise well for usefullness in a mission field."

These most general references and the very short letter from Narcissa herself satisfied the board, who considered Christian commitment and piety the major qualifications for missionary life. Narcissa's experience teaching school and Sunday School and her academy education assured the board that she would be able to manage a mission school. Narcissa's background in terms of family, education, and religious conviction seemed quite similar to that of other female candidates for missionary assignments. The prospect of her marriage to Marcus removed what could have been the major drawback to sending her to the West sometime in the future.

By late March, the board informed Narcissa that they had accepted her application. Nothing was said of her possible marriage, merely that she had been appointed as assistant missionary for some tribe "west of the State of Missouri." The particular tribe and location could not "of course be stated definitely," since the board's exploring party had not yet even started out from St. Louis. The board left the matter of accompanying the Powells to "the future indication of providence," but could see no problem with that scheme.

Narcissa's proposal, as was so often the case in the nineteenth century, when marriage determined a woman's future, gave her life a focus. The board's letter reinforced it. Yet she still faced uncertainties. The board's letter was vague. No one could foresee the results of Parker's expedition. But some of the ways of Providence became clear soon enough. Mrs. Powell discovered she was pregnant, and the couple postponed their trip west. Narcissa, eager to begin her missionary work, was disappointed that she would not be setting out with them. In the one existing letter to Marcus during his absence of over nine months, Narcissa not only expressed her impatience with the delay but also suggested that she could have accompanied Parker and Marcus on their trip across the mountains that very spring. Of course, the ABCFM had never given any hint that it would accept such an arrangement. Nevertheless, Marcus writing in late April from Missouri, had decided that the rigors of the trip had been much exaggerated. "I should have been entirely willing, if not anxious, that you should have accompanied us. . . . We have the most flattering account of the health of such a trip. Perhaps no tour could do as much for an invalid."

The months of Marcus's absence crept by. Narcissa now could not expect to be setting out herself for the frontier for some time. Nor could she expect to receive news from Marcus once he and Parker had left civilization. Life went on much as usual. Narcissa visited relatives in Onondaga. Sometime during the summer, she moved with her family from Amity to Angelica, six miles distant, where her brother Jonas had opened a dry-goods store. Angelica was the county seat, "the largest village in the county," with a newspaper, common schools, and several churches. A relative visiting the family in September found Narcissa cheerful and happy. Festive family occasions included Jonas's marriage the following month.

As usual, she was at the center of the church's evangelical activities. She liked Angelica's Presbyterian minister, Leverett Hull, who was "of strong mind and ardent temperament" and who was well aware of women's spiritual talents. He favored "the stimulating and arousing methods then in vogue, and classed himself among new measure men and radical reformers." As Narcissa worked with the "sinners" during the revival, she must have been thinking of those with whom she would labor in the future.

While outward appearances were calm enough, Narcissa later hinted that her final year at home was a time of heightened emotions. Some of these, no doubt, grew out of the excitement of the revival. At times, however, she became disheartened about the indefiniteness of her future—if indeed she really had a future as a wife and missionary—and her powerlessness to determine it. Writing to Sarah Hull, the wife of Angelica's minister, probably during the summer of 1835, Narcissa was depressed, "well-nigh crushed with an unsupportable load." "Clouds of darkness" and obstacles threatened to overwhelm her. She found herself unable to push off her depression, too weak even to "roll it upon the Lord." It was even hard "to pray effectually for . . . mighty objects." She asked for Sarah's prayers.

Narcissa thought the board was reluctant to proceed with the mission and wondered whether their hesitation stemmed from lack of funds, workers, or even "want of faith and prayer in the churches?" Of one thing she was sure—"the obstacles cannot be with the Indians, when they have sent over to us and invited us to carry them the Word of Life."

If Narcissa was reading the *Missionary Herald* carefully during the months of Marcus's absence, she would have had even more reason to wonder about the future of her proposed venture. Several articles appeared on new ABCFM missions among the Indians, including the mission to the Ojibway tribe near Lake Superior. Unlike the settled eastern Indians so often described in the evangelical press during the 1820s, the Ojibways were nomadic. ABCFM missionaries described the frustrations of working with "unsettled" Indians, the difficulties of learning the native language, the medicine men's opposition to truth. The Indian character also presented problems: a reasoned argument about religious matters, the missionaries concluded, was ineffectual with Indians, who valued only what they could see and feel. Pawnee missionary John Dunbar made similar points. "I have not yet discovered that their religious duties extend any further, than they are accompanied by some sensual gratification."

If Narcissa read these reports, they seemed less important than the repeated appeals for workers. "Can none be found to pity the Indians, once the sole possessors of this extensive and happy country. Are the eyes of all who devote themselves to preaching the gospel to the heathen under the patronage of the Board, turned to the eastern world. . . . Tell them here are souls perishing, and now is the time, and probably the only time, to save them"; "when will the work be done?—how?—by whom?"

It was not until early December that Narcissa heard Marcus's first hand impressions of the Indians and news of his exploring trip with Samuel Parker. In August, Marcus had left Parker to complete the western tour alone while he returned to recruit a mission party to leave the following spring. Arriving in St. Louis in early November, Marcus and two Nez Percé boys he had decided to bring east with him made their way to New York State. In early December, Marcus had a brief visit of a day or so with Narcissa.

Marcus's decision to let Parker go on alone so that he could return and organize a mission party highlighted his enthusiasm and his positive evaluation of the opportunities for missionary work among western tribes. On their exploratory tour, Marcus and Parker had accompanied the American Fur Company to its annual rendezvous at Green River in present-day Wyoming. There they had met Flathead and Nez Percé chiefs who assured the two men of their interest in having missionaries among them. Marcus came home knowing that the Indians eagerly awaited the arrival of white missionaries and convinced that women could manage the journey. His news was cheering to Narcissa, who had spent long months wondering and worrying about her future. In early January, the board authorized a mission among the Flathead Indians.

This hurried visit was an opportunity not only for recounting the events of the past ten months but also for planning for the new mission. There was not much time to gather a party, for Marcus calculated that it would be necessary to leave the East by the end of February. The recruiting effort would be a strangely haphazard undertaking. The board informed Marcus of a few people who had expressed interest in going to "remote western tribes." Narcissa had already had a letter from one of them, a Daniel Clark, an agent of the American Bible Society living in Seneca Falls. Some of these possible missionaries Marcus contacted himself; others were approached by the board or by its agent Mr. Eddy.

During the visit, as Marcus and Narcissa discussed potential missionaries, Narcissa must have told Marcus about Henry Spalding, her former classmate at Franklin Academy and rejected suitor. Henry and his wife, Eliza, had been appointed as missionaries to the Osage tribe in Kansas but had not taken up their posts because of Eliza's pregnancy. In October, Eliza gave birth to a stillborn child in Prattsburg. Narcissa heard the news. Now there were no obstacles preventing the Spaldings from embarking upon their missionary career. Possibly they would agree to go to the Far West rather than to the Osages. When Marcus wrote Henry a letter of inquiry, Henry replied that he would consider changing his plans if the board approved.

While Narcissa remained in Angelica preparing for her eventual marriage and her journey west, Marcus frantically tried to secure the missionaries necessary to allow them to start out that spring. The board had authorized a party consisting of an ordained minister, a teacher, a farmer, and a mechanic. With the exception of the Spaldings, none of the possible missionaries materialized. Narcissa waited, not knowing the date of her wedding, her companions, or the day of her departure—if there was to be a departure.

By early February, Marcus was discouraged. While the Spaldings had expressed some willingness to go to the newly proposed mission, the ABCFM was reluctant to release them from their obligation to the Osages. Writing to Parker's brother-in-law, Marcus admitted that "the present prospect is poor for going next spring. Our only other method is to have the destination of Rev. H. H. Spalding changed from the Osages to the Nez Percés." The board continued to equivocate but finally told Marcus to proceed west. "If you should not obtain any associate, . . . you had better proceed . . . at least as far as Council Bluffs & then go further or stop among the Pawnees, as Providence may seem to direct. I much regret this perplexing embarrassment & delay," Greene wrote, "but know not how to remedy it."

Marcus took matters into his own hands. He hurried after the Spaldings, who were on the way to the Osage mission and begged them to join the Oregon expedition. The couple agreed, and Henry communicated their assent in a letter to the board. Promising to wait for Narcissa and Marcus in Cincinnati, the Spaldings continued their journey. They apparently stopped at the Prentiss household in Angelica to let Narcissa know what had happened.

The meeting was not entirely satisfactory. At some point before Henry agreed to join the Oregon mission, he had said in public, "I do not want to go into the same mission with Narcissa Prentiss, as I question her judgment." Others had described Henry as "sometimes too much inclined to denounce or censure those who are not as zealous and ardent as himself." Perhaps his sense that Narcissa was insufficiently committed to the missionary cause arose from personal experience or from bitter feelings at his rejection as a suitor. In any case, his remarks reached the ears of the Prentisses and offended Narcissa. Before the Spaldings left Angelica, Stephen tried to mediate between the two. It appeared as if peace was made, but the incident left hard feelings. Probably neither Henry nor Narcissa spent much time worrying about the future relations between members of the mission family, but it was ironic that Narcissa would have as a missionary companion the very man she had turned down years before.

Within a matter of days, Marcus returned to Angelica for his marriage. He and Narcissa had spent less than a week together since their engagement. Now they were to set out with only a few companions to begin a lifetime of mission work.

The night before her wedding found Narcissa anxious about the enormous challenge she was undertaking and sorrowful at the prospect of leaving her family and home for good. Friends, including Reverend Hull, gathered at the Prentiss house to spend what was, for Narcissa, a "memorable evening." She confessed that she "felt deeply in view of the obstacles that appeared to be in the way of our undertaking this journey and of the success of this mission." Some of her worries, she confided to Hull and another guest, were about the journey itself. What Marcus had initially written to her about the trip had suggested its rigors were exaggerated. Some of his experiences had tempered that optimistic evaluation. Now Narcissa wondered if she could successfully meet the challenges of the trail. Used to middle-class comforts, she had had no experience to prepare her for the rigors of overland travel. She told the two men "that if we ever got over the mountains it would be in answer to your prayers."

The next evening, after a ceremony that included the ordination of her father as a church elder and a communion service, Narcissa and Marcus were married. The wedding party was somberly but fashionably attired, Narcissa in her best black bombazine (a silk and wool cloth) dress, the rest of her family also in black. Since the marriage of missionaries was an event of community interest, many gathered in the church's large box pews to witness the ceremonies and to donate twenty-six dollars toward the pair's expenses.

As was customary on such occasions, Hull probably addressed his sermon to the newlyweds. Perhaps, like Philadelphia's Reverend Price, he talked about the necessity of bringing benevolence to the world. He must have emphasized how this marriage rather than symbolizing withdrawal from the world represented an entry into it. In later years, Narcissa would meditate upon it, finding cheer in its truth and "blessed promise."

Oral tradition suggests that the evening service ended on a highly emotional note. The congregation sang a missionary hymn whose words played upon the sadness of departure and the noble purpose that justified abandoning loved ones. "Can I leave thee, can I leave thee, / Far in heathen lands to dwell?" the refrain asked. The congregation dissolved into tears as the hymn continued. Narcissa's experience of singing at highly charged times stood her in good stead as she finished the hymn alone.

> In the deserts let me labor,
> On the mountains let me tell,
> How he died—the blessed Saviour—
> To redeem a world from hell!
> Let me hasten, let me hasten,
> Far in heathen lands to dwell.

The newly married couple did not linger. The next day Narcissa parted tearfully from her family and friends. Bidding them farewell was the first hint of what sacrifice in the mission cause meant. Yet the departure with her chosen companion represented the beginning of her life's work, the start of all she had dreamed about.

The couple hastened first to Ithaca, where Marcus had left one of the Nez Percé boys with Mrs. Parker and her family. Now that they were a missionary couple, they both had obligations there. On Sunday, Marcus had the more important task of addressing the congregation that had sponsored Parker's initial efforts to establish a mission in the Far West. As his helpmate, Narcissa spoke in the Sabbath school. Her experience with children was apparent. Parker's son recalled her "gentle pleasing manner" and the way she spoke easily to the Sunday school students at their "reading comprehension" level.

From Ithaca, Marcus and Narcissa went on to Rushville, where Narcissa met Marcus's family. There were practical tasks to do. Narcissa had Marcus's brother Augustus make her a pair of men's boots for the trip, while the ladies of the Rushville church sewed shirts for Marcus. Church members also contributed two hundred dollars toward the expenses of the trip.

In early March, still on schedule, Narcissa and Marcus set out for the frontier. At Williamsport, Pennsylvania, they joined up with other ABCFM missionaries assigned to the Pawnee tribe. Dr. Satterlee was a medical missionary; his wife, Martha, accompanied him. With the couple was Emeline Palmer, who planned to marry Samuel Allis, who was already at the mission station.

Mrs. Satterlee was ill, and the group spent Sunday in Williamsport. After a day in bed, she seemed better, and the missionaries went on to Pittsburgh, where they planned to take a steamboat down the Ohio. There, on Sunday, Marcus appeared in church, this time with the two Indian boys. Narcissa had a headache and stayed behind in the hotel room.

The next day was Narcissa's twenty-eighth birthday. She must have spent some of the previous day in the hotel reviewing the course of her life, the events that had brought her to Pittsburgh. All had been preparation for this moment, or so it must have seemed. Ahead lay the millions of perishing heathen. The immediate and not-so-immediate future was daunting, but her work was finally clear.

CHAPTER 3

Was There Ever a Journey Like This?

ON Tuesday, March 15, 1836, the mission party left Pittsburgh on the riverboat *Siam*, headed for Cincinnati, where they would join the Spaldings. From there, they steamed to St. Louis and then to Liberty, where the long overland trek would begin. Their route was one that thousands of Americans in the 1840s and 1850s would follow to the Pacific Northwest, but in the 1830s, as Narcissa knew, it was an "unheard [of] journey for [white] females."

At some point on the day they left Pittsburgh, Narcissa started the travel journal that her mother had suggested she keep. While she often thought of the "proposal concerning keeping a diary," she found it impractical "while traveling by land." Now, even though the motion of the boat made writing somewhat disagreeable, she began the record of her travels, which she continued until early November. She wrote several letters to family and friends as well. Her journal and letters together provide a detailed picture of this transitional period in her life when she was poised between the familiar routines of a small village in New York State and the unknown challenges of missionary life in Oregon.

As a female missionary, Narcissa realized that she had become a public figure of sorts and that her correspondence would not be private. As the conclusion of a popular novel entitled *The Wife for a Missionary* made clear, missionary wives should write "simple, matter-of-fact letters," not "for the public journals. No, let . . . husbands labor in that field," but for all the residents of towns and villages who needed to be stirred up about the missionary cause. Narcissa's letters would be read by family and friends, and even shared with strangers. She acknowledged as much when she told her sister Jane, "This letter is free plunder. . . . I will write to you again but on reflecting what I say to one I say to all."

Conscious of an audience, Narcissa shaped material with some of her readers in mind. She described fording rivers for her sixteen-year-old brother Edward and making fried biscuits for her sisters, her chatty tone often suggesting informal speech rather than epistolary art. When she described using buffalo chips as fuel on the prairie, she imagined that sister Harriet "will make a face at this, but if she was here she would be glad to have her supper cooked at any rate, in this scarce timber country." Most often, she thought of talking to her mother. "Now Mother if I was with you by the fireside, I would relate a scene that would amuse you." She sent many messages to particular friends and relations at home and asked about their news.

Some matters were too private to share with everyone, and she held them back. But even though there were "many things which I cannot write," Narcissa's journal and letters suggested much about her character and concerns. Her energy, resilience, and interest in what was going on around her come through clearly. So too do feelings that she only unconsciously revealed, misgivings about her vocation, an increasing ambivalence about the Indians she had come to save. A close reading of her journal also shows that, like most Protestant missionaries and many later apostles for the American way of life, Narcissa was so tightly enmeshed in her own culture and so sure of its verities that she was ill prepared for the realities of working in another with very different values and mores.

During the early days of traveling, however, the destination seemed very far away. To her surprise, Narcissa's worries about the rigors of travel proved groundless. As she steamed west, she discovered not toil and privation but diversion and novelty. She was delighted by the boat's "passing so rapidly down the waters of the beautiful river," the "varied scenes . . . [and] beautiful landscapes." The accommodations were good, sometimes excellent, with "enough to eat," and "servants, who stand at our elbows ready to supply every want." When the boat stopped, there were curiosities to see and to collect.

Narcissa was finding the trip an exciting adventure. Upon leaving Pittsburgh, there were moments of high drama when the missionaries' steamboat jockeyed with another vessel for position on the river, and the passengers feared that "injury would be done by their coming in contact." But luckily the missionaries' boat avoided harm, and "we passed her unhurt." In Cincinnati, she heard the famous Presbyterian churchman Lyman Beecher preach. Having grown up thinking of Beecher as one of the great men of the day, she was amazed to discover him merely ordinary in his person. "Dr. B. appears the same in the pulpit that he does at a distance—I mean he is a small man, quite indifferent in his appearance, I could hardly believe it was he when I saw him come."

Narcissa wanted her family to visualize the interesting aspects of the trip. So she listed for them the items purchased for the journey: the life preservers, plates, knives, forks, and tin cups. As she told sister Mary Ann, she would provide a more vivid picture of prairie travel later. "When we are under way, I will describe the whole process to you. When I see it before my eyes & can give a better description, for I shall have a better understanding."

There were even incidents that Narcissa included to suggest that the trip had its humorous moments. Sometimes the amusement was mostly in retrospect and probably appreciated by only her family. Sometimes, the fun was more immediate. Western speech was, in Narcissa's opinion, "singular . . . I could scarcely understand them, yet very amusing. In speaking of quantity they say 'heap of money, heap of water, she is heap sick, &c.'"

While Narcissa never came right out and said so, she was gratified by all the attention directed at the band of missionaries. The "deep interest . . . taken in the missions" on the Sabbath spent in Cincinnati spilled over to include herself. Detailing how "especially our two Indian youths attracted the gaze and admiration of a crowd on Sabbath evening," she hinted that the missionary women so bravely heading west also received their share of admiring gazes. Another "most delightful" Sabbath spent in Chester, Illinois, inspired that town's aged minister to declare, according to Narcissa, that the mission family's presence "seemed like angels' visits." She made sure to tell her family when the abolitionist Elijah Lovejoy visited Marcus with an invitation for dinner and his intention to publish news of their wedding in the newspaper. Throughout the trip, Narcissa artlessly suggested how much she enjoyed attention each time she described how people made much of her. The fuss served as a form of approval of her new status and the choice she had made. But it also reassured Narcissa that she enjoyed the affection and appreciation she had always craved and not always been able to find in her large family.

Narcissa was in good spirits, but by the time she reached St. Louis at the end of March, she was hoping for a letter from "home, home, sweet home, and the friends I love." Though she tried to convince herself that she "was not sad" when there was no news, she was obviously homesick. Her disappointment was natural, but the seemingly inexplicable negligence set off old fears. "Why have they not written, seeing it is the very last, last time they will have to cheer my heart," she wondered. In an attempt to stifle her feelings, she declared that her mind was "completely occupied with present duty and passing events."

Narcissa had never been very far from home, and the journal shows her first reactions to new people, new places, and an unfamiliar culture. In Prattsburg, she had learned to use strict evangelical norms of behavior and belief to evaluate others. Faced with diversity for the first time in her life, like many other travelers, she turned to familiar standards as she sorted out her impressions.

As committed Christians, the missionaries were under no illusions that they were ordinary Americans. On shipboard, thrown in with all sorts of people, Narcissa began her journal by noting that the mission party held itself somewhat aloof, having "a stateroom where we can be as retired as we wish." The decision to spend the Sabbath on shore rather than on the steamship further indicated the distance the missionaries felt from the other passengers. "We felt it our duty not to travel on the Sab. and determined to leave the boat altho many on board tryed to persuade us to remain and to have preaching . . . and of the number one was a Presbyterian minister from New York." At each stop along the way to the frontier, the party eagerly sought out the company of sympathetic evangelicals.

It was in St. Louis that Narcissa confronted one of the most troubling and revealing experiences of those early weeks. The ABCFM agent for Illinois and Missouri called on her and took her to visit the handsome classical revival Roman Catholic cathedral. A high mass was in progress, and the service shocked Narcissa. "I wish I could describe the feelings I had in viewing their worship, if it may be so called," she wrote. Her sense of not being able to describe what she was feeling soon became a theme in Narcissa's writing. When she experienced powerful emotions, as she did at the cathedral, she often could not or would not analyze them. What lay behind this pattern of avoidance of what Narcissa was actually feeling can only be surmised. Here, in St. Louis, her general attitude was hardly in question. Like most evangelical Protestants, she regarded Catholicism with distaste. The mass struck her as "a form of idolatry." But she took in all its sensuous details, the altar boys, the embroidered robes, the golden staff, the music "of a character . . . very different from our church tunes," some sung by nuns "in an unknown tongue . . . sound without articulation." Altogether, she concluded, "splendor and show characterized the place."

Narcissa's response to the service owed much to the standards of the Prattsburg Presbyterian community. But it may be that her intolerance was connected to the strict and controlled way in which she had been raised, as modern studies on the origins of prejudice suggest. And it is possible that her condemnation of the sensuous nature of the mass was related to the attraction that fleshly things held for her, that she was attributing to others tastes and impulses that she found unacceptable in herself. If so, her revulsion during the service reveals more about her fears than it does about the flaws of the Catholic worshipers.

Narcissa's response to a faith closer to her own than any Indian religion also suggests that at some level she believed that people knowingly embraced error. She did acknowledge that the young altar boys were not responsible for their training "in such a school of destruction," and that "dellicate [sic] fingers . . . had been employed innocently perhaps" in "preparing vestments for such hypocritical characters." But her concluding reflection revealed a tendency to blame disbelievers for their disbelief and conveyed her righteous certainty in the Protestant way. "What cause of gratitude, have I that I am not of the number who *willfully* shut my eyes to the truth, *deceiving* and being *deceived*."

During these first few weeks of traveling toward the frontier, as Narcissa was seeing many new places and people, some of them shocking, she was also falling in love with her new husband. The missionary engagement was not supposed to resemble that of secular couples, and Narcissa had accepted its limitations. But she was not immune to the notion that an affectionate courtship was appropriate. Now on shipboard, Narcissa revelled in Marcus's company as the two talked, strolled on the deck, or admired the scenery. Like other middle-class women, she hoped for a loving marriage and a companionable intimacy, something that, though she did not yet recognize it, her new husband was not well equipped to provide. For the time being, she was happy, so happy that she actually regretted it when Henry Spalding interrupted their evening walk with his summons to evening prayers. She concluded Marcus was "one of the kindest Husbands and the very best [in] every way," "so excellent." Narcissa found the first year of her marriage one of her happiest.

She said nothing about her introduction to sex. It would have been surprising if she found it pleasurable. After years of conditioning about the virtue of female purity and chastity, many nineteenth-century brides found it difficult to enjoy sexual relations with their husbands. Some may not have expected much gratification, so used were they to thinking of themselves as asexual. Whatever Narcissa's experience was, it did not diminish her general satisfaction with her husband and her wish to share it, to "whisper in Mother's ear. . . . If I could only see her in her room for one half hour."

Narcissa admired her husband's competence and energy, his kindness and consideration for her comfort. She liked the way he took the lead and pictured herself as being sheltered under his wing. At a time when some ministers' and missionaries' wives were expanding the definition of a woman's role in a clerical marriage, Narcissa was not seeking a partnership. Not only did Narcissa accept Marcus's desires and priorities as more important than her own, but she also conceded moral leadership to him. Dependent on and missing her mother's guidance, she allowed Marcus to play Clarissa's part. "He is just like Mother in telling me my failings," she wrote. "He does it in such a way that I like to have him, for it gives me a chance to improve." While she did not always "confide in his judgment and act under him," as she ruefully admitted when she gathered prickly pears against his advice, she allowed Marcus to become her instructor and guide.

In the early weeks of travel, her emotional satisfaction with Marcus was more apparent than the mutual commitment that had drawn them together. She rarely mentioned the missionary imperative. Her diary does not suggest that she was thinking much about the future, wondering, as was Henry Spalding, about her worthiness for the task ahead, or meditating, as was Eliza, on religious matters. Nor were the "benighted heathen" whom she hoped to save much in her thoughts, at least as she wrote them down. Rather, she told Jane, "if you want to be happy, get a good husband as I have got and be a missionary."

Although Narcissa was putting Marcus in her mother's place and leaning on him as she had on her mother, the new relationship did not entirely compensate for the absence of her family, as her disappointment over finding no letters in St. Louis so clearly indicates. Marcus had early learned about loss when his mother had sent him off after his father's death and had lived on his own for years. Narcissa had had neither of these experiences. While her brother Stephen's abandonment of his family had been embarrassing and perhaps shameful, Narcissa was not particularly close to him, and it was not traumatic. Her absences from home had been of short duration. Now Narcissa was assailed by loneliness, especially for "Dear, Dear Mother" to whom she addressed her journal and referred regularly. Frequent comments about her younger siblings, especially Jane, Harriet, and Edward, suggest how she longed for them and the easy intimacy of family life, the shared conversations, perhaps while resting in a cool room in the heat of the day or sitting in mother's room for a chat. She could visualize such scenes so vividly that she forgot the present altogether.

Missionary tales suggested that women like Harriet Newell who left their families in order to do God's work were especially valiant. Although Narcissa was attracted to heroic images, it was an indication of how closely tied she was to her family that she was already thinking at the beginning of April of how they might be reunited. She imagined them joining her. "Mary [Ann], I wish you were with us. You would be happy as I am . . . . I think it would do your health good as well as [your husband] Lyman and Brother J.G. too."

Like many later female emigrants, Narcissa had "peculiar" feelings as she passed "the very borders of civilization" after leaving St. Louis in early April. It was at this point in the trip that women confronted the full meaning of leaving home. Here, as familiar signs of life disappeared, Narcissa realized the import of her decision to become a missionary. No delightful shipboard comforts, no servants standing at her elbow to offer her tempting dishes could distract her.

Ordinary women were free to admit in their journals how sad they were to leave family, friends, and home behind, but like most missionary women, Narcissa could not express herself so openly. Her letters would be read at home and in monthly concerts; others would pray for her success and admire her unfaltering conviction. Jane would have her journal published. The constraints on expression must have made it one of the trials of missionary life and made it all the more difficult for those who had chosen it.

While there was no way Narcissa could directly acknowledge her feelings, they often slipped out indirectly. Had she been aware of how revealing her omissions and denials were, she probably would have monitored herself even more carefully than she did. She would have been dismayed to realize that, at what she considered to be the border of civilization, her misgivings and doubts about the future were implicit in her reassurances to her family. "I have not one feeling of regret at the step which I have taken but count it a privilege to go forth in the name of my Master," she announced. She would make similar statements over and over again. "I often think of my Dear Parents but do not regret coming." Had she not been apprehensive about her future, denials would hardly have been necessary.

Narcissa's journal was pointedly silent on some things. In mid-March, the mission party had joined Henry and Eliza Spalding in Cincinnati. After the frantic efforts Marcus had undertaken to ensure that the Spaldings would join the Oregon mission, Narcissa surprisingly devoted few words to the meeting. "Found Brother Spalding. Said he had been waiting for us anxiously for a fortnight." Later, in the same diary entry, which covered an eleven-day period, she mentioned that Henry Spalding, on March 26, had "preached in the forenoon."

This reticence was certainly not based on the fact that the Spaldings had no interesting news to communicate. In fact, Henry had met the painter George Catlin in Pittsburgh, and the two men had discussed the mission and the danger of taking white women west. Spalding reported to the ABCFM that Catlin had been positive about the success of the mission "if we begin right. Says they are doubtless the most friendly, interesting Indians in the continent." Catlin had been less sanguine about taking white women west, for he thought their presence would provoke "unrestrained passion" among the Indians. Eliza, however, was undaunted and determined to trust in God and go forward. Narcissa included none of this interesting information in her diary. Nor did she mention Eliza until April 4, two and a half weeks after the two couples had met.

The silence about Eliza was curious. Eliza's upbringing was quite similar to Narcissa's own. She had spent much of her life in New York State and had attended academies and taught school. Converted during a revival at the age of nineteen, Eliza had, like Narcissa, dreamed of a becoming a missionary. At the urging of a friend living in Prattsburg, she had begun corresponding with Henry. It led to courtship and marriage.

Unlike Narcissa, who had stayed at home and awaited the leadings of Providence, Eliza had seriously and actively prepared for a missionary life. While Henry attended Lane Theological Seminary in Cincinnati, Eliza kept boarders, found time to study Greek and Latin, and listened to Lyman Beecher's weekly lectures on theology. The Spalding household became the center for a group of young people who wished to devote their lives to the missionary cause. When the two applied to the American Board, Cincinnati minister Artemas Bullard judged Eliza to be "one of the best women for a missionaries wife with whom I am acquainted." Eliza's history and vocation should have made her a sympathetic figure for Narcissa, especially since she was lonely for female companionship.

Actually, it was Narcissa's misfortune to be paired with such an unusually gifted and single-minded missionary, if only because historians have compared her with Eliza and found her wanting. The fervor of her new companion was, in fact, Narcissa's first missionary trial. Eliza's qualifications and intense spirtuality surpassed Narcissa's (and many other women who went to the mission field) and suggested a greater and more independent commitment to the mission cause. Narcissa had had many reasons over the years to see herself as qualified to be a missionary. Now Eliza's zeal raised questions about her vocation and perhaps even of her own inner resources for what lay ahead.

Narcissa could hardly help comparing herself with the saintly Eliza. Her rivalry with her younger sisters as she was growing up had nourished her sense of competition. Now Eliza's presence and her husband's behavior fueled competitive feelings. As the son of one of the later Oregon missionaries recollected, "Spalding liked to show off his wife, and Mrs. Whitman got the notion that he did it just [to] aggravate her." Artemas Bullard had also noted certain character traits that could have contributed to the awkwardness between the two women. Henry was "sometimes too much inclined to denounce or censure those who are not as zealous and ardent as himself." In this case, he might well have found Narcissa neither so zealous nor so ardent as his wife.

The nature and pattern of Narcissa's comments revealed the rivalry she felt. Her first reference to Eliza was her longest. After reporting on her own good health, she assessed her chances of bearing the strains of the trip. "I think I shall endure the journey well, perhaps better than any of the rest of us." Her thoughts then turned to Eliza, who in contrast, "does not look nor feel quite healthy enough for our enterprise." She continued, "Riding affects her differently from what it does me. Everyone who sees me compliments me as being the best able to endure the journey over the mountains from my looks." In the area of physical fitness at least, Narcissa could feel confident of herself.

After having affirmed her own superiority, Narcissa characterized Eliza as "resolute, no shrinking with her. She possesses good fortitude. I like her very much. She wears well upon acquaintance." She followed this positive assessment with more ambivalent judgments. Eliza was "very suitable" and had just "the right temperament to match" Henry. Considering past relationships between Henry and Narcissa and his negative comments about going west with her, Narcissa's evaluation could just as well have been derogatory as complimentary. Finally, Narcissa ended with extravagant praise of Marcus. "I have such a good place to shelter, under my husband's wings." The comparison between the two men was implicit but obvious: Marcus was strong, Henry was not. In the Spaldings' marriage, Eliza had the fortitude, not her husband, which would have been more appropriate. Narcissa was the lucky one, with a "good husband," cherished, happy, and protected.

Elsewhere in the journal, Narcissa made other references to the Spaldings—that the entire party, including the Spaldings and Whitmans, would sleep in the same tent at night, that Henry preached, or that Eliza and Narcissa shared a wagon or canoe. But in comparison with overland diaries written by women later, in which the female circle figured so importantly, this journal contains very little about Eliza, who was her sole white female companion after the ABCFM missionaries assigned to the Pawnee station departed. Whatever Narcissa felt, it was certainly not the easy intimacy she had enjoyed with her female relatives and friends.

More puzzling is the long silence about Martha Satterlee. Her illness had caused the Whitmans and Emeline Palmer to delay in Pennsylvania early in the trip. While Martha had recovered enough to continue the journey, she had not been well. The waters of the Ohio gave her diarrhea; she improved during the few days in Cincinnati, then began to fail as the party steamed toward St. Louis. Only on April 4, a full month after the Whitmans had joined the Satterlees and Emmeline Palmer, did Narcissa mention having "a sick one with us all the way. . . . Mrs. Satterlee has had a very bad cough and cold which has left her feeble. She is now recovering and is as well as can be expected. She is en famalle [sic]."

Several days later, the missionaries, including the ailing woman, left St. Louis and steamed onward toward Liberty, Missouri. Here, they were joined by William Gray, a "good teacher, cabinet maker and housejoiner, from Utica," whom the ABCFM had recruited at the last minute to assist the mission. The party spent several weeks procuring supplies and livestock for the overland journey. Eliza and Narcissa made a tent for sleeping on the way.

Martha Satterlee probably had tuberculosis, and in Liberty it became apparent that she was dying. Henry Spalding, William Gray, the two Indian boys, and two hired hands had already set out with the stock and wagons to meet up with the American Fur Company, with whom the missionaries expected to travel to that year's rendezvous. Marcus was planning to put Eliza and Narcissa on a steamboat that would take them up the Missouri to join the American Fur Company at Belleview and then overtake Spalding and Gray at Fort Leavenworth. Left to minister to Martha, then, were the Whitmans, Eliza, Martha's husband, and the newly married Allis couple. One of them had to inform the young woman that she would die, for she "had thought she should recover." All sat around her bed to sing hymns, question her about her faith, to read the Bible, to pray. Late in the evening of April 30, as Eliza wrote in her diary, "after affectionately exhorting us to be faithful in our Master's service, she bade us farewel [sic] . . . [and] fell asleep (we trust) in the arms of Jesus."

Martha Satterlee's death was one of the missionaries' first examples of what their sacrifice might entail. Marcus wrote of the incident to the ABCFM, as did Dr. Satterlee. Eliza mentioned Martha's ill health several times in her journal and described her moving death. But Narcissa was silent until late October. Writing to Mrs. Parker, an Ithaca friend of Martha's, from Fort Vancouver, Narcissa made her second reference to Martha. "Never was I so rent at the death of any one," she said. "Our care of her on the way, and at Liberty, Mo. enlisted us in her, and when we came to give her up to die, it was like a sister taken away."

If her affection for Martha was so strong, it is surprising that Narcissa hardly mentioned her in the journal and travel letters. It is possible, of course, that a letter did not survive in which she discussed the illness or that Narcissa was too preoccupied with novelty of the

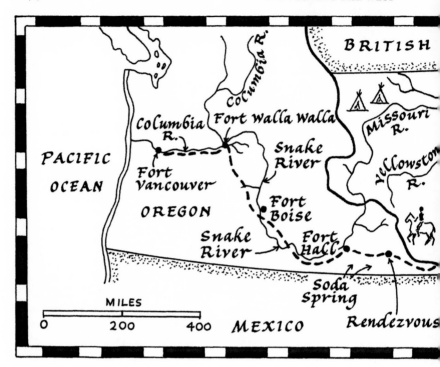

The missionaries' route west.

trip to pay much attention to Martha Satterlee. Certainly she was caught up in the excitement and gratification of courtship, which must have made it hard to think much about the other missionaries. But it is also possible that she did not want to worry her family by talking of the death of the young missionary wife, or that the reality of a missionary's "heroic" ending filled her with such powerful emotions that she chose not to record them.

The day after Martha Satterlee's death, the missionaries held her funeral. As the service began, the fur company steamboat, which Narcissa and Eliza were to take to Belleview, came into view. The missionaries hailed it, but the captain, shouting that the boat could take no more passengers, refused to put ashore.

Dismay and frustration mingled as the missionaries saw the boat disappear from view, but they continued with the funeral service.

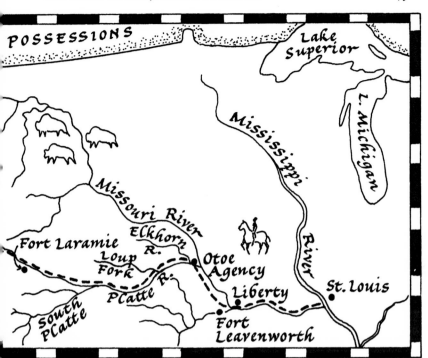

They were stranded in Liberty without any transportation. The American Fur Company would, most likely, set off to the yearly rendezvous without them. The trip across the prairies was considered too dangerous to undertake without protection. After so much effort, the missionaries might not get to Oregon in 1836 after all.

Marcus was determined not to fail. He hastily hired a team for the baggage and horses for Narcissa and Eliza. The three began the arduous trip that Marcus had hoped the women would not have to undertake. He expected to catch up with Henry Spalding and Gray at Fort Leavenworth, where Spalding had agreed to wait for him. But when the party arrived, they discovered that the men had already gone onto the prairie. Marcus was understandably provoked by Henry's thoughtlessness.

It took nine days of hard traveling, with the women riding horseback and sleeping out in the open for most of that time, before the party was reunited. Despite the need to press on, the missionaries agreed to spend Sunday, May 15, in camp. This satisfied their consciences, but since the fur caravan left Belleview on that same day, the stopover made it even more unlikely that they would overtake the company.

There were further problems. Marcus was called away to care for a sick man at the Otoe Indian Agency and rode on ahead to the American Fur Company camp to ask them to delay. The caravan's leader, Thomas Fitzpatrick, told Marcus that he planned to break camp within three days. Hurrying back to meet the others at the Platte River with this hopeful news, Marcus found no one there. The missionaries had lost their way and did not reach the Platte until the following day. Crossing the river turned out to be a far greater ordeal than anyone had anticipated. The water was high, and it took time to get stock and wagons across.

Narcissa shared the perplexity of the rest of the party, although it was the men's responsibility to deal with the difficulties. Here was a trial indeed, the first about which she wrote, and she was only an onlooker. She did not find it easy to observe "husband . . . so completely exhausted with swimming the river . . . that it was with difficulty he made the shore the last time swimming it." The pleasant evening strolls and chats with her husband were things of the past. Henry was sick, the hired men "good for nothing."

The next few days were exhausting as the missionaries forded several more "difficult streams" and pushed themselves and their stock hard. One night's supper was nothing more than a cup of milk. "Our blankets upon our saddles with our Indian rubber cloaks was all we wished for bed," Narcissa wrote.

Finally, at one o'clock in the morning, on May 26, just at the point in Nebraska where the traders would pass the Pawnee villages, the Oregon-bound missionaries caught up with the fur company. They had been traveling hard since the beginning of May.

Life took on a less frantic pace. The missionaries were now in a large company, which Narcissa aptly described as "really a moving village—nearly four hundred animals with ours, mostly mules and seventy men." There were nine wagons, all told, and one cart. To her brother, she wrote, "Now E. if you wish to see the camp in motion, look away ahead and see first the pilot and the Captain Fitz-

patrick, just before him—next the pack animals, all mules loaded
with great packs—soon after you will see the waggons and in the
rear our company. We all cover quite a space. The pack mules always
string along one after the other just like Indians."

This part of the overland route took the travelers over the rolling
prairies along the Platte River in present-day Nebraska. The two
women had contrary responses to the landscape. Narcissa, who was
intrigued with describing people and animals, found it "mostly barren," while the contemplative Eliza thought it "delightful country"
and was struck with its "beautiful flowers and roses . . . delightful
scenery to the eye of the traveler."

Late May marked the real beginning of overland-trail life for the
missionaries. In many ways, Narcissa's travel experience was like that
of the thousands of women who would go west later across these
same trails. She rose early "to get our breakfast in a hurry and eat it"
and was ready to start "usually at six—travel till eleven, encamp, rest
and feed, start again about two—travel until six . . . then encamp for
the night." Probably she did much of the unloading and loading of
the wagons, unpacking and packing up what was needed for eating
and sleeping. As she told her mother, "Since we have been in the
prairie, we have done all our cooking." She had to learn by trial and
error how to prepare food out of doors, finding it awkward at first,
but "very easy" once accustomed to it. The buffalo dung for fuel had
to be gathered. She washed under the beating sun only three times
during the trip and gathered berries along the trail to supplement
the daily diet.

Like many emigrant women, Narcissa prided herself on her ability
to use her domestic skills in the wilderness. "Tell Mother," she told
Harriet and Edward, "I am a very good housekeeper in the prairie.
I wish she could just take a peep at us while we are sitting at our
meals." Dinner, though taken on the ground, offered some opportunity for laughter, for "it is the fashion of all this country to imitate
the Turks" by reclining to eat. The setting featured a rubber table-
cloth, tin dishes, and iron spoons and knives. The missionaries took
breakfast and supper in the tent that she and Eliza had made in
Liberty.

While Narcissa was not enthralled by prairie landscape, like many
later overland travelers, she duly admired the wonders of the trip and
the trail's curiosities. She found the first sight of buffalo especially

memorable, so much so that "Sister Spaulding and myself got out of the waggon and ran upon the bluff to see him. Husband was quite willing to gratify our curiosity since it was the first."

In some respects, Narcissa's trip was easier than it would be for many later emigrants. Traveling with a sizable company of trappers and traders who were familiar with the terrain and its inhabitants provided many advantages for the missionaries. Day and night the company posted guard, which protected the "animals from the approach of Indians who would steal them" and which gave the missionaries security from real or imagined dangers. In the company experienced hands hunted for the abundant wild game. Instead of the ubiquitous bacon, beans, and coffee of later years, the party lived on fresh and then dried buffalo meat for some weeks. The diet initially pleased Narcissa, who wrote, "I never saw anything like buffalo meat to satisfy hunger. We do not want any thing else with it." The missionaries' cows also provided fresh milk, which Narcissa pointed out "is a luxury in this country."

Because there were so many men, the women did not have to take on male tasks as the trip wore on. Men herded the livestock, stood guard, and drove the wagons. Narcissa and Eliza rode in the wagons as passengers for much of time, although they had horses and side saddles. The men took over some of the cooking. The women baked, but Marcus was the expert at preparing buffalo meat. "He has a different way for every different piece of meat," Narcissa reported. "I ha[ve had but little] to do with cooking."

The caravan also provided Narcissa with compensation for the lack of female companionship. As Narcissa told her family, there were several gentlemen in the group who were "going over the Mountains for pleasure." With their servants, dogs, and "extra fine horses," the Englishman and Scottish nobleman were certainly the grandest people she had ever met. The foreigners and the gentleman from St. Louis made themselves agreeable to the women. While William Gray found one of the men lacking signs of "mental improvement" and judged the gentleman from St. Louis "a gallant," Narcissa was impressed and flattered by their attention. "We had a few of them to tea with us last Monday eve," she reported, obviously pleased with such presentable guests.

After the exhausting effort to catch up with the fur company, Narcissa was once again finding the trip pleasurable. Her resilience returned. She concluded, "Our manner of living is far preferable to any in the States. I never was so contented and happy before." Her health was better than it had been for years. The route itself was "astonishing," and "I think I may say easier traveling here than on any turnpike in the [States]." Even though the wagon had no springs, seats on the baggage provided ample cushioning from the shocks of the trail. Marcus considered this part of the journey difficult because of the need to keep the missionaries' cattle moving at the company's speed, but Narcissa found the pace tolerable. There was even a respite when the caravan paused for eight days at Fort Laramie. Narcissa was finding herself far more comfortable than she had ever anticipated. As she wrote to Marcus's brother and wife, "We feel that the Lord has prospered us in our journey beyond our most sanguine expections."

One of her worries had been that she would go hungry during the months of travel. Instead, she found that there was plenty to eat and that even though the diet was restricted to buffalo meat, "I do not wish anything else." In one of her rare references to Eliza, she commented that the reliance on buffalo meat had adversely affected Sister S., however, who "has been quite sick."

Marcus still was the best husband in the world. He was always properly solicitous about her welfare and comfort. "If I had looked the world over I could not have found one more careful and better qualified to transport a female such a distance," she told her family. Sometime in mid-June, probably during the stop at Fort Laramie, which presumably afforded the couple some privacy, she became pregnant.

As the trip progressed, however, she discovered Marcus was not always willing to gratify her. Although she pressed him to correspond with her family, he wrote only "one hasty letter" to her parents. She excused him. He was very busy; she had "no disposition to complain." Her comment, however, suggested that she was annoyed at his intransigence.

For her part, she was learning the feminine strategies that were necessary when power relations were lopsided in marriage. Trouble began when Marcus decided to lighten the baggage by discarding his shirts, black suit, and overcoat. At first Narcissa "could not believe him in earnest," but she soon realized he was determined to get rid of his best clothes. Care for a husband's clothing was a wife's responsibility, and Narcissa attempted to exert her wifely authority. But "all the reasons" she could think of failed to move him. Only when she threatened to throw out all her own clothes and to write his sister, Julia, who would "plead" with Marcus, did her husband soften. "It would not do," he told Narcissa, "to act against or contrary to . . . [Julia's] wishes." This was not the only time that she had to appeal to others when she and her husband differed. She rallied assistance to keep Marcus relatively clean during the trip, William Gray reported, by taking "sides with Mr. Parker . . . and with the assistance of Mrs. Spalding."

Narcissa's journal during the weeks of June and early July focused on the daily events and experiences of trail life, rather than spiritual concerns or her calling. She did express gratitude for God's mercies in facilitating the journey and mentioned the missionaries' habit of daily "worship after sup & breakfast" as well as a refreshing visit with a Baptist missionary family on the prairies. But she gave few signs of introspection or intense spirituality. The absence of introspective writing does not mean that Narcissa did not reflect privately. But her habit of telling her family that they could better imagine her feelings or thoughts than she could describe them suggests that she was not very practiced in self-contemplation. Possibly she hoped her omissions would make her family think about her and what she might be experiencing.

On July 4 the caravan reached the South Pass of the Rocky Mountains. The first leg of the wilderness journey was almost over. That evening the missionaries had a scare when "some ten Indians and four or five white men, whose dress and appearance could scarcely be distinguished from that of Indians . . . came in sight over the hills . . . [and] all gave a yell, such as hunters and Indians only can give; whiz, whiz, came their balls over our heads." Fear gave away to relief when the travelers saw a white flag flying from one of the rider's guns. When the wild shouting and firing ended, the missionaries met the party who had ridden out from the rendezvous to give them this raucous welcome. Some of them were Nez Percé Indians whom Marcus had met the previous year, and the missionaries invited them to share their evening meal.

Two days later the caravan arrived at the Green River, in present-day Wyoming, the site of the rendezvous. Hundreds of Indians (largely from the Flathead, Nez Percé, Snake, and Bannock tribes) and perhaps two hundred whites (trappers, traders, and observers like the missionaries) encamped for this annual meeting. Narcissa had never seen anything remotely like this exotic gathering, but she wrote very little about it. Perhaps she was thinking of the instructions that the ABCFM had sent to Marcus as they were setting out. David Greene had warned that traders might be courteous and kind, or passionate and uncivil. "Let your conduct be unblameable, examplary & free from the appearance of evil," he counseled. "Do not feel it necessary to be the forward reproofer of everything wrong among this class of persons."

Others reported that Narcissa seemed pleased by the attention she received from the mountain men, who rarely saw white women. Twenty-six-year-old Joseph Meek went out of his way to spend time with her, and she enjoyed his adventurous tales and colorful company. Even though Henry Gray thought some of the "rough mountain hunter[s]" were "absolutely ridiculous" in the way they touched their hats to Narcissa, she took their admiration in good humor. As Gray concluded, "All the refined education and manners of the daughter of Judge Prentiss, of Prattsburg . . . found abundant opportunity to exhibit the cardinal ornaments of a religious and civilized country."

What Narcissa emphasized in her accounts of the ten days spent at the rendezvous was the opportunity it offered to do the Lord's work. Up until this point in the journey, her faith had given her strength and comfort, delight and rest. At home, however, her faith had been active; she had undertaken many "labours of love for His sake who has died for us." Now she was on familiar and seemingly safe ground; "Wherever we go we find opportunities of doing good." The traders and trappers were coming "for tracts & bibles. . . . We have given away all we have to spare." Once the men returned to their cabins they would have time for reflection and reading, "which might result in the salvation of their souls." Had the missionaries "packed one or two animals with bibles & testaments we should have had abundant opportunity of disposing of them." Whereas Gray saw Narcissa socializing, she reported herself laboring for the Lord. Both perspectives had some truth.

There was one other aspect of the rendezvous that impressed her deeply. In writing to one of Marcus's brothers and his wife, she related a particular that Marcus had failed to mention in his own letter home. Upon her arrival at the rendezvous, "I was met by a company of native women, one after the other, shaking hands and salluting me with a most hearty kiss. This was unexpected and affected me very much."

Up until this point, Narcissa had made very few references to Indians. Early on, she saw Indians only infrequently. But she did write about John and Richard, the Nez Percé boys, who were returning to the West with the Whitmans. She was "very much interested in the . . . lads," finding them affectionate, eager "to please us in every way." As time passed, she became increasingly attached to Richard, and Narcissa slipped comfortably into a maternal relationship with him. "He calls me Mother. I love to teach him, to take care of him and hear them talk."

In mid-June, still hastening after the fur caravan, the missionaries had encountered a large party of Pawnee Indians. Narcissa reported their surprise and pleasure at seeing white women. "Many of them had never seen any before." Later, other Pawnees visited them "both noon and night. We ladies were such a curiosity to them, they would come and stand around our tent—peer in and grin in their astonishment to see such looking objects." Narcissa's careful reporting suggests their interest and attention were far from burdensome. And the Indians made a favorable impression on her. "They are a noble Indian—large, athletic frames, dignified countenances bespeaking an immortale exhistance within." But the missionaries did not meet many other tribes on the prairies. Correctly, Eliza Spalding had concluded that "the natives who once roamed over these vast and delightful plains are fast fading away."

Now at the rendezvous, Narcissa again reported being "in the midst of [a] gazing throng" and hearing protestations of friendship. "They all like us and that we have come to live with them." Their courteous behavior helped to balance any anxiety stimulated by their wild greeting and the display mounted by hundreds of warriors "carrying their war weapons, bearing their war emblems and . . . implements of music . . . skins drawn over hoops with rattles and trickets to make a noise." She noted approvingly and perhaps with relief the polite way one of the chiefs introduced his wife, the "pleasing" meeting between Richard and John and their friends. "When they met each took off his hat and shook hands as respectful as in civilized life."

The rendezvous was Narcissa's first introduction to the Indian tribes she had come to save, and she was favorably impressed. But, pleased by her attentive male callers, she spent far less time with them than did Eliza. Fired by an unusually strong missionary vocation, Eliza was intent on learning the language quickly so she could begin her work. Not surprisingly, Eliza seemed to be a favorite of the women.

At the rendezvous, the missionaries had to decide how they would proceed to Oregon. They discussed the possibility of traveling with the Indians but were reluctant to subject their wagon to the rigors of the Indians' route. Moreover, the Indians were planning to do some hunting before returning home.

Luckily, a small group of Hudson's Bay traders, led by John McLeod and Thomas McKay, had come east to the rendezvous and agreed to escort the mission party to the company's post at Fort Walla Walla. John McLeod's hospitality impressed Narcissa the very day that the missionaries joined his camp. "On our arrival Mr McL came to meet us led us to his tent & gave us a supper which consisted of steak (Antelope) broiled ham biscuit & butter tea and loaf sugar brot from Wallah Wallah This we rellished verry much as we had not seen anything of the bread kind since the last of May." The missionaries were again in good hands.

About two hundred Indians had decided to accompany the expedition as far as Fort Hall (in present-day Idaho), which they reached on August 3, sixteen days after leaving the rendezvous. During this time, Narcissa was forming more definite impressions of the Indians, particularly of Indian women. Like most American missionaries, Narcissa never doubted that white Anglo-Saxon Protestant women enjoyed the highest status in the world. She pitied "the poor Indian women," who were always on the move, who had none of the comfort[s] that Narcissa so thoroughly enjoyed. Seeing them collecting wood, cooking food, pitching the lodges, packing and driving animals, she concluded that the women did all the work. John's father had given the missionaries "a few messes of Antelope," and Narcissa was eating dried buffalo meat purchased from the Indians. But like most whites, Narcissa did not consider hunting to be work. Indian women, she decided, were "complete slaves of their husbands."

Despite her disapproval and dismay at the women's apparent subserviency, Narcissa was "making some little progress in their language" and longed "to be able to converse with them about the Saviour." For their part, the Indians continued to appear eager, even "anxious to converse with us & to be understood by us."

After two weeks of traveling, the group arrived at Fort Hall on the Snake River. It was time for the Indians to depart. Now Narcissa saw a tiresome and less attractive side of Indian character. All were "exceedingly anxious" for the missionaries to continue on with them. The Indians used not only "every argument they can invent to prevail on us" but also "stratagem." Either weariness or disapproval led her to dismiss their appeal. "We all think it not best. We are very much fatigued & wish to get through as soon as possible."

After the rendezvous, the journey became more challenging for the travelers. While the Indians rode along with them, the party did not pause for a noon break, and Narcissa missed the opportunity to rest. Once the Indians had departed, the pace was slower but still exhausting. The route over the deserts of southern Idaho and the mountains of eastern Oregon was the most difficult part of the entire journey. The high sun of late July and August beat down on the humans and beasts alike. Now Narcissa found the trip tedious and the heat oppressive, and she felt almost sick from fatigue and the weather. Although the traders were skilled hunters and shared their game with the missionaries, there were times when Narcissa was hungry. And their staple—dried buffalo meat—no longer pleased her. Narcissa found it "so filthy" she could scarcely make herself eat it.

She worried about her husband's health. Marcus was driving himself hard, making great efforts to bring the cart safely into Oregon. Accidents were common, and potentially dangerous. On one occasion, "both the cart & mules were capsized in the water and the mules entangled in the harness . . . a desperate struggle to get them ashore." As she told her mother, "It is not very greatful to my feelings to see him wear out with such excessive fatigue as I am obliged to." At this point, she felt closer to her mother, whom she counted upon to know "what my feelings are," than to her husband who could not or would not take them seriously. As a result of his exertions, Marcus had a bout of what he diagnosed as rheumatism, making him so lame that he could scarcely move.

She became less sympathetic with the struggle with the cart. When its axle broke, she hoped that it would be left behind. She was careful to veil her wish in general language, however, so that she would not appear to be directly opposing her husband. But "our rejoycing was in vain," for the cart was repaired. "They are so resolute and untiring in their efforts they will probably succeed," she concluded.

Although she still insisted that she was content, Narcissa wondered whether she had the "patience to endure." At times she was finding it difficult to maintain the demeanor appropriate for a Christian female. "Long for rest, but must not murmer," she wrote on July 27. Occasionally, as in late August, she had moments of rebellion. Then she admitted that "sometimes my wicked heart has been disposed to murmer, thinking I should have no rest from the heat when I stoped [sic]." But her excellent husband always provided her with some shade, thus unknowingly reproving her "by the comfort and rest I received under these circumstances." Her determination, she insisted, did not waver. "I never have wished to go back. Such a thought finds no place in my heart."

Narcissa did not like privation, however—the absence of middle-class comforts such as good food and plenty of rest. As she did without, she fantasized about home—the "houses to shelter . . . from the scorching heat of the noon day sun," the "sofas on which to recline." She waxed enthusiastic about "Mother's bread & butter" and "pork & potatoes." All these things that she had taken for granted seemed especially desirable now.

Still, there were good moments as well—the occasions of good eating: "turnips & fried bread which was a luxury," or McLeod's present of "fresh Salmon, also a plate of fried cakes . . . Believe me I relish these." There were curiosities like Soda Springs to visit, berries to pick along the way. And there were cherished moments of privacy with Marcus. The best times for Narcissa involved talking about home and friends there. These moments of "sweet repast" "sweetly decoyed away" the "tedious hours."

There was the slightest hint, however, that even these sweet moments might have a sour side. A comment Narcissa made in a letter to Marcus's brother and his wife suggests that he may have thought Narcissa too attached to home. Perhaps he enjoyed the talk about Narcissa's home and friends, whom he knew only slightly, somewhat tiresome. Narcissa wrote that Marcus found her "a little selfish" in not writing to his relatives but always to Angelica. If there was implicit criticism and the suggestion of a lack of empathy, Narcissa chose not to make much of it. For Marcus had "been pressed above all measure with care, labours, and anxieties, all the way." The pattern of the overbusy husband whose work was so important that he stood above criticism was already being established.

As the trip grew arduous, each day calling for endurance and strength, Narcissa began to meditate more often on her faith and on the meaning of the journey. Hers was not an anxious soul. Her moments of religious satisfaction were "calm and peaceful" times when she felt a "sweet communion" with Christ, or "a freedom in prayer for my beloved Parents." Even on a Sabbath devoted to travel, she enjoyed "a melting sense" of Christ's presence that rested her soul and made her grateful for her privileged access to "a mercy seat." It strengthened her resolve. "It is good to feel that he is all I want & all my righteousness, & if I had ten thousand lives I would give them all to him. I long to be more like him, to possess more of his meek Spirit."

During the days and weeks after leaving the rendezvous, Narcissa began to picture the journey not just as an exciting adventure but as an event with a larger significance. Signs of God's favor became apparent in the events of daily life. Good grass for weary animals and presents of food from McLeod were indications that "the Lord provides and smooths all our way for us, giving us strength." An invitation to tea was yet another sign of blessings "gather[ing] thick around us." Even feeling strong and rested enough to survive a difficult ride suggested the promise "Lo I am with you alway." The band of missionaries she likened to the ancient Israelites, following the pillar of cloud by day and of fire by night. "Was there ever a journey like this, performed where the sustaining hand of God has been so manifest every moment?" she asked herself.

Her own part in this heavenly drama became clearer. She offered a revealing insight into her vocation with her comment that her parents had offered their daughter as a sacrifice "for his Name Sake," a sacrifice Narcissa hoped would prove acceptable. Although she was not the only member of the mission party, Narcissa began to visualize herself as a "weary and solitary Missionary." But while she was imagining herself as part of a missionary drama, the character of the drama itself was still vague and uncertain. None of the missionaries had spent enough time with the Indians to allow them to understand what missionary work might entail.

The final weeks of traveling were interrupted by two stops. In early August, the party spent a day and a half at Fort Hall, on the Snake River, in present-day Idaho. Like later trail travelers, Narcissa found herself immensely cheered when the fort came into view, for "Any thing that looks like a house makes us glad." She delighted in the hospitality and relative civilization and provided all the details for her family—the delicious dinner, the "cool retreat of an upper room," the garden, even the "stools to sit on," perhaps not so good as the "very comfortable chairs" at Fort Laramie, but still a luxury.

About two weeks later, the party arrived at Snake Fort, located on the Boise River. This was Mr. McKay's post, and they received a "hearty welcome," lingering for several days to wash and rest.

There Marcus left the cart. The animals were so weak that they might not be able to pull it over the Blue Mountains, which lay ahead. Narcissa regretted abandoning the cart after having "taken it so near through." Now she was realizing what "a useful article [it was] in this country."

On August 26, soon after leaving Snake Fort, the Spaldings and Whitmans parted company. The Spaldings, with the help of hired men and a Nez Percé, planned to bring the animals slowly over the mountains and down to the Hudson's Bay trading post, Fort Walla Walla, while the Whitmans and Mr. McLeod moved at a faster pace toward their destination. The separation, Narcissa explained, was a practical one. But more than a concern for the animals was involved. The couples wanted to be apart for a few days. Tension and conflict had simmered during the long months of travel and flared out into the open on several occasions.

All the missionaries concealed the signs of strife. Narcissa, who realized that many people might read her journal and who was, consciously or unconsciously, justifying her decision for a missionary life, avoided mention of any friction between the two couples. Acknowledging conflict or angry feelings could damage the mission cause and tarnish her own commitment. Eliza's journal was silent about relations between the four missionaries. Nor did letters from Henry and Marcus to the ABCFM draw attention to the personal difficulties of the mission party. Only in 1840 did Henry Gray tell the ABCFM that the two men had three serious quarrels during the journey.

Personality differences certainly contributed to tensions. While many have blamed Henry Spalding for most of the mission's problems, all of the missionaries were joined together in the new relationship, which they likened to a family. Just as no one member of a family causes all of a family's problems, but rather each person is involved by virtue of his or her position and role within the family, no one missionary caused the mission's difficulties. Marcus had plenty of reason to be exasperated and short tempered with Henry Spalding, whose poor judgment had almost prevented the party from meeting up with the American Fur Company. Narcissa, loyal to her husband, "one of the best the world ever knew," shared his perspective and was no admirer of Henry herself. Eliza's sickness and frailty were a burden for the others, while her piety and missionary zeal were a silent rebuke to Narcissa. Narcissa's love of company and desire for attention raised questions in Henry Gray's and probably Henry Spalding's minds.

Beyond personality differences were structural problems in the mission family. In a real family, each person occupies a particular position that carries with it certain expectations about role and function. While issues of power and authority are often not entirely resolved, it is generally acknowledged that parents are entitled to make the important decisions while the children are young and to resolve conflict between them. In the mission family, however, members called each other "Brother" and "Sister," a form of salutation that suggested only the basic gender distinction—men could vote in mission meetings while women could not. But no hierarchy other than that of gender existed, and the allocation of power was unclear. Decisions were supposed to be reached in the spirit of Christian love and harmony. But if there were disagreements among the missionaries, who would establish mission goals and policy? Henry, the only ordained minister, or Marcus, the organizer?

These troublesome issues were put aside for the time being as the Spaldings and Whitmans went on toward their destination separately. For Narcissa, the last few days of traveling into eastern Oregon were especially pleasurable. Since leaving civilization, she had found most of the scenery indifferent. Now as the party approached the Grande Ronde Valley, where the Cayuse and Nez Percé tribes gathered camas root, and then the Blue Mountains, she found scenes to delight her senses. The valley, with its great ponderosa pines and coursing stream, was "a beautiful place." The Blue Mountains, "covered with timber through which we rode all the afternoon," was a most "agreeable change."

The key to Narcissa's response was that the landscape was familiar. "The scenery reminded me of the hills in my native county Steuben" and home. "I frequently met old acquaintances," she wrote, "in the trees & flowers & was not a little delighted. Indeed I do not know as I was ever so much affected with any scenery in my life. The singing of the birds, the echo of the voices of my fellow travelers, as they were scattered through the woods, all had a strong resemblance to bygone days."

Despite the repeated protestations that she was glad that she had come and her growing sense of herself as a missionary, she had natural regrets about the wisdom of her choice. Home and homelike things moved her powerfully. Recollections diverted her attention from the present and perhaps kept her from thinking about the future responsibility, which was relentlessly coming closer and closer. She explained to her mother how restless and weak she had felt during these days. "But see! how I have been diverted with the scenery and carried out of myself in conversation about home & friends."

On September 1, after a breakfast of cold duck and coffee, the Whitmans hastened toward "the desired haven" of Fort Walla Walla at a gallop. The long journey was over. In Gray's opinion, "Mrs. Whitman has indured the journey like a heroine." Although she once again suggested that her family could better imagine her feelings than she could describe them, Narcissa's excitement and delight at the end of months of travel were apparent. She reveled in civilization and its comforts. She first noted the garden two miles from the fort, "the first appearance of civilization"; the salutations of Mr. McLeod, Mr. Pambrun, "the gentleman of the house," and others; then the delight of sitting in "cushioned armed chairs." The ample breakfast of fresh salmon, potatoes, tea, bread, and butter," which followed, the barnyard animals—hens, turkeys, hogs, and goats—the room with its beds, feasts of melon—she itemized them all. Finally, there was dinner of "pork, potatoes, beets, cabbage, turnips, tea, bread & butter, my favorite dinner, and much like the last dinner I eat [ate] with Mother Loomis."

The next day, Narcissa informed her mother, she was unpacking and then repacking her trunk for a visit to the Hudson's Bay Company's major trading post, Fort Vancouver. Marcus was going to consult with the company's powerful chief factor, John McLoughlin, and she wished to be with him. The trip by water would be agreeable, and she felt remarkably well rested and vigorous. Indeed, she was "as well able to engage in any domestic employment as I ever did in my life."

When the Spaldings came up the following day, Narcissa's thoughts turned to the goal of her trip, still somewhat vague in her mind. "Surely my heart is ready to leap for joy, at the thought of being so near the long desired work of teaching the benighted ones a knowledge of a Savior." Thanksgiving and dedication to the future characterized the Sabbath spent at the fort. "Feel to dedicate my[self] renewedly & unreservedly to his service, among the heathen & may

Narcissa found Fort Walla Walla, here sketched by Paul Kane as it appeared in 1846, an oasis of comfort and hospitality after the rigors of the trip west. Stark Museum of Art, Orange, Texas. Stark WWC62; CR IV-355.

the Lords hand be as evidently manifest in blessing our labours among them as it has been in bringing us here."

The entire mission party decided to go to Fort Vancouver, since it was necessary to wait for the Indians to return from their summer hunt before choosing locations. The trip down the Columbia River was a "pleasant change," reminding Narcissa of her travels on the Ohio five months earlier.

The missionaries took almost a week to reach Fort Vancouver. During the voyage, Narcissa had another opportunity to study the Indians, who, she had been encouraged to believe, were eager for salvation. Her views became progressively less favorable. The Indians who were assisting the party in making portage did remind her of pictures she had seen at home. But unlike Indians in a picture, these real Indians were intrusive, and she no longer was so pleased with their attention as she had been at the rendezvous. She was glad to reembark and move further down the river "to get away from a throng of Indians." Eliza, who also wrote about the Indians they saw along the river, found the natives wretched enough. But her burning zeal inspired her with the hope that they might "soon be blest with the light of the Gospel of our Lord . . . & with the means for securing a more comfortable subsistence for this life."

It was not long before Narcissa had the chance to observe the Flatheads, the very tribe featured in the stirring article published in the *Christian Advocate* in 1833. Months before, Narcissa had found the Pawnee Indians noble, with signs of immortal life within. Now she was not impressed. The Flatheads' "eyes have a dull & heavy expression." The habit of binding infants' heads was pitiful, cruel, and self-indulgent, done only "to please a father and mother." It was obvious to her that Indians lacked normal family feelings. Twice she wrote about the shocking story of a baby buried alive by its grandfather.

Narcissa was experiencing her first round of culture shock. Certain sights made her shudder, increasing her awareness of being "on heathen ground." Even Richard and John, left behind at Fort Walla Walla, began to figure differently in her imagination. While Narcissa still claimed to love both the boys and to feel interested in their welfare, the relationship was becoming conditional. We "shall treat them as our own," she decided, "so long as they deserve it."

On September 12, the missionaries arrived at Fort Vancouver, located near the juncture of the Willamette and Columbia rivers. The fort was the main trading post of the Hudson's Bay Company, Britain's political and economic agent in Oregon country, and the headquarters for the Columbia region. Here furs from all the areas west of the Rockies were sorted, cleaned, and prepared for shipment to England, while English trade goods were available for purchase or exchange. Two of the company's six ships, "dressed in complete regalia from stem to stern," were visible as the missionaries approached the fort, over which the flag of St. George waved in the breeze.

After weeks in the wilderness, it was not surprising that Fort Vancouver appeared to Narcissa as the "New York of the Pacific Ocean." The stockaded fort spread over two acres and had about forty frame and log buildings clustered around two squares, a two-storied governor's residence, a school, and a chapel. It had all the bustle of civilized life—"the sound of hammars, click of the anvils, the rumble of carts, with tinkling of bells"—and an exotic mix of people and languages—Indians, mixed bloods, French Canadians, English, and Scottish all mingled at the fort. Beyond the stockade, settlement extended for almost five square miles. There was a "neat village" housing company employees several hundred yards from the fort itself and an impressive farm "fenced into beautiful corn-fields—vegetable-fields—orchards—gardens—and pasture-fields . . . interspersed with dairy-houses, shepherds' and herdsmen's cottages." The company employed hundreds of workers for its agricultural, fishing, lumbering, and trading activities.

Presiding over the post and the Columbia department was Dr. John McLoughlin. The fifty-two-year-old Canadian had been chief factor since 1825, and it had been under his talented leadership that Fort Vancouver had grown to be the bustling center of Oregon Territory. Tall, physically impressive, with a head of white hair that caused the Indians to dub him "white-headed Eagle," McLoughlin had, like many company officials, chosen a woman of mixed blood as his wife.

McLoughlin cordially greeted the missionaries and paid special compliments to Eliza and Narcissa for their heroism in traveling the overland route. Naturally hospitable to visitors and genuinely pleased to have the missionaries at the fort, McLoughlin, nonetheless, probably was not entirely delighted by the arrival of the Americans. The treaty provisions between the United States and Great Britain for joint occupancy of Oregon had been extended to 1838, and Mc-

Loughlin likely wished to keep the American presence at a minimum. The arrival of ABCFM missionaries could herald growing American interest in the territory.

There was nothing in McLoughlin's behavior that revealed his possible misgivings. He escorted the visitors inside, "seated us on the sofa," Narcissa reported, and introduced them to the ladies of the household. The tour of the garden that followed seemed a wonderful contrast "to the rough barren sand plains," and Narcissa admired not only the abundance of fruit and vegetables but the way in which the garden was "very neat & tastefully arranged with fine walks . . . [with] a good Summer house covered with grape vines."

Narcissa was charmed by all the amenities of civilization and impressed by the lavish way of life. Her middle-class rural upbringing had hardly prepared her for the table set by the McLoughlins, with its great variety of food, "at every new dish . . . a clean plate," the silver marked with the McLoughlin crest, the mahogany chairs and table that could sit twelve. The opportunities for genteel society was a happy surprise. "This is more than we expected when we left home," she wrote, "that we should be privaleged with the acquaintance & Society of two English Ladies."

One disappointment was the absence of Samuel Parker. Parker failed to keep his promise of meeting the missionary party at the rendezvous. Now they learned he was not waiting for them at Fort Vancouver but had decided to return home by sea. Of course, the most significant consequence of his departure was that the missionaries would not have the benefit of his "counsels & advice . . . concerning location character of the Indians &c." But Narcissa's response showed that home was uppermost in her mind. Now that Parker was gone, he could not bring news of their arrival to "our dear Parents & friends at home," or the special messages or curiosities she might wish to send. The reconnection with her family would be delayed.

McLoughlin invited the women to remain at the fort for the winter while their husbands found locations and built houses for their wives. Narcissa realized she would be more comfortable at the fort than at a new mission site, for her child was due in the spring. Yet she did not want to be apart from Marcus at that time. It was finally decided that the men would choose locations and start building and return for Eliza and Narcissa within a few weeks.

Once this matter was settled, Narcissa settled down to enjoy her

stay at Vancouver. She must have been surprised to find that Mc-
Loughlin had a wife of mixed blood, but she kept her feelings to
herself. The McLoughlin household was the grandest she had probably ever visited, and the chief factor and his wife were cordial and
kind. She liked them and found herself a favorite. It was easy to
interest herself in the domestic operations of the household, dairy,
and gardens. She took weekly rides with Mrs. McLoughlin and even
made a featherbed from wild fowl feathers, as was the custom at Fort
Vancouver. She continued to appreciate the good living, which she
described in some detail and sampled eagerly. "If Mother could see
me now she would not think my cheek bones were very promenant.
We have every comfort we can ask for here, enough to eat & drink."

Narcissa also spent some time tutoring and teaching singing. Mc-
Loughlin indicated his good opinion of Narcissa when he asked her
to hear his daughter's lessons. Both Narcissa and Eliza, at his request, also helped in the school for children of company employees.
The previous winter, Parker had taught the children hymns. Now
Narcissa spent about an hour every evening teaching the children
"new tunes." McLoughlin warmly praised her efforts, saying that the
songs were helping the children learn English. These compliments
Narcissa proudly passed along to her family. She said nothing about
what Eliza did in or out of the school.

There was one bit of unpleasantness that Narcissa left out of her
journal and letters. The story was embarrassing, petty, and somewhat humiliating socially, the kind of news that Narcissa had begun
to omit when she wrote home.

Herbert Beaver, the Anglican clergyman appointed by the company, had only arrived at the fort a week earlier than the missionaries. He believed his appointment gave him full authority in the
school and considered that Eliza and Narcissa were infringing on his
prerogatives. He informed McLoughlin that he wished the children
to be "strictly prevented from receiving any [instruction] not authorized by myself." "It . . . [was not] . . . usual," he insisted, "for the
Clergy to take the *partial* management of any school." He told Eliza
and Narcissa much the same thing, asking that "the Ladies . . . refrain from teaching, in any respect, the children of the School at
Vancouver."

The women, rather than confronting Beaver directly, brought
their letter to McLoughlin. As a Roman Catholic, McLoughlin did
not appreciate Beaver's Anglican zeal or the implication that the

chief factor was not the ultimate authority at Fort Vancouver. Beaver raised another issue that touched McLoughlin deeply. For Beaver the traditional fur-trade marriage "à la façon du pays" was nothing more than concubinage, and Mrs. McLoughlin, therefore, a "kept mistress." The chief factor's angry response to Beaver's letter to Eliza and Narcissa probably had as much to do with the minister's labeling his wife a concubine as it did with the "deliberate insult" Beaver had offered the two missionary ladies.

For the two women the school was not the only issue. Beaver was a snob. His letter contained condescending references to the "various customs" that "prevailed in different countries" but not in England. Certainly the comments hurt Narcissa, who had been looking forward to genteel English society. Being the daughter of Judge Prentiss did not make Narcissa a suitable companion for Beaver's wife, whom he considered superior to all the other women at Fort Vancouver. Narcissa probably also sensed that Beaver did not think much of her husband, either, whose medical credentials he airily dismissed.

Beaver's behavior was obnoxious enough that John McLoughlin intervened. He forced Beaver to apologize "gladly" and to assure the women "that not the slightest insult was intended."

During these weeks, as this small drama was playing itself out, Narcissa was also busy buying and ordering domestic goods. Although the company store did not have many articles for convenience or any "Fancy articles," Narcissa was able to "find here . . . every article for comfort & durability we need." All the goods were English, "of the best quality." Company craftsmen made what the store did not provide. Narcissa ordered tinware, "six large milk pans Coffee & Tea pots, Candle sticks & moles. Covered pails & a baker, very good, the first of the fashion seen here, &c, &c." While Narcissa found "a few deficiencies in the cloth line," she bought up all the bleach linen for her sheets. Because there was no cotton batting for quilts, she secured white blankets for the beds. To ensure further their warmth during the winter, Marcus acquired a heating stove from Mr. Pambrun at Fort Walla Walla. Narcissa began her married life in more comfortable circumstances than many emigrant families who followed her west, who would have only what they carried across the plains with them.

Narcissa was also preparing for her garden. "I save all the [grape] seeds of those I eat for planting & of apples also. This is a rule of

Vancouver." She also intended to take "some young sprouts of apple peach & grapes & some strawberrry vines &c from the nursery here." The Whitmans were going to start life in the wilderness as comfortably as possible, and McLoughlin was generous in helping them out. Even though the ABCFM had wondered "how you can in your families keep up even the forms of civilized life for the first year or two," Narcissa was intent on doing her best.

In contrast to the domesticity Narcissa was planning, Eliza was preparing to set up housekeeping on a somewhat simpler level. Since Narcissa had bought up all the bleach linen, the Spaldings would certainly not have white sheets.

The visit to Fort Vancouver revealed much that was novel to Narcissa, and she was impressed by many of the trappings of British upper-class life. But she found no reason to modify her narrow evangelical views. She disapproved, for example, of wine at table and the toasts the gentlemen made to one another. "We belong to the tetotal Society," Narcissa reminded herself, and since the gentlemen knew this, they did not even offer the missionaries wine. Unfamiliar food like the "black pudding" (haggis) was sent from the table untouched. "It is not a favourite dish with us Americans."

Narcissa also found much to criticize in the domestic arrangements she observed at the fort. She deplored, for example, the confusion of gender roles and the domestic sloppiness she saw. "The wives here are not first rate housekeepers," she explained; they had mistaken views of female responsibilities and an "over nice" sense of gentility. She knew her parents would laugh, but it was even considered impolite to use spittle to seal a letter. At the same time, "it is not very fashionable for women to do any kind of work. This is done by men & servants." Not unexpectedly, with the wrong people doing the housekeeping, "all kinds of work is done at the greatest disadvantage having no conveniences or any one who knows how to make things as they should be." Narcissa noted a similar confusion of gender roles in Mrs. McLoughlin's preference for "riding gentleman fashion." Even though many claimed that riding astride was easier, Narcissa had "never seen the necessity of changing our fashion."

Despite the awkwardness with Beaver, she enjoyed the "privaledge" of two Sabbath services, held in McLoughlin's house. "The singing . . . was done by the children. Some of their tunes were taught them by Mr Parker. . . . [Some] by Mr Shepherd of the Methodist Mission." Other aspects of the service were less satisfactory than the music. While the Anglican service was obviously not in the same class as the Roman Catholic mass she had witnessed in St. Louis, it was deficient in terms of her Congregational-Presbyterian values. "To contrast it with the preaching at home, I find a great want of plainness and heart. He is a great way behind the times. The standard of piety is low with him. . . . He seldom draws the line of distinction between the righteous and wicked, and when he does it is so faintly that it is scarcely perceptible." Beaver's defect was that he was not an evangelical Protestant who taught his congregation to make the essential distinctions betweeen those who were saved and those who were doomed.

Beaver was not the only one she judged deficient. The other residents of the fort, even "professors . . . from the Kirk of Scotland," were equally wanting. She could not find the important signs of commitment in this ostensibly Christian community. "Do not see much evidence of real piety among them; no family worship, no social prayer meetings; yet at the same time all think themselves Christians, safe enough; at least they appear so." Fort Vancouver, she concluded, needed "a minister of the right stamp."

As she was observing the life and people around her, Marcus was hunting for a proper mission site. Weeks earlier, at the rendezvous, both Nez Percé and Cayuse Indians had begged the missionaries to settle with them and had almost come to blows in their eagerness to secure a missionary presence. When Marcus and Henry left the fort in late September, they had decided on separate sites, one with each tribe. Tensions between the two families contributed to the decision. As Henry Gray reported later, Spalding explained that he would not "have come here all alone, a hundred and twenty miles, if I could have lived with him and Mrs. Whitman." Separate sites, for the time being, seemed to resolve the leadership issue. On October 18 Henry returned with the happy news that the men had selected stations. Marcus was already at work with Gray building a house.

Narcissa found it cheering that they would be able "to make a beginning in our pleasing work soon." The Whitmans' mission among the Cayuse Indians would be about twenty-five miles east of Fort Walla Walla. Marcus described it as a good spot for crops, "no want of good land for cultivation & herding."

The departure date was set for early November. Narcissa reminded her family how lovable and worthy their daughter was with her news that "all regret my leaving." The doctor urged her to stay all winter;

Mrs. McLoughlin "wishes to go & live with me." So too did her daughter and Mrs. Douglas, the wife of Dr. McLoughlin's assistant, Sir James Douglas. When the mission party set off on November 2, the children whom Narcissa judged to have "improved much in their singing & learned very many tunes" sang a farewell.

One person did not regret Narcissa's departure or join in the farewell. "When the missionaries went from the Fort the other day," Beaver reported, "I was shocked, not as being present, but at hearing that the scholars, by command, had been paraded on the River Beach, and sung there an hymn. Sacred music should only be used on solemn occasions, but it is made here a common entertainment of an evening, without the slightest religious feeling or purpose."

Letters written to Mrs. Parker, to Mr. Parker, and to her Angelica minister, Leverett Hull, and his wife a few days before she set out for her new work set the long trip and the tasks lying ahead in some perspective. To Mrs. Parker, Narcissa said that she had no regrets at having taken the overland route west. While there had been a "little suffering and fatigue . . . the fatigue is entirely forgotten," and there had been many pleasures along the way. For the most part, she had survived with buoyant good spirits. "I believe I was prepared for the worst, but happily have been disappointed." There was ample reason to thank God for his mercy.

The very mercy God had shown increased the missionaries' obligations to labor among the Indians. And although she did not say so, God's favors made the thought of failure unacceptable. To Mr. Parker, she stated, "Our desire now is to be useful to these benighted Indians, teaching them the way of salvation . . . and the beauties of a 'well ordered life and godly conversation'; and to answer the expectations of those who sent us here. It is a great responsibility to be pioneers in so great a work. It is with cautious steps that we enter on it."

She told Parker she was aware of her insufficiency and solicited his prayers. Her caution and sense of inadequacy were appropriate for one facing the beginning of missionary life. But like her companions, as yet she hardly knew what external challenges she might face. Certainly she did not dream that her careful upbringing or her tastes, values, and personality might complicate the mission that she had been contemplating for so many years.

While she was anxious, however, she was also ebullient. Had she not mastered the trip? Was she not beginning the life for which she had so long hoped, with an excellent husband and a child on the way? Given her world and evangelical culture, how could she recognize her intolerance of others as a problem? Perhaps she could have examined her shifting feelings about the Indians, but they were heathens, after all—benighted beings. Her love of comfort and genteel life seemed reasonable enough. And why think the missionary endeavor might come to grief, when the Spaldings would be so far from the Whitman mission?

This was not the time for these daunting questions. "We are all safely over the Rocky Mountains and in health," she wrote the Hulls. "We want to see the hand of God as evidently in blesssing our labors here, in answer to your prayers, as we have seen it in leading us safely through this journey."

CHAPTER 4

Alone, in the Thick Darkness
of Heathendom

AS the children of Fort Vancouver sang a farewell hymn, the heavily loaded boats of the missionary party pushed away from the river beach and started up the Columbia River at about noon on November 3, 1836. It was late in the year to be moving to a primitive home. Narcissa and Mr. McLeod, an unexpected but welcome traveling companion, were in one boat, the Spaldings in another. That afternoon it started raining, and the gloomy weather continued for the next few days. But Narcissa was in good spirits. She was not thinking about the Indians as she had during the voyage down the river. Instead, she noticed the details of traveling. In comparison to the long trek across the country, this trip was comfortable and even enjoyable at times. Even though the rain was steady, the boat's oilcloth covering kept her dry. At night, the party camped on the shore, and with the tent, the great fire, blankets in profusion, and the featherbed she had made at the fort, Narcissa found all "pleasant & comfortable."

The party reached Fort Walla Walla early on the Sabbath, nine days after setting out from Fort Vancouver. The Pambruns again made the missionaries welcome. Narcissa was cheerful and eager to see Marcus after a separation of over a month and a half.

When Marcus came to the fort six days later, however, Narcissa learned that the men had not quite "succeeded in making a comfortable place for me." Pierre Pambrun encouraged her to remain at the fort for a few more weeks, and Narcissa, several months pregnant, agreed. He and his "interesting" family made her "contented & happy," and Narcissa decided that "a very kind Providence" had arranged for the Pambruns "to be situated [so] near" to her future home.

If the Pambruns also urged Eliza to remain at the fort until her husband had completed their house, she refused. Eliza longed for "the glorious, blessed, but responsible work of laboring to introduce the blessing of that Gospel . . . among this benighted people" and was undaunted by the thought of primitive accommodations. In late November, she set out for Lapwai to "live in a skin lodge untill her house is built & this too in the dead of winter."

Always conscious of how she measured up to Eliza, Narcissa assured her family that she would also have preferred going to her mission site rather than staying at Fort Walla Walla. In reality, she found the Pambruns' attention flattering and life in their comfortable household appealing. Although Henry Gray regarded the Pambruns' house a "rude specimen of half-native, half-French dwelling," with plank floors, rough-hewn lumber doors, and simple furniture, it was far more civilized than a tent, partially finished house, or Indian lodge. Having experienced the pleasures of domestic life after the hard months of travel, Narcissa was in no hurry to begin housekeeping in inconvenient and uncomfortable circumstances. And she was hesitant about beginning her work as a missionary.

During the weeks in the Pambrun household, Narcissa became further acquainted with the mixed racial world of the Hudson's Bay Company. Like many company wives, Catherine Pambrun was descended from two generations of white men who had taken Indian women as partners. Although Catherine was acquainted with certain aspects of white culture, she retained habits and customs learned from the Indian side of her family. Stories suggest she smoked an Indian clay pipe; Narcissa noted that Catherine had bound her first two babies to a cradleboard, Indian fashion.

By the mid-1830s, changes within fur-trade society were putting pressures on métis women like Catherine, who stood between two cultures, to adapt more thoroughly to white ways. Her French husband apparently tried to bribe her to give up her pipe. Doubtless, he was the one to suggest that Narcissa instruct his wife and daughter in English while she was at the fort. Narcissa agreed, and mother and daughter made good progress.

Narcissa worked easily with the Pambrun women, and Catherine, only three years her elder, eventually became a friend. While Catherine knew much about Indian life that might have been helpful to the new missionary, Narcissa, like most whites, viewed cultural transfer as a one-way process. Indians were low on the ladder of civilization and needed to abandon their way of life and learn how to be like white people. Even after she left the household, Narcissa continued to instruct Catherine on the white way of doing things. Cathe-

Lapwai, the site of the Spaldings's mission. Photograph by Julie Roy Jeffrey.

A Cayuse papoose. Narcissa reported proudly that she had saved the Pambrun child from the sort of carrying board pictured here. National Anthropological Archives, Smithsonian Institution.

rine had Narcissa to thank for knowing how to wash clothes in a tub of water rather than in a stream. Later Narcissa was especially proud that she had persuaded Catherine to free her new baby from the tyranny of the Indian cradleboard.

Teaching the Pambruns reinforced Narcissa's confidence in her abilities as teacher and cultural guide. But the experience with the métis women did not necessarily prepare her for the duties lying ahead. Full-blooded women living within tribal groups would find far less reason to discard native ways than Catherine, who had white relatives and a white husband. Nor would they necessarily interpret Narcissa's behavior with Catherine Pambrun's appreciation.

In early December, Marcus brought Narcissa to Waiilatpu, her new home and the scene of her future labors. The stark landscape that turned brown and dusty in the summer, the sky, and the sense of vast spaces could hardly have been more different from the wooded rolling hills and green valleys of New York State. It was a place that could seem far emptier and lonelier than any other Narcissa had ever known. But at the moment of arrival, it seemed "a lovely situation," with its vistas of "plains & mountains." Soon a heavy snow blanketed the ground, where it remained for weeks.

The almost-completed mission building stood close to the north bank of the Walla Walla River. About three hundred acres suitable for farming stretched back from the river, while small hills covered with bunch grass offered grazing for animals during the winter. Along the river poplars, willows, birch, and alder trees mixed with brambles would create touches of color in the warm weather. Marcus had chosen an excellent spot for a post that was supposed to become self-supporting, but whether it would prove to be well situated for missionary work was yet to be seen.

Visible from the mission were the winter lodges of one of the bands of Cayuse Indians who had invited the Whitmans to settle at Waiilatpu. Like their neighbors, the Nez Percé, who lived to the east and north, the Cayuse were a powerful and fierce group of horse-breeders and traders who had grown prosperous supplying the fur companies with their steeds. At one time, the Cayuse, who called themselves "Te-taw-ken," or "We the People," had spoken their own language. By the time the missionaries arrived, however, the small tribe had so intermingled with the Nez Percé that they had adopted Nez Percé as their own tongue. The two tribes shared many other cultural characteristics as well.

The Cayuse were known for the excellence of their horses. National Anthropological Archives, Smithsonian Institution.

Narcissa's happiness at being reunited with Marcus colored her first view of her new home. Her heart leaped for joy when she saw the adobe house and log lean-to that Marcus, Henry Gray, two Hawaiian laborers, and an additional helper had constructed. When it was done, the house would have a room heated with the Pambruns' stove for Marcus and Narcissa at one end, a kitchen in the center with a fireplace, and a pantry and small bedroom at the other end.

Narcissa happily described her domestic arrangements in the journal she was still keeping for her family. As she realized, her home in Waiilatpu was probably more comfortable than her parents' early log cabin in Prattsburg had been. Narcissa had a heating stove, furniture (a table, three chairs, two with deerskin bottoms, and a bedstead nailed to the wall), her tinware and other goods from Fort Vancouver, bedding, and soon even glass in the windows. Catherine Pambrun sent her a barrel for the washing. Narcissa speculated that "probably mine with Mrs. Pambran [*sic*] are the only two this side of the Rocky Mountains . . . she never knew the use of one untill I suggested it." She even had a "dog and good cat." "These may appear small subjects to fill a letter with," she explained, "but my object is to show you that people can live here, & as comfortably too as in many places east of the mountains."

There was, of course, a good deal of domestic work involved in setting up the household. Though she was an accomplished housekeeper, Narcissa wished for her father's carpentry skills "in many things difficult & perplexing to hands unacquainted." For more ordinary chores, she used less skilled hands. But she soon discovered to her surprise that it was fruitless to rely on Indian women for household assistance; they "do not love to work well enough for us to place any dependence upon them." Eventually she concluded that the Cayuse regarded "all who work . . . [as] slaves and inferior persons."

In part, she was right. Cayuse women saw little reason to add the burden of a white woman's housework to the tasks they already performed. Although Narcissa had decided during her trip west that Indian women were enslaved by their husbands, the fact that they did not do domestic work as she understood it led her to conclude that they were too lazy and proud to labor for her. This habit of using her own standards to judge the Indians almost always led Narcissa to find the Cayuse deficient. Few whites would have faulted her assessments. But her critical evaluation may well have encouraged the haughty and reserved demeanor she adopted when dealing with tribal women.

Although Narcissa did not get much household help from women of the Cayuse tribe, after her first months at Waiilatpu, she almost always had some domestic assistance. In April 1837 Dr. McLoughlin sent an orphan girl of sixteen to help her. Narcissa called her Sarah Hull, keeping her promise to the wife of Angelica's minister to name a child after her. Since Sarah did not speak English when she arrived, it was at first "difficult . . . to realize any benefit" from her. Eventually Sarah became "a great comfort" to Narcissa. She was the first of several teen-aged girls in the Whitman household. From the beginning, there were also Hawaiians who often worked as laborers in Oregon in the 1830s. They helped with the outdoor chores; Narcissa found they also made "excellent cooks and house servants," and the men sometimes prepared meals for her.

While Narcissa vividly described her domestic arrangements, suggesting thereby the enormous signficance she placed on re-creating familiar surroundings, she wrote nothing about the Cayuse during those first few weeks at Waiilatpu. She did not mention that the Whitmans had started a worship service. One would not know from reading her December journal entries that she was a missionary at all. Finally, on January 2, a universal fast day, she paid a visit to the Indian village. She devoted only two brief sentences to that event. She passed on none of the intimate details of Indian life but merely informed her family that "all seemed well pleased as I had not been to any of them before."

Why had Narcissa been so long in paying her visit? Possibly the snow, domestic chores, or her pregnancy prevented her from leaving her house sooner. But more likely, her reluctance stemmed from the discomfort she felt when confronted by a different race and culture. Her reaction to the Roman Catholic mass in St. Louis, which she found exotic and threatening, had hinted that her tolerance for difference was limited. Now her environment was far stranger than it had been in St. Louis. Rather than gorgeously clad priests, she saw Indians dressed in animal skins, adorned with beads, shells, and claws, their faces and even their hair sometimes painted in vivid colors, their horses decorated with strange designs. Instead of tinkling bells and Latin hymns, she heard Indian music, with its wild, harsh sound of rattles, drums, flutes, and whistles. No wonder it was hard to leave the house that shielded her from this new and uncertain world.

Like most newcomers to the mission field, Narcissa was finding the realities of heathendom disturbing. As Lucia Holmans, an ABCFM missionary in Hawaii, pointed out, "Could any female know before she left her home, *all* the trials and afflictions through which she must inevitably pass, she would not of *herself* have strength or grace to enlist in so great an enterprize." Narcissa must have had similar thoughts. Her reticence about the visit to the village was a clue that she was experiencing emotions too powerful to express.

Another clue was her entry for January 2, a day she was spending "in heathen lands . . . widely separated from kindred souls, alone, in the thick darkness of heathenism." The repetition of the word "heathen," the association of heathendom with a thick darkness, and her description of herself as alone betray her complex but primarily negative emotional response to the Cayuse, so different from herself and other "kindred souls." In striking juxtaposition to this description of darkness, Narcissa wrote several lines about the separate room that the Whitmans had finished for themselves, cozy with the stove, comfortable, and as civilized "as heart could wish." This was a place familiar and safe, a room where Indians would never be allowed to come. This is the room where Narcissa felt at home, a refuge from her alien surroundings.

Narcissa, of course, was not at all unusual in her response to a group of people who were classified both as savages and as pagans. Few nineteenth-century Americans admired the many forms of native life they discovered as they came to know other parts of the world. Even modern anthropologists have been surprised to find themselves harboring negative feelings about the people they are studying. Certainly missionaries, like other emigrants, routinely found the "heathen" distasteful. Rev. Henry Perkins, a member of the Methodist Oregon mission, whose wife, Elvira, would become a dear friend of Narcissa's, revealed his own initial reaction to the Indians more openly than Narcissa did, but the two were in accord. "That I did not love the savages was apparent to myself the moment I saw them. Their appearance was revolting. Dirty, oily, almost naked in their squalid deformity, how could I love the savages for their own sake." Mary Parker, a Hawaiian missionary, flatly stated that the Hawaiians were "naked, rude, and disgusting to every feeling."

In a sermon to departing missionaries published in the *Missionary Herald* at the very time the Whitmans were heading west, Reverend Bird discussed some of the trials of missionary life, the conflict between dreams based on reading and dreaming in "our comfortable closets" and the harsh realities. "Missionary zeal," he cautioned, "is not quickened by exile, and by a long and near acquaintance with heathenish abominations." Nevertheless, "you must love the heathen in spite of their hatefulness." This was Narcissa's—and all missionaries'—paradoxical and almost impossible challenge.

If the directive to love the Cayuse was a difficult one, the challenge of loving her little daughter was no trial at all. In mid-March, a

Long Hair, photographed at the turn of the century, was born during the years of the American Board mission effort. National Anthropological Archives, Smithsonian Institution.

month and a half after her first visit to the Cayuse lodges, Alice Clarissa was born. It was, remarkably, the evening before Narcissa's own birthday and within days of her own mother's. The timing of the birth and the choice of Clarissa as a second name reinforced special bonds between the generations of women in Narcissa's family. Marcus's dominance within the marriage, however, is suggested by the fact the child's first name was that of his mother, Alice.

Although Narcissa had contracted a rash and Marcus had bled her repeatedly only days before the birth, the delivery went smoothly. Narcissa was in labor for two hours and was alert enough to notice the baby being dressed. After the first two wakeful nights, she was able to get her usual rest, for the baby often slept through the night. It was not long before she was able to take a walk out in the pleasant March weather.

Like other western women, Narcissa yearned for her female relatives, who, at home, would have gathered around her bed to give her support and companionship during the hours of her labor and delivery. The way in which she dramatized her situation in her letter home revealed that she felt more solitary than she was in fact. The costs of her independence were high, and she was sorely missing her family's attention and sympathy. "Thus you see Beloved Sisters how the missionary does in heathen lands," she wrote. "No Mother, No Sister, to relieve me of a single care."

Actually, she had a far easier time of it than her image of the solitary care-laden missionary suggested. Catherine Pambrun and her two children came to stay with Narcissa, and she also had her "affectionate Husband" by her side. Since Catherine was not well, Marcus acted as "Physition & nurse," as well as cook and laundress.

The Indians' great interest in the new white child gratified the new mother. "The Little Stranger is visited daily by the Chiefs & principal men in camp & the women throng the house continually waiting an opportunity to see her." On the day after the birth, a friendly Indian called and "said she was a Cayuse Te-mi (Cayuse girl) because she was born on Cayuse wai-tis (Cayuse land). . . . The whole tribe are highly pleased because we allow her to be called a Cayuse Girl."

As Narcissa was adjusting both to the realities of missionary life and to motherhood, she kept her family supplied with information about the Cayuse tribe. With perhaps more time, fewer distractions, and greater interest in writing than Marcus, Narcissa tended to give fuller descriptions of Indian life than did her husband.

Narcissa's first report on the Cayuse suggested some fundamental, if not yet recognized, obstacles to the success of the missionary endeavor. Like other Indian tribes of the Columbia plateau, the Cayuse followed a cycle of annual activities organized around the search for food. For thousands of years, men as hunters and fishers and women as gatherers and processors of food had contributed to survival of family and kin in the area between the Bitterroot and Cascade mountains.

During the winter, Indians lived in small groups in villages usually located near the water. The small village near the Whitman mission was one of perhaps eight winter villages inhabited by the Cayuse. In the spring, the yearly cycle of travel and food gathering began as men left the village to hunt, while women searched for tender spring roots. Near the end of May, fishing and preserving salmon became the main focus of economic activity. During the summer, tribal bands moved on to fish, hunt in highland meadows, and visit one another. In late July, many bands, sometimes from different tribes, joined in highland valleys to gather and prepare the camas root. This was a time when women worked as their men whiled away the hours socializing, gambling, and racing their horses. In the fall, the men stalked mountain deer and elk and fished for more salmon before returning to the winter villages, while women made clothes, baskets, and mats. Winter was a time to live off the stored caches of food, to tell stories, and to wait for the coming of spring.

The wandering life of the Indians meant that unless the missionaries accompanied them on their travels, they would only have a few months a year in which to teach Christian doctrine. The efforts that Marcus was making to establish a mission farm and the necessity to make the mission self-supporting meant that he was already ruling out the possibility of itinerancy.

Narcissa also described the Cayuse as not "well united." She probably was referring both to the dispersed settlement pattern of the tribe and to the absence of any overarching political structure. Although she correctly perceived the lack of tribal unity, Narcissa and the other missionaries misunderstood the leadership structure at the village or band level. Narcissa spent some time discussing "young Chief Towerlooe . . . more properly the ruling chief" and "Old Chief Umtippe," whose winter quarters stood nearby. Rather than being powerful political figures, these men were usually the headmen of local councils. Since tribal decisions were made by voting, the so-

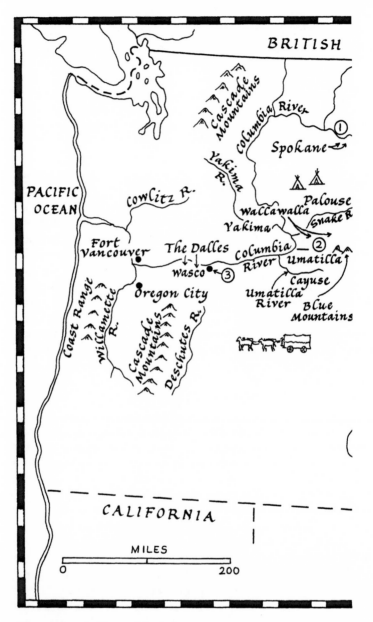

The missions in Oregon Territory.

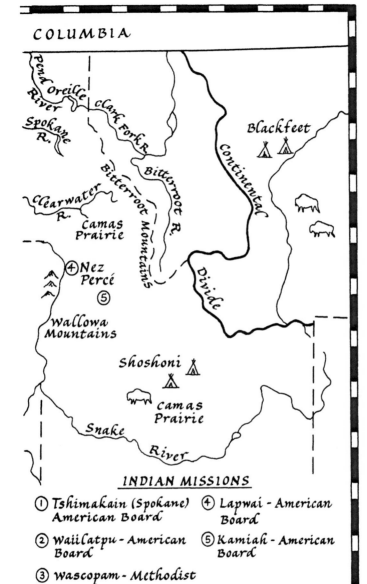

COLUMBIA

Pend Oreille River

Spokane R.

cCark Fork R.

Bitterroot

Blackfeet

Continental

Clearwater R.

Bitterroot Mountains

Bitterroot R.

Camas Prairie

④ Nez Percé

⑤

Divide

Wallowa Mountains

Shoshoni

Camas Prairie

Snake River

INDIAN MISSIONS

① Tshimakain (Spokane) American Board

② Waiilatpu - American Board

③ Wascopam - Methodist

④ Lapwai - American Board

⑤ Kamiah - American Board

called chiefs had no special authority to impose their will on others. In Hawaii, the ABCFM mission was having that organization's most spectacular success by concentrating on converting the rulers, who then swept their followers into the church. In Oregon, however, the missionaries could not rely on a hierarchical political structure to trigger similar mass conversions.

Old Chief Umtippe epitomized for Narcissa many of the traits that she was coming to identify as Cayuse. Unaware of Indian cultural norms that shaped behavior, Narcissa found many of the early personal exchanges puzzling. Judging Umtippe by her own standards, she found him untrustworthy, "full of hypocracy [sic] deceit and guile." Furthermore, he was "a mortal beggar as all Indians are. If you ask a favour of him, sometimes it is granted or not just as he feels, if granted it must be well paid for."

Like most outsiders, Narcissa misunderstood the pattern of exchange that characterized Indian society. Although the Indians were not above taking advantage of whites and certainly expected to receive some material benefits from the missionary presence, they regarded the act of giving as a demonstration of friendship that should be reciprocated. To fail to do so was to break the bond of friendship. To Narcissa, favors did not need to be "paid for," and Indians should not beg for "pay." Like the other missionaries, she hoped to make the Indians her brothers and sisters in Christ at the same time that her behavior suggested a rejection of any form of kinship.

At the commencement of the missionary venture, what Narcissa most admired about the Cayuse were the ways in which they seemed most like Christian white people. She praised their strict observance of Christian practices they had learned from a Hudson's Bay Company trader, the way in which they prayed every morning and evening and celebrated the Sabbath with Christian hymns, prayers, and a talk by the chief. As January wore on, Narcissa found herself "more & more interested" in the small band living near the mission. Although the Cayuse did not yet understand the need to change their hearts rather than their outward actions, they seemed to have partial knowledge of the Bible and understood something of the notion of sin.

The practices that the Cayuse had already adopted suggested a willingness to incorporate new elements into tribal religious life. Even before whites arrived as traders, missionaries, and settlers, Indian prophets had warned the plateau tribes that "soon there will come from the rising sun a different kind of man . . . who will bring with them a book and will teach you everything." Certainly many tribes wanted to learn more about Christianity, if only because they thought it would provide them with some of the great spiritual power that whites apparently possessed. They saw white goods and technology as a reflection of this power, and they wanted to share in it. It was not surprising that the Nez Percé and Cayuse vied over the white missionaries or that the Cayuse had allowed one of their young men, Halket, to attend the Anglican mission school at Red River in Canada.

When the Cayuse and the Nez Percé invited missionaries to settle among them, they had no idea that the missionaries would demand that they reject all their sacred rites and beliefs and many ordinary customs as well. After all, they knew almost nothing about evangelical Protestantism and its rigid definition of faith and salvation. Chants, songs, and other rituals had long played a central role in native religion, and the addition of the Christian practices Narcissa observed did not require substantial changes in outlook or customs.

The missionaries, of course, had definite expectations of their own great task. As Narcissa explained, "Our desire . . . is, to be useful to these benighted Indians, teaching them the way of salvation." Unless the Indians followed the way the missionaries pointed out, they would surely perish. As a contemporary manual for clergy wives pointed out, "Do not suffer yourself to believe that . . . the mercy of God will rescue the heathen. It is not in the nature of holiness to make the unchanged heart happy."

With little understanding of Cayuse belief or culture, Narcissa could not realize the profound differences separating Cayuse and Christian religious perspectives. One of the few surviving Cayuse myths suggests the distance between the two traditions and the difficulty, if not impossibility, of achieving the goal the missionaries sought.

Like the Book of Genesis, the Cayuse myth describes a time of beginnings, but few other similarities between the two stories exist. The Cayuse tale shows an unfinished world where humans, birds, and animals live without fire, which the Creator has entrusted to a demon who keeps it in Mount Hood. The absence of fire does not harm the living creatures and certainly not the people, who can change into animals at will. One fall, however, while the people feast and dance without their skins, an eagle sent by the Creator carries away the skins. Without their warm coats, the people grow cold and begin to kill their animal brothers for their skins. They tire of raw food. Finally, two braves decide they will steal the fire from Mount Hood. They succeed, but avenging fire demons race after them. The braves call upon the Creator for help. "The Great Spirit . . . willing the children should have the fire they had stolen" transforms the demons into pine trees. He changes one of the braves into a beaver and the other into a "little gray woodpecker" whose tap shows that there is fire in the wood.

Such a myth pictures a Creator neither perfect nor all-powerful. His relation to his people appears almost casual, though in the end he saves the two braves from the demons' wrath and allows the people to keep the fire. While the demons are unfriendly to humans, they are in no sense the Creator's rival. Nor are they identified with evil. The demons do not end up in hell but on the earth as beautiful pine trees.

The myth shows how human beings participate in both the human and the animal world. No sharp line divides human from animal, spirit from flesh. As another Cayuse story explains, all "beasts, birds, reptiles, & fish were once a race of men" and therefore retain the ability to speak to present-day humans. While the myth presents important truths about the creation of the world and its inhabitants, unlike the Book of Genesis it contains no particular moral lessons or explanation of why evil exists. Its tone is cheerful and nonjudgmental.

The Nez Percé and the Cayuse viewed the earth, spawned by Coyote, as their sacred mother; the grass was her hair, stones her bones. The gifts of nature, then, came from the sacred mother. Indians owed reverence not only to their mother but to all things—every tree, every animal, every inanimate object—for each possessed a spirit. Marcus's comment that the Cayuse had once been idolators captured the enormous gap between the Christian belief that God alone was sacred and the Cayuse perspective that all of creation was sacred. "Many of their traditions are evidences of . . . worship of some Animals & Birds."

Like Christians, the Cayuse sought to make personal connections with the sacred world. The rituals of connection did not focus on guilt, confession, and conversion, however, but on the relationship with the *weyekin*, or guardian spirit. At the age of ten or eleven, Indian youths left their village on a quest for their special *weyekin*.

The spirit could be an animal, a growing thing, even a rock or storm cloud. Whatever it was, the spirit would reveal the taboos or special observances that had to be followed in exchange for spiritual guidance. If, in later years, an Indian fell ill, the sickness was a sign that the guardian spirit had fled because taboos had been neglected or because a powerful person's bad magic had driven it away. Disease was a spiritual disorder that called for the *tewat*—the medicine man, who dealt with spiritual ills.

As the emphasis on taboos suggested, the Cayuse considered the outward act, properly performed, as vital to spiritual well-being. Winter dances placated the spirit world. Appropriate burial rituals assured entry into the shadowy world of the dead. Given their perspective on the importance of ritual, the Cayuse would expect that careful performance of Christian practices would please the Whitmans and also ensure a happy afterlife. The Whitmans' explanation that an interior change of heart was necessary for salvation, however, must not have made much sense to the Cayuse and contributed to their frustration and eventual anger with the Christian message.

Despite early promising signs, the cultural differences between the Indians and the missionaries and the Whitmans' conviction that they were there to transform the Cayuse, not to change themselves, made the missionary enterprise problematic. Certainly, the endeavor would prove to be far more difficult than either Marcus or Narcissa had ever dreamed in their comfortable closets at home and far more difficult than they realized in the first months at Waiilatpu. The Spaldings, too, would find missionary work daunting, but since they were more flexible and more willing to strike out in new directions than the Whitmans, they were marginally more successful.

The general goal of conversion was clear; the puzzle was exactly how to proceed. Even though Marcus had many worries—finances, building, agriculture, medicine—Narcissa shrank from asserting herself. She once again let him take the lead as she had allowed him to take the lead in their marriage and her mother in her religious development. This habit of dependence seems to have distinguished her from many women who became ABCFM missionaries or clergy wives. Perhaps at home in a more predictable and controlled environment, Narcissa would have followed the advice of new marriage manuals urging each clergy wife to "be a helpmeet for her husband, and besides this exert an independent influence." But in this heathenish place, she wished others to make the decisions. As Narcissa told her new friend Elvira Perkins in a letter of July 1838, she had no plan apart from her husband's.

Marcus and Narcissa gradually set up a familiar schedule of Christian worship and education. First, they established a family service in the evening. Without much fluency on either side, music was an important means of communication. Both Marcus and Narcissa taught the congregation, usually men and boys, how to sing hymns in English. Later there were Nez Percé hymns as well.

Narcissa was surprised at the role music played in missionary work. She had long been used to using her voice in evangelical work, but at Waiilatpu she was not comfortable enough with the Cayuse to do without Marcus's help. "Indeed I should not attempt to sing with them, were it not for the assistance my Husband renders." While he had not been much of a vocalist in New York, Marcus had apparently improved. "Now he is able to sing several tunes & lead the school in them. This saves me a great deal of hard singing."

The Sabbath services were mainly Marcus's responsibility. Although he was a medical missionary and not a minister, he led the Presbyterian exercises and delivered the sermon. Narcissa helped with the singing. In addition, there was often a Sabbath school.

Narcissa's main duties lay in the school that met in her kitchen. Here, in her own kitchen, in the familiar roles of teacher and surrogate mother, she was most comfortable. Both models seemed appropriate in the new situation, where Narcissa would be dealing with children or with adults who often struck her as childlike.

At first, she conducted the classes in English, probably in much the same way as she had in New York. Teaching the students to read was an important part of missionary work, for unless they were literate, they could not study the Bible and other religious works. She also tried to mold her students' characters. The ambitious hopes lying behind the seemingly modest school were revealed by Narcissa's habit of providing the children with new identities. She named the scholars after her younger brothers and sisters, as well as New York State friends. The names symbolized new identities for the Cayuse children and the character of Narcissa's relationship with them.

Many missionary wives started boarding schools for native children, believing that this was the only way to wean them away from native culture. The Whitmans occasionally took in children "willing to labor." But as Marcus explained in a letter to the ABCFM, "my plan for teaching the children is not to take them to board but let them live with their parents & come for instruction." Certainly Narcissa agreed with his plan, for she found it troublesome to have children in the house, even on a daily basis. "We have had a school," she wrote in March 1838, "and my kitchen has been filled with children morn and eve, which has made my floor very dirty."

It was, of course, impossible to have an active ministry among a people who understood only a little English, unless all the missionaries learned the local language quickly. Eliza Spalding had begun her studies at the rendezvous, but then Narcissa had been otherwise occupied. Once at Waiilatpu, she was very slow to pick up Nez Percé. She may have had no natural facility for languages, but more likely her ambivalent feelings about the Indians made it difficult for her to learn.

Whatever the reasons for her ignorance, she was reluctant to admit it. In January 1837, she wrote her family that she and Marcus were beginning to succeed in the language and in "communicating the truth to them." Over a year later, she assured them that "we are becoming familiar with their language." That September, however, she admitted, "I cannot do much more than stammer yet in their language." To Elvira Perkins, she confided, "Nothing is more difficult than for me to attempt to convey religious truth in their language, especially when there are so few, or no terms expressive of the meaning." As late as October 1839 she still did not have command of the language and could not "converse satisfactorily with them hardly in the least degree."

As Narcissa struggled to find her way in missionary work, she discovered that another well-known evangelical approach was of limited use to her. At home she had been active in revival work and had successfully encouraged the conversion of friends and relatives. This experience hardly seemed relevant in Waiilatpu. None of the Cayuse resembled friends, relatives, or kindred souls. Nor did Narcissa seem quite like the old Narcissa, for she was more self-conscious in the presence of those who stared at her and more awkward because she could not easily speak to them.

Beyond her public labor of teaching and her occasional work copying manuscripts for publication, Narcissa spoke of having some kind of "gentle influence" on the heathens. This vague comment suggested how difficult it was for her to imagine how to proceed in this strange new setting and of how unprepared she was for the realities of missionary life. The ABCFM operated on "the presumption that whom the Lord calls to this work he will endow with the requisite physical, mental, and spiritual abilities," but their faith must often have been misplaced.

When Marcus was away on mission or medical business, however, Narcissa sometimes had to take sole responsibility. She did not like acting on her own or the sense that the Indians depended upon her. In early February, Marcus was at Fort Walla Walla, and Narcissa had "to sustain the family altar, in the midst of a room full of native youth & boys." After the service, they gathered around her, "as if anxious I should tell them something about the Bible. I had been reading the 12th chap of Acts, & with Richards help endeavoured to give them an account . . . as well as I could." On this evening, she felt helpless, frustrated by her inability to speak Nez Percé. She was glad of Richard's assistance.

As time passed, she grew only a little more confident about having "all the care and responsibility" rest on "poor feeble me." Despite her role in church services at home, she particularly found "the worshiping part" difficult. Even on an ordinary Sabbath, she felt the "weight of responsibility [of dealing with the instruction of the heathen] almost insupportable." When she had to deal with tragic circumstances, she felt even less competent. In the summer of 1838 her serving girl, Sarah Hull, died. Again, Marcus was away, and Narcissa handled the funeral with Catherine Pambrun's assistance. "If ever I felt the presence of my husband necesary to sustain me, it was while passing through such a scene," Narcissa wrote. Although she stumbled through the service, "sung, prayed and tried to talk a little," she habitually felt like a poor weak female when Marcus was not there to guide her.

The general problems Narcissa was encountering in missionary work were not unusual, although her timidity in overcoming them was. Other American missionary women working in foreign cultures wanted a missionary partnership and managed to carve out a role for themselves. The *Missionary Herald* described missionary wives who worked closely with native girls and women. At The Dalles, her close friend Elvira Perkins, the Methodist missionary, held special meetings with native women and wrote to Narcissa asking her what she was doing for women. Narcissa replied somewhat defensively, "We have done nothing for the females separately; indeed, our house is so small, and only one room to admit them, and that is the kitchen.

It is the men only that frequent our house much . . . women are not allowed the same privileges with the men. I scarcely see them except on the Sabbath. . . . I have frequently desired to have more intercourse with them, and am waiting to have a room built." In fact, the room for women was never built. Although Narcissa did report in 1840 that she held daily Bible classes with women, she had to abandon them because of ill health. There is no evidence that Narcissa undertook a consistent program of visiting the women in their own lodges.

Despite her years of picturing herself as a missionary laboring among the heathen, despite her earnest desire to bring the Cayuse to Christ, Narcissa was making the terrible discovery, if not admitting it, that she was not really suited for missionary life. The mismatch between her talents and the reality of her work with the Indians was not surprising, given the casual methods of recruiting female missionaries. In fact, despite the heroic tales Narcissa had read about Protestant missionaries, very few were able to cross what one historian has called the "vast cultural gap" separating them from the heathen they had come to save. In thirty years of effort at the ABCFM missions in Hawaii, all of the missionary women continued to feel "shocked and alienated" by the native people.

At the same time, however, many were more active and bolder than Narcissa seems to have been. Now, some 150 years later, it is difficult to know why Narcissa was more passive than others in similar settings. She did lack the intense spirituality of some of the extraordinary female missionaries whose faith presumably helped them to cope with native life. But one wonders whether the commanding role Narcissa's mother had played in encouraging her vocation and structuring her upbringing may not have contributed to the daughter's timidity, dependence on Marcus, and inflexibility. The language of sacrifice was often used to describe a missionary vocation, and Narcissa herself had spoken in these terms. One also wonders if the thought ever crossed her mind that she herself had indeed been sacrificed to the missionary life by her pious mother.

No missionaries could really accept heathens as they were, for the whole point of missionary work was to transform them. But beyond recognizing a few positive traits—the Cayuse's careful observance of certain religious practices, their occasional attentiveness to the Whitmans' teaching, for example—Narcissa found far more to condemn

Grizzly Bear; his clothing suggests some of the alterations in Indian life and culture produced by the Cayuses' interaction with Americans. National Anthropological Archives, Smithsonian Institution.

than to admire. She endowed the Cayuse with clusters of negative qualities, ranging from what she considered to be bad habits to dangerous and excessive passions.

Narcissa, like others, used familiar gender expectations as standards for judging the men and women. The women failed as wives, housekeepers, and mothers. In Narcissa's eyes, they were abjectly subservient to their husbands, lazy, and proud. They were dirty and bad housekeepers. Moreover, Cayuse women failed rather spectacularly as mothers; Narcissa reported their children often died from "neglect etc."

As for the men, they invaded her house, her refuge, and violated her sense of privacy. She never felt comfortable with Indian notions of sociability or their sense of hospitality. If Indian lodges had no structural barriers like doors to keep people out, Indians should understand that her house did. She longed to have a room that would keep them from the main part of the house, a clear physical boundary between her space and theirs. Beyond their prying habits, however, there lurked other more dangerous qualities. The Cayuse men had threatening and excessive passions—anger, rage, villainy, bloodthirstiness.

The lopsided nature of Narcissa's response to the tribe that others found handsome and clean, if warlike and proud, shows the powerful feelings the Indians inspired in her. What she saw as the Cayuse's weaknesses and flaws were the very ones that she feared most in herself. Some of the criticisms others would make of Narcissa and she would eventually acknowledge were the very accusations that she mounted against the Cayuse.

At the beginning, however, like many new missionaries, both Narcissa and Marcus were optimistic about missionary prospects. The Cayuse, who were familiar with sacred chants, enthusiastically adopted hymn singing. Narcissa thought she recognized "a strong desire . . . in them all to understand the truth & to be taught." Despite the language problems, Narcissa was sure that the Cayuse were seeking the very truth the missionaries possessed and on the very terms that they offered it.

The Cayuse were also eager to come to school. Reading and writing were some of the white powers they wished to acquire. When the tribe was present, the kitchen was filled with children. They seemed "very much attached," and Narcissa wrote in April 1838 that she hoped soon to begin teaching them to read in their own language. Since her own language skills were still weak, they would be learning together.

In general, Narcissa concluded that "we appear to have every encouragement missonaries could possibly expect, for the short time we have been here. We see a very great improvement in them." Even Umtippe, that "selfish, wicked, cunning and troublesome old chief," had become quiet and attentive by the summer of 1838.

Marcus also reported that the mission was making progress in civilizing Indians. Unlike the Hudson's Bay Company, which did not attempt to transform tribal life, the ABCFM missionaries encouraged the Indians to adopt settled agricultural life. No more sensitive to Indian culture than was his wife, Marcus thought many of the Cayuse were ready to cultivate the land and assumed that "when they have plenty of food they will be little disposed to wander." His plan, however, did not take into account the power of Cayuse culture or preferences.

The Cayuse were hardly as ready to become agriculturists as Marcus predicted. Some Indians did take up farming, but others held back. Normal agricultural procedures like plowing violated the belief that the earth was mother. Others regarded farming, like root digging, as women's work. None considered agriculture as a replacement for the tribe's traditional food-gathering activities. Just as they had added buffalo hunting on the plains to their annual cycle when they had acquired horses in the eighteenth century, now some of the band added agriculture to their yearly rounds.

Even in these first optimistic days, there were glimpses of the strength of Cayuse culture and tradition. During the first summer, there was an outbreak of lung disease. Having already experienced the devastating illnesses of white people, the Indians probably associated this new outbreak with the arrival of white missionaries.

The traditional Cayuse understanding of sickness called for spiritual remedies. But the Whitmans' presence had already divided the Indians living at Waiilatpu. Some of the sick turned to Marcus and his medicine. But others resorted to the *tewat* or first tried the *tewat* and only then Marcus. Given American doctors' limited knowledge about various illnesses and the drastic cures they often used, Marcus was probably not much more successful than the *tewat*. But both Marcus and Narcissa saw the *tewat* as a fake who gave "no medicine . . . relying solely upon incantations." His treatment, attended by "horrible" singing, the beating of sticks, bodily contortions, and "incoherent" speech, repelled them. The contest involved more than physical health, since the Whitmans believed that the *tewat* trafficked with the devil.

Sensing the divisions within the tribe, Narcissa interpreted this "trying crisis" not as a battle between cultures so much as a battle between generations. If younger Cayuse men came to the fore, "a new character would at once be given to the whole tribe." For the young men "naturally possess a different disposition, and manifest

Quieetsa, photographed in the early twentieth century, holds the blanket and staff of a *tewat*, or medicine man. The Whitmans saw *tewat*s as major obstacles to their conversion efforts. National Anthropological Archives, Smithsonian Institution.

an eager desire to adopt the manners and customs of civilized life."
It may well be that the presence of whites divided the Cayuse along
generational lines, with the young men eager for white medicine.
But Narcissa occasionally realized that the cultural reality was more
complex. Even an "excellent" Indian had returned from root digging
in May, sick, uneasy, and talking of *tewats*, she wrote. While she was
convinced that "sensible" Indians recognized the *tewat* as a fake,
many "no doubt feel it a great struggle in their minds, to entirely
renounce that in which they have so long had implicit confidence."

In the spring and summer of 1838, there was no sickness, and the
headman, Umtippe, appeared more friendly toward the Christian
message. Now the missionaries learned how hard it was to evaluate
progress. How much did Umtippe understand of "the atonement"?
Did he have "any correct views of salvation through Jesus Christ"?

As Marcus acquired the language and was "able to give them a
greater amount of the truth," however, there were signs that a few
understood all too well and were rejecting the notions of sin and
damnation that the missionaries felt compelled to tell them about.
The Cayuse regarded life as good. Now they were hearing that life's
pleasures were sins. "Some feel almost to blame us for telling about
eternal realities," Narcissa observed. "One said it was good when
they know nothing but to hunt, eat, drink and sleep; now it was
bad." Despite her mixed feelings about the tribe and the signs of
division and resistance, however, Narcissa still held herself to the
missionary goal. "We long to have them know of a Saviour's pardon-
ing love."

Another disconcerting event also hinted at the limited power of
the missionaries to transform Indians into model Christians. Marcus
reported, in a letter written to the ABCFM in May 1837, that the
Whitmans had thrown the Nez Percé boy Richard out of the house
for "bad conduct." Narcissa never told her family that her attempt to
play a mother's part had not succeeded. She may have been ashamed
at her failure and must have also been angry at Richard for resisting
her efforts at acculturation and failing to appreciate all the Whitmans
had done for him. It would not do to relay these feelings along to
her family and whoever else was reading her letters at home.

During the second summer, however, the missionaries could report their most positive news so far. But their success was not with
the Cayuse but with those more attuned to the Christian message:

the mission's Hawaiian laborers, a Scottish visitor, and a French Canadian Roman Catholic settled nearby.

Because she had grown up with the stirring story of the famous Hawaiian convert Obookiah, Narcissa was far more ready to accept the Hawaiians who worked at the mission than she was the Cayuse. The Hawaiians' "kind and tender feelings" and their Christian practices (learned from the ABCFM missionaries in Hawaii) reminded her of the pious young Obookiah. Missing the support of an organized religious community, she found solace in hearing them pray. "You cannot imagine how it strengthened our hearts . . . notwithstanding we could not understand a single word."

When a married couple, members of a native church in Hawaii, came to Waiilatpu in the summer of 1838, their fervor spread. One of the Hawaiian workers was "melted to tears" while the Roman Catholic Campo, who had settled near the mission, was so affected that he joined the new mission church. A boy of around twelve, Mungo Mevway, also gave "pleasing evidence of a change of heart" and lisped "his desires to God in prayer" like "an infant child." Jack H. gave his heart to God, abandoned tobacco, and changed his appearance.

These moving events appeared to affect "two or three of the Indians" who were "unusually serious." In a burst of enthusiasm for the Cayuse, Narcissa reported in October 1838 that they were an "interesting" people, whom she loved.

Despite a few encouraging signs of progress during the first two years at Waiilatpu, Narcissa was not finding her missionary labors rewarding. But motherhood was. Little Alice became Narcissa's "treasure invaluable" and the center of her emotional life. The child compensated both for the frustrations of missionary work as well as the limitations of her marriage. At the beginning of her marriage, when she and Marcus spent time together strolling and admiring the scenery, Narcissa had hoped that her husband would be her best friend, her mother's replacement. It is doubtful that Marcus's own family background and his years of independence prepared him to play this part for his wife. His brusque character—those who knew him described him as a person of few words, always in a hurry—made the intimacy and emotional empathy for which Narcissa yearned difficult. Besides, Marcus was often away on medical or mission business for weeks at a time. If she felt angry or dissatisfied when he disappeared, she kept these feelings to herself. Like many other nineteenth-century women, Narcissa rarely criticized her husband or faced the reality of a limited marriage. But she hungered for connection.

In such a context, Alice became Narcissa's "great comfort." She alleviated loneliness and "melancholy hours." She was "pleasant company," "my own little companion from day to day, and dear daughter." Narcissa slept with Alice every night for over two years and nursed her until she was at least twenty months, longer than was customary in the nineteenth century. Both practices effectively kept her from getting pregnant again. Having the child in bed with her may also have meant that she did not have sexual relations with her husband for a period of more than two years. If this was the case, Alice had literally replaced her father in her mother's affections.

Born so soon after her arrival, Alice provided another yardstick by which to measure the Cayuse. As she compared Alice with the Cayuse children, Narcissa saw that she was larger, stronger, and more active than the Indian children. In contrast to the Cayuse, she was making rapid religious progress under her mother's careful direction. At a year and a half, she loved to sing, "especially Nez Percé hymns . . . & most of her talk is about Jesus Christ & the Savior as she has learned to lisp his blessed name." When she was just over two, she was able to repeat a Bible verse at family worship and appeared "to take a part in worship as if as old as her mother." To her proud mother, Alice's development was additional proof of the superiority of the white race and Christian civilization.

But motherhood, taken so seriously in American culture, also made Narcissa uneasy. When Alice was a year old, Narcissa, as her own mother had done when she was a baby, made "an unreserved consecration of her to God." She pledged "to train her up for His glory." But this commitment produced feelings of incompetence. Like most missionary wives, Narcissa found the obstacles to raising Christian children in "heathen lands, among savages," without "one savory" example to guide her, dismaying. Narcissa begged for prayers from maternal associations and devoured the issues of *Mother's Magazine* that Jane sent her. Eventually, she wrote to Eliza Spalding, suggesting that they observe periods of contemplation and prayer for their children. A Maternal Association was formed at Waiilatpu in 1838.

The Cayuse's early interest in little Alice created the possibility for a relaxed and friendly relationship between Narcissa and tribal members. But Alice's constant contact with the Cayuse troubled Narcissa. She carried Alice in her arms until she was almost a year old because the Indians made the floor so dirty. She had never much liked having Indians in the house; now she discovered that Alice was "much inclined to imitate and talk with them, or they with her." The Indians were pleased with Alice's facility with the language, which was so different from her mother's.

Correspondents at the Hawaiian mission and Mr. Hall, a visiting Hawaiian missionary, fed her anxiety. Members of that mission, troubled by the Hawaiians' easy attitude toward sex, feared the corruption of their children. They were horrified to see how quickly their young ones learned about the culture their parents judged inferior and godless. It was hardly surprising that the Hawaiian missionaries warned Narcissa about "the evils of allowing" Alice "to learn the native language." Although the Whitmans were not sure "what is our duty concerning her," Narcissa concluded, "in order to prevent it, it appears I must take much of my time from intercourse with the natives." Rather than bringing her closer to the Cayuse, motherhood reinforced her natural reluctance to engage with them and justified keeping them at a distance.

In early November as their first year at Waiilatpu ended, the three Whitmans made the six-day trip to Lapwai to be with Eliza Spalding when she delivered her baby. They stayed for three weeks, and the visit was cordial. After a year, Narcissa was glad to see Eliza and Henry. Still, the underlying distance between the women remained. When additional missionaries came to Oregon in 1838, one of the women would report that "Mrs. [Spalding] likes Mrs. Whitman as well as any of us." As for Narcissa, she had far more to say about the trip to Lapwai than her visit with Eliza. Nor did she mention Eliza's recovery, merely that they "had the pleasure of seeing her up about the house before we left." In his account of the visit for the ABCFM, however, Marcus revealed that all had not gone so smoothly. "We prolonged our visit for Mrs. Spaldings recovery as in a former sickness she had a protracted & tedious recovery." When Henry asked Marcus to help him with a house-building project the following year, Narcissa's comment suggested that all was not well between the Spaldings and the Whitmans and that she disapproved of Marcus's putting the Spaldings' concerns before their own. "Mr. Spalding . . . quite persuaded my husband to believe that he needed a house more then we did, and prevailed on him to go over and assist in building, notwithstanding he had more work on hand than he could possibly attend to."

Despite the energy that it took to adjust to motherhood and missionary life, home was often in Narcissa's thoughts. The separation from her family continued to be painful. True, there were often crowds at Waiilaptu, but they were all of the wrong sort. Although Narcissa had correspondents, she longed for the opportunity to pour her heart out to her mother. A husband did not replace a mother, especially now that Narcissa was a mother herself. She also hungered for all the particulars about the people in Angelica and the progress they were making toward salvation. Missing the rhythms of organized religion and the fellowship it had afforded her, she craved comforting details about familiar people and events.

At first the act of writing home was almost enough. But as time wore on, and Narcissa heard nothing, she felt lonely, discouraged, and fearful—"perhaps you have all forgotten me." She wanted "consolation in a desponding hour. This *long*, long silence makes me feel the truth of our situation, that we are far, very far removed from the land of our birth and Christian privileges. I am weary of writing so much about ourselves without receiving a response, and yet I am anxious that father and mother should know all about us."

Only in July 1838, over two years after leaving home, did Narcissa receive her first letters from Angelica. Some had been written six months after her departure; probably others were lost on the way. But never would there be enough letters to allow Narcissa to feel secure in her family's affections. "I am still one of your number," the devoted daughter reminded them, "and desire and sympathize with you in everything."

Once communication with home was reestablished, Narcissa's letters took on a new tone. Gone was the somewhat flip and humorous advice to Jane that if she wanted to be happy, she should marry a missionary. She knew that her letters were circulated and that Jane had had her journal printed. She learned that her missionary career had helped to inspire revival activities at home. Now she slipped into the role of spiritual mentor, giving advice and inquiring after the spiritual and temporal health of family and friends. She urged Jane to come "and spend your life in the same work in which we are engaged, and not only you, but many others I know of." She encouraged her married sister Mary Ann and her minister-husband to come, "for there is work enough for all to do." "Dear father and mother" received the same advice.

She tried most to influence Edward, who at the age of eighteen, was contemplating a career as a minister or missionary. But when Narcissa received letters from home in 1838, she learned that he had been wavering. She was quick to give her opinion. "How I am disappointed in not hearing that Edward, by this time, is prosecuting his studies for the ministry and missionary work. I shall never feel as if all was right at home until more of the dear ones are thus wholly given up to the work of the Lord."

While it was natural for Narcissa to assume the part of advice giver and spiritual guide, her willingness to play the mentor role further constrained what she could reveal to family and friends in her letters. Mixed feelings about missionary work or frustrations at the lack of progress were hardly appropriate subjects to discuss with those who looked to her as a symbol of missionary commitment and source of spiritual advice.

Narcissa regarded her persistent efforts to encourage members of her family to join the missionary cause—at Waiilatpu—as laudable attempts to hurry the work of salvation along. But at one level, the encouragement represented not the love of missionary life so much as the wish to surround herself with familiar, loved ones rather than with the benighted heathen. Since she had already claimed that she was not sorry to have left home and would never return, her only alternative was to lure her family westward.

Still, 1838 was hardly a good time to be encouraging others to contemplate the missionary life. In 1837 the missionary organizations were feeling the adverse affects of the financial panic of that year. Contributions shrank, making cutting costs necessary. In January and again in July of 1837, the ABCFM wrote to the Oregon missionaries that they were "much embarrassed for want of funds" and that the Whitmans and Spaldings must reduce their expenses "or the Committee will feel obliged to discontinue" the mission. The American Indians would have to receive the gospel economically. In a shift from much that had been said to the missionaries and to the public at large in the *Missionary Herald*, Greene announced that ambitious efforts with American Indians were out of the question "so long as many more densely peopled portions of the world remain unenlightened."

By the spring of 1838, Whitman and Spalding received the first letter pointing to a shortage of funds and suggesting the possible scaling back of Indian missions. Spalding was inspired to respond to the ABCFM with a grandiose vision of the mission's obligations and a defense of the missionaries' expensive policy of teaching the Indians to farm. He called for 110 missionaries and their wives and for supplies, confident that "you have only to make the request known & the men & money are at your command at once."

Marcus signed the letter, for while there is no indication that he shared Narcissa's ambivalence about missionary work, the many demands on him seemed excessive. As a physician, he was caring not only for the Cayuse but for the other missionaries and Hudson's Bay Company acquaintances as well. Each visit demanded travel and often gobbled up weeks of his time. He was also to put the mission on a self-supporting basis, teach the Cayuse the elements of farming, and introduce them to Christianity. Only a few months after their arrival, Narcissa noted with dismay that the pace was affecting Marcus's health. By March of 1838, Marcus informed the board that he was having trouble managing the secular affairs at the mission. "I have no one who understands how to labour without much supervision [and] I am obliged to spend much time in manual labor." The complaints continued. The next year he wrote, "I do not think it proper for me to hold the most difficult & responsible station in the mission . . . and have to discharge all the duties of Minister & Physician to the Mission." In 1840 he asserted that it is "to much for one man to fill so many trusts as I am called to here."

What with the depressing news about the need for economy and the importance of more populated pagan countries, the missionaries were surprised in the late summer of 1838 by the arrival of reinforcements. Henry Gray had returned to the East in the previous fall, found himself a missionary bride, and persuaded the ABCFM, whose financial situation had somewhat eased, to send out three couples to the Oregon mission. The board selected the Walkers and Eellses, originally assigned to Africa, and the Smiths, who had expected to go to Siam. When the Eellses, Smiths, and Walkers passed through Cincinnati on their way to join the Grays at the frontier, they met Cornelius Rogers, a young man who was a member of Lyman Beecher's church. On the spur of the moment, Rogers decided to go with the missionaries, even though he did not hold a board appointment.

The Whitmans learned of the reinforcements only a few days before the main party arrived in late August, just in time for the mission's annual meeting. Narcissa and Marcus gave the travelers a most cordial reception. Myra Eells found that the Whitmans "appear friendly and treat us with great hospitality." Mary Walker appreciated the feast of "melons, pumpkin pies & milk" and that evening's "fine dinner of vegetables, salt salmon, bread, butter, cream, &c." Sarah Smith also enjoyed the Whitman's kindness and found herself "glad to eat once more some nice potatoes, milk & vegetables."

The newcomers' descriptions of the mission showed the successful results of two years of effort. The adobe house was still rough. "Some of the floors are nailed & some of them loose boards & all unplaned," the windows and doors "sawed by hand and put together by no carpenter." The furniture, too, was "very primitive. The bedsteads are boards nailed to the side of the house, sink fashion, then some blankets and husks make the bed." Yet the women all recognized that "compared with traveling accommodations," the mission house was a good one. In fact, Sarah Smith decided that the Whitmans were "provided with many of the comforts & even the luxuries of life."

The mission farm still had no fences and needed more agricultural implements. Since there were no carts or wagons, oxen dragged the corn up to the house on brush, or Indian women carried it on their backs. But despite the lack of equipment, about seventeen acres of wheat, corn, potatoes, and turnips as well as a garden filled with melons and "all kinds of vegetables" stood near the house. Asa Smith estimated that the Whitmans would harvest at least one thousand bushels of potatoes and reported that the corn and wheat crops had been fine.

The arrival of three white couples and Mr. Rogers drew the Cayuse to the mission house. No sooner had the missionaries sat down to eat their first melons than "the house became thronged with Indians & we were obliged to suspend eating & shake hands with some 30, 40, or 50 of them." Asa Smith, whose sense of privacy was much like Narcissa's, found he disliked the Indians' habit of looking into the windows.

The newcomers were eager to assess the Cayuse's spiritual progress after almost two years of instruction. Mary Walker was impressed with the Indians' behavior during worship. "Before breakfast & supper the Indians were collected. In the morning one prayer was offered in English & one in Indian laguage. It was truly affect-

Paul Kane's *Falls on the Upper Pelouse River* captures the stark character of plateau landscape. Stark Museum of Art, Orange, Texas. Stark WOP22; CR IV-349.

ing to witness what two years had accomplished among these people. The exercises in the P.M. were out of doors. Dr. W. & Mr. Spalding addressed first, then the other gentlemen addressed them & Mr. Spalding interpreted. Several of the chiefs replied." But Asa Smith was more critical. He judged the Cayuse to be strangers to true or inner piety but seekers after truth.

At the general meeting of the mission, the men decided that the Walkers and Eellses would locate among the Flatheads. The Grays were to join the Spaldings at Lapwai, while the Smiths stayed at the Whitman mission. By the beginning of October, Walker and Eells had selected a site and begun building. But the two families would spend the winter with the Smiths and Whitmans at Waiilatpu.

The small adobe house and lean-to became quarters for the newcomers, who, as it turned out, had bickered their way across the country. Their problems suggested that Narcissa's difficulties with Eliza and Henry Spalding were hardly unique. No matter how keen the missionary commitment might be, virtual strangers thrown together for a demanding trip and a challenging assignment were likely to experience tension and to disagree. The absence of any leadership structure contributed to dissension. During the general meeting, tempers flared. Walker, Eells, and Smith "said respectively and decidedly they would not be associated with Mr. Gray." Over time, the pattern of hostile and friendly feelings would shift, leaving former enemies friends, and friends enemies.

Narcissa knew nothing of the hard feelings at first. She was initially delighted to have all the "excellent" helpers at Waiilatpu and expected the newcomers would be friends. Sarah Smith reminded her of her sister Clarissa, if "not quite as tall." The fact that Sarah's sister was the missionary "Mrs. Tracey, of Singapore" impressed Narcissa favorably. Mary Gray was "a most excellent person, and will, no doubt, be a great blessing to our missions." Narcissa told Mary Walker privately that she had a "partiality" for Mary and her husband. She was happy to have social prayer and regular services with a minister. Such favors "almost make us forget we are on heathen ground."

But Narcissa's delight with her visitors was short-lived. In mid-September, only a few weeks after the newcomers' arrival, Marcus left Waiilatpu for several weeks. As usual, he had an excellent reason to be away; he was going to buy mission supplies at Fort Vancouver. Mary Walker noticed that Narcissa seemed upset as Marcus bustled around getting ready to leave. The strain of overcrowding and incompatible temperaments was already beginning to show, and Narcissa must have felt angry at being left alone to cope with the visitors. "Finally he got himself in such a fret," Mary wrote, "that his wife began to cry which brought him to himself. He went on more calmly until he got ready to start."

Petty tensions between the newcomers contributed to Narcissa's growing disillusionment. Mary Walker was driven to distraction by Myra Eells's habit of snuffing and thought the women were inconsiderate in letting her do so much of the housework in her advanced stage of pregnancy. Sarah Smith claimed to like Mary Walker and Myra Eells better than either Mary Gray or Narcissa. But she may have shared her husband's scorn for Mary, whose baby was conceived almost immediately after her wedding day. Cushing Eells complained about Mary Walker's late hours. Clearly, the house was too small for all the missionaries to be in it together.

As usual, Narcissa concealed bad and embarrassing news from her family at home, where her letters would be read and circulated. To Elvira Perkins she wrote of "so much company and so many cares."

She hinted at problems with "our sisters here," who "have nothing else to do, comparatively speaking."

There was, of course, plenty to do at Waiilatpu: cooking, washing, churning, candle making, soap making, and a host of other domestic chores. A total of almost thirty people were living at the mission. Narcissa's serving girl had just died, leaving Narcissa without her assistance and saddened by the event itself. Alice was sick, and Narcissa was tired and worried. While Mary Walker tried to help out, it appears as if the others did not. Mary wrote in her diary near the end of November that Narcissa "has less help from the other ladies than she ought."

As mistress of the household, Narcissa quite naturally felt the other women should take on some of the household work. Used to being the eldest daughter in her own family and now the wife of the man who had been responsible for establishing the Oregon mission, Narcissa also expected a regard from the newcomers that they were unwilling to give to her. Because no formal distinctions existed within the mission family, some of the women felt they owed no special deference to Narcissa. When Sarah Smith asked Myra Eells to help her work on a dress of Narcissa's, Myra "declined because she pretended she did not like the fashion. She said too that Mrs. W. wrote all the time & her writing was of as much consequence as hers etc. Just as [if] she did not feel under the least obligation & had as good a right to the house as Mrs. W." Mary concluded that Myra "does not seem to like Mrs. Whitman very well."

While Narcissa had good reason to resent carrying the burden of domestic responsibilities, she seems to have contributed to the deteriorating situation. Nothing had prepared her to handle a group of fractious missionaries. When she had contemplated the missionary life, she had doubtless imagined her work with the heathen rather than her interactions with her coworkers. Now she did not have enough sympathy, patience, and tolerance to deal with conflicting personalities and aims.

Almost as soon as Mary Gray arrived at the mission, Narcissa suspected the new bride was pregnant. Perhaps in an attempt to show she was in charge, Narcissa pressed Mary Gray to reveal her situation. Although Mary did indeed think she was pregnant, Narcissa's prying was intrusive and offended her. When someone, possibly her own husband, spread the news of Mary's pregnancy before she wished others to know, she was convinced that Narcissa had be-

trayed her forced confidence. As late as February, Mary Gray revealed that the two women had not "succeeded in settling their
difficulties."

Mary Walker's comments suggest Narcissa's behavior was alternately avoidant and aggressive. At times, Narcissa held herself apart
but then was "not sparing of hints to others when they do not suit
her." Her comments were not well received. Narcissa offended Myra
Eells by telling Cushing Eells that "he thought of nobody but his
wife." In early October, "Mrs. W. has said and done many things
that do not suit Mrs. S. today." In mid-November, Mary just observed that "Mrs. W. appears to feel cross at everybody." One evening the two women talked. But Narcissa said little that helped Mary
understand her behavior. Mary could only conclude, "She seems
in a worry about [something]." With Marcus away, Narcissa was
doubtless taking out some of her resentment toward him on her
guests. But her behavior also had deep roots in her past. Her desire
to be the most important, her anger at those competing with her for
that prize, feelings first experienced in childhood, surged up in this
difficult situation to color her relationship with the mission women.

Certainly, if Mary Walker is to be believed, Narcissa's behavior
toward Mary changed dramatically as the weeks wore on. Initially
Narcissa had assured Mary that she favored the Walkers. Unlike the
other women, Mary seems to have tried to do her share of housework. But she was critical of Narcissa's behavior and thought Narcissa should be more explicit about what she expected others to do.
Instead of directing the household, however, Mary reported that
Narcissa withdrew. "After breakfast Mrs. W. went [into the] other
room and there remained through this whole day without concerning how or what was done," Mary wrote on November 17. "I know
not, I am sure, what she wishes or thinks, but think her a strange
housekeeper."

When Mary had her baby in December, relations between the two
women apparently worsened. By this time, Narcissa was in no condition for any more problems from her uninvited guests, whom perhaps she had never dreamed would spend the winter in her small
house. Mary had trouble nursing the baby. Her milk caked up, and
she had to have her breasts steamed, drawn, then covered with stick-
ing plaster. She needed extra care and attention, and so did the baby.

At first, Narcissa nursed the new baby as well as Alice. But perhaps
in another attempt to prove who was in charge, Narcissa weaned

Alice and refused to let Mary give her newborne a bottle. Mary reported that Narcissa accused her of not loving her baby, "not nursing it when I might if my heart had only been big enough or I had a mind to." The cruel words, which blamed Mary for not having sufficient milk to nurse her child, suggest that Narcissa had forgotten the rules of hospitality and charity and was abusing her power as hostess and nurse.

Once Mary was on her feet again—feeding the baby with a bottle and relying on Indian wet nurses—relations between the two women remained poor. One morning, Mary came to breakfast to find there was no cloth on the table. "This fresh mark of disrespect as I deem it" so insulted her that she was tempted not to eat. "If she does not begin to put away her hard heart soon I am resolved to call her to account or if I have wronged her know what my offence is. Tomorrow is our Maternal meeting and if she wears as much of Cain's countenance as usual I do not think I will unite with her in prayer."

For this tangled and cheerless situation, all bore some responsibility. Almost everyone annoyed someone else at one time or another. But the problems were also symptoms of unresolved issues in the mission family. First, there had been the conflict between the Spaldings and the Whitmans that stemmed from the fact that no one was really in charge of making mission decisions. The arrival of newcomers, of course, made matters worse. Without any leaders to establish clear goals and direct the mission's energies, competing interests and conflicting personalities caused ill will. Theoretically, the mission was to reach decisions by consensus. Though decisions were made, they were reversed with some regularity, as one or another of the missionaries refused to abide by what had been agreed upon.

Narcissa had problems with the men as well. She exchanged bitter words with Asa Smith on many occasions, especially when Marcus was away. He criticized what was in her pantry; she thought he drank too much milk and ate too much sugar. He was dissatisfied with their uncomfortable accommodations in the rooms used for worship with the Indians. Elkanah Walker chewed tobacco and spit into the fireplace.

Narcissa also struggled with Asa Smith over who was in charge at the mission. Although she was content to follow her husband's lead when he was at home and actually failed to organize her women guests effectively, she was not willing to defer to Asa Smith. With

Marcus away in Vancouver, Asa was overseeing the harvest. He seems to have thought that he was entitled to make all kinds of decisions, including ones that Narcissa considered her own to make. On one occasion, he sent for a melon to give to boys who were pounding corn. Reasonable as the reward was, "Mrs. W. countermanded." On another occasion, he refused to let the Hawaiian worker Jack help her. "Mrs. Whitman was quite out with Mr. Smith" as a result. While the differences were over petty matters, feelings were bitter.

There were also disagreements in the mission that mirrored controversies within the denomination at large. Narcissa was used to praying aloud, as she had done at Prattsburg. The new ministers disapproved of the custom, and since their wives were silent, so too was Narcissa. They also favored wine with communion, which was against Narcissa's teetotal principles. Narcissa regarded her guests as lacking in "high toned piety"; they were not "warm-hearted revival Christians." On many occasions, Narcissa retreated into her room for a day or more. At least once, she went down to the river to cry.

Mary Walker claimed that the "other ladies are as much perplexed as myself" by Narcissa's behavior. Yet there were so many problems between all members of the missionary party that after a monthly concert of prayer, "Dr., his wife & Mr. E. & wife, husband & self sit up till midnite talking about Mr. S. & G. Mrs. W. gets to feeling very bad, goes to bed crying." When the Smiths moved out of the house in early December into a finished room of the new house that was under construction, things improved, but only slightly.

Marcus, who had returned from Fort Vancouver in mid-October, was also having difficulties with the newcomers. Doubtless he was feeling the same household strains that provoked Narcissa's outbursts and retreats to her room. Asa Smith was critical of both Marcus and Henry Spalding, claiming that they had neglected to study Nez Percé. "They are not men who do much in the study. Dr. W. & Mr. Spaulding are both western men & partake of the peculiarities of western men." By the end of November, Mary Walker thought "Dr. W. quite out of patience with Mr. Smith." In February, Asa had decided that he could not stay at Waiilatpu but had to have his own mission station. At a special mission meeting called at the end of the month, it was decided that the Smiths should stay at Waiilatpu and the Whitmans should find and move to a new and more central location.

So trying did both the Whitmans find the situation at Waiilatpu that when the opportunity presented itself, they abandoned their guests at the mission. The Spaldings were holding a protracted meeting with the Nez Percé, and in the third week of January 1839, the Whitmans set out to join them. Narcissa was not only glad to be away from home but was moved by the meeting itself. Henry Spalding was having great success with the Nez Percé, although Asa Smith would criticize him for being too tolerant of the Indians and too lenient in his standards. Some of the Nez Percé Indians had already learned the appropriate evangelical behavior. Timothy "broke the silence with sobs weeping" and publicly acknowledged his black heart. His brother and their wives followed, with others showing "deep feeling; some in sobs and tears, others in anxious and solemn feeling." Although Jane could not catch Narcissa's full meaning, Narcissa told her sister she had not "realized so much enjoyment for a long time."

At the Waiilatpu mission, the Whitmans were not missed, or at least Narcissa was not. As Mary Walker put it, "Mrs. W. has dealt so largely in powder & balls of late that perhaps her absence will not detract much from our happiness." After three weeks away, the Whitmans returned refreshed. Narcissa was at first "in good humor . . . but at supper table & even before she began to show out."

Matters rapidly reached the exploding point. Mary wanted an explanation. Narcissa, perhaps because of her attendance at the protracted meeting, was increasingly troubled by her own behavior, which departed so radically from good manners and Christian love. During the first few days home, she stayed in her room. Then at Tuesday's prayer meeting, "in the greatest agitation," she begged Cushing Eells to pray for her. "After prayer she confessed to those present that she had abused them and intreated their forgiveness." Since Mary Walker had not been at the meeting, Narcissa sought her out for forgiveness too. Mary brought forth all her grievances. "I told her plainly that her treatment of us had been such as to render our residence in the family very unpleasant, that we felt we were wished out of the way." She brought up Narcissa's behavior over nursing. "But although she confessed she had done wrong and wished forgiveness yet she was disposed to justify her conduct in every particular! She said we did not know her own heart. That we thought her out of humor when it was anxiety for the salvation of sinners caused her to appear as she did. . . . This rather troubled us and we almost felt that she designed to make a cloak of Religion. Can it be, we thought, that anxiety for sinners can cause one to appear so petulant morose and crabbed? We almost felt worse than before." Eventually, Narcissa went to bed, with issues no more resolved than they had been at the end of the prayer meeting.

Mary Gray was equally perplexed when she tried to clear up what she considered her "trifling difficulty" with Narcissa. As she had done with Mary Walker, Narcissa "justified herself and pretended . . . that she was the injured party." Mary Gray observed that "she seems willing to settle difficulties when she can do so & justify herself [but] she seems unwilling . . . even [to] express sorrow that she has injured . . . feelings." Forced into relationships with people she had not chosen as her intimates, Narcissa simply could not cope. "Had I known her better," Mary Gray concluded, "I should have let her alone."

Narcissa dealt with her problems in the way many nineteenth-century women handled unpleasant realities: by claiming to be ill and staying in her room. When letters came from the Spaldings inviting the Whitmans to yet another protracted meeting, however, Narcissa was up and around. She was determined to accept the invitation, and the Whitmans left the mission a few days later. By the time they returned, the Walkers and Eellses had set off for their station at Tshimakain.

What was Narcissa thinking and feeling during the months when the missionaries were living at Waiilatpu? Mary Walker's diaries and letters present her own side of the story, which must have been colored by the difficulties she was having in her marriage. Mary Gray's letters lend support to Mary Walker's observations, but she was not a disinterested observer, any more than was Mary Walker. But while the two women's accounts may be exaggerated and overly critical, they suggest that Narcissa's behavior was erratic and that she was emotionally distraught. Unfortunately, aside from the brief references to her guests in her letter to Elvira Perkins, Narcissa did not discuss what was really going on at the mission until months after the events had taken place. In her letters home between August and March, she maintained that all was well with the reinforcements. The long trips away from the mission she described as attempts to learn the language. Finally, in a letter to Jane that she warned "had better be kept to yourselves," she admitted some of the difficulties at Waiilatpu. She placed the blame squarely on Cushing Eells and Elkanah Walker, who did not like "too many meetings, too many prayers," or women praying aloud, and who argued for "the necessity for wine, tobbaco, etc; and now how do you think I have lived with such folks right in my kitchen for the whole Winter? If you can imagine my feelings you will do more than I can describe." "So much care and perplexity," she explained, "nearly cost me a fit of sickness." In a dramatic appeal for sympathy, which revealed the depth of her unhappiness and her sense of injury, she declared, "I do not know but it would have taken my life had it not been for the journey I was permitted to take."

Narcissa's tendency to blame others rather than herself suggests that Mary Walker may have been right when she judged that Narcissa did not know her own heart. Certainly, Narcissa's habit of letting others imagine her responses rather than describing them herself suggests her inability or reluctance to examine herself too closely. And while she knew she had not borne up well under the strain of the visitors, there were other reasons not to probe too deeply. Conscious that she had been urging Jane to become a missionary, how could she admit the lapses in her own behavior or point to serious problems at the Oregon station? As a missionary and as a model for others, she was constrained in what she could reveal to others, even when it was to be "kept to yourselves."

When the Walkers and Eellses left Waiilatpu in March 1839, the status of the Whitmans' station was unclear. Marcus rode out early that month to seek a new mission site. He and Smith could not agree on who would go where. Narcissa, with her house to herself once more and a new and larger house under construction, was unwilling to leave Waiilatpu. Smith was annoyed. "It is very evident that the Dr. & his wife were not so willing to leave this place as was pretended. . . . I lament that I ever consented to remain here." In April it was resolved, finally, that the Smiths would go to Kamiah (in present-day Idaho) to study Nez Percé.

The arrival of the reinforcements might have started off a new and more vigorous missionary initiative. Instead, it resulted in weakening of the missionary enterprise as the missionaries argued and scattered to different stations. At the same time, at Waiilatpu, the Whitmans were beginning to recognize the obstacles that hindered conversion. When Marcus and Narcissa returned from the Spaldings' protracted meetings with the Nez Percé, Marcus "spent more than usual time in worship and instructing" the Cayuse who had returned for spring planting. But "instead of yielding to the truth, they oppose it vigorously, and to this day, some of them continue to manifest bitter opposition."

The Cayuse had now heard enough of the Whitmans' teaching to realize that a few new additional observances would not satisfy the missionaries. What the missionaries sought was nothing less than the abandonment of Cayuse religious beliefs as well as the rejection of "sinful" tribal practices such as dancing, gambling, and horse racing. But what the Whitmans held out as a replacement for comforting traditions was both unappealing and cheerless. While the missionaries talked about eternal life and heaven, they seemed to be offering the Indians hell and eternal suffering. Many of the Cayuse rejected this offer.

Disenchantment and discouragement were difficult to live with, but Alice helped to compensate her mother for all the frustrations. That source of contentment ended on a quiet Sabbath afternoon in June 1839. As was their habit, Marcus and Narcissa were reading. So absorbed was Narcissa in her book, that she only vaguely noticed that Alice had climbed out of Marcus's lap, taken two cups from the table, and announced that she would get some water. Suddenly realizing that she could not hear Alice, Narcissa sent her domestic helper, Margaret McKay, to look for the child. The Hawaiian boy, Mungo, reported finding two cups down by the river bank, alerting Marcus and Narcissa to the awful possibility that Alice had wandered down to the river by herself. "In wild dismay" the parents rushed to the river and searched up and down its banks. Finally, an Indian jumped into the river near the place where Mungo had found the cups and discovered Alice's body a short distance away. "It was too late; she was dead. We made every effort possible to bring her to life, but all was in vain."

Without a moment's warning, Narcissa lost the emotional center of her life, her ray of cheer in what often seemed a cheerless existence. Overwhelmed with grief, she asked herself why the Lord had seen it "necessary to afflict us." In her child's death, she saw the terrible truth that she and Marcus had loved Alice too much. "You know the blessed Saviour will not have His children bestow an undue attachment upon creature objects without reminding us of His own superior claim upon our affections."

For a few dreadful moments, Narcissa agonized over Alice's spiritual fate. She had grown up believing that the unconverted were destined for hell. When her servant girl Sarah Hull had died, Narcissa had not discerned clear evidence of a change of heart. Toward the end of her illness, Sarah had "seemed . . . more sensible," but Narcissa was not confident that the girl had escaped the fires of hell. What then of little Alice, who was not even three?

Narcissa's love for her child proved far stronger than the orthodoxy that had shaped her understanding of life and death, though her position on infant death would soon become typical of mainstream Protestantism. Remembering the way in which she had consecrated Alice to God, the earnest prayers she had offered up when she had seen her daughter's heart "defiled by sin and in need of the cleansing efficacy of the Saviour's blood," and the child's "thoughtfulness and relish for worship and particularly her own attempts at prayer," Narcissa convinced herself that even without Alice's own conversion, the child's spirt was "at rest in the bosom of the blessed Jesus." The leniency she could extend to her own child, however, she would never be able to extend to the Cayuse.

This belief that Alice was in heaven helped her survive the terrible days following the accident, when she was without the support of family or intimate friends. The news went out to the Spaldings, who hurried to Waiilatpu to help with the funeral. As for the Walkers and Eellses, they "did not deem it expedient to return."

As they waited for the Spaldings, Narcissa washed the body, prepared the shroud, and sat by her dead child for three days. "This proved to be a great comfort to me, for so long as she looked natural and was so sweet and I could caress her I could not bear to have her out of my sight." When the Spaldings arrived, the body had begun to decompose, and Narcissa was ready to accept the burial. "I wished then to put her out of my sight and felt it a great privilege that I could put her in so safe, quiet and desirable a resting-place as the grave—to see her no more until the morning of the resurrection."

After the funeral, the Whitmans returned with the Spaldings to Lapwai for a short stay. The Grays were now living at that station. The Whitmans, who were humbled by grief and a sense that God was chastening them "to bring them where they ought to be and to teach them their duty," had no defenses to explain away the missionary troubles. Narcissa and Marcus made apologies for the past and asked for pardon.

When they came home, a letter from the Eellses awaited them.

Myra was seriously ill. Marcus set off immediately. Abandoning his wife at her moment of greatest need, Marcus left Narcissa to face "the trial . . . upon me which I had dreaded more than anything else—to have my husband go from home and leave me alone. It was then that I realized the full reality of my bereavement." Narcissa could scarcely function. She kept thinking Alice was in the house, kept hearing "her footsteps all day long." Although two Indian children were dying of dysentery, she could not bring herself to sit with them in their last hours. She managed to oversee the funeral, but "all these things together made me feel as I never felt before . . . at times lost sight of my supporter." When Henry Perkins unexpectedly arrived from the Methodist mission at The Dalles, it was like "an angel's visit." Elvira's letter was "a cordial" to Narcissa's "afflicted heart."

Narcissa did not recover quickly or easily from Alice's death. As she grieved and coped with "excessive feeling," she tried to make sense of the sad event. Like most parents in an earlier time, she saw God's hand in what had happened. But reflecting a newer understanding of childhood, she began to see that her daughter, while not free of sin, had been of "too delicate material to remain here longer and be subject to the ills of this cruel and unfriendly world." The conviction that "Jesus' love for her was greater than mine" replaced the idea that God might be punishing too-affectionate parents. A year after the event, her heart still bleeding at "fond recollections," she had concluded that Alice had been taken away because "our situation and responsibilities require that most of my time should be spent in teaching school, which I could not do without her having been exposed to the contaminating influence of heathenism and very much neglected." She comforted herself with the thought that in her own way, Alice had died for the missionary cause and was heartened by her belief that Alice was in heaven.

There was another terrible truth that Narcissa was unable to confront fully—that her own inattentiveness had been responsible for the accident. Having blamed Cayuse mothers for their negligence, she had paid more attention to her reading than to her daughter. Now her child had been the one to die.

In the end, although Narcissa accepted some of the implications of newly emerging ideas that a child's welfare depended more on a mother's care than on the decision of an all-powerful God, she could not hold herself accountable. To her mother, she explained, "Perhaps you will think we cast reflections upon ourselves for neglect, or as being the cause of dear Alice's death. We cannot do it, although we see now how it might have been prevented, could we have known or anticipated it. What I have to say more is, do pray for us."

In the months following Alice's death, Narcissa continued her daily routine, teaching the children to read Nez Percé, sometimes with Marcus's assistance, and overseeing domestic chores. There were also new guests. Waiilatpu was becoming a stopping point for secular visitors as well as "the missionaries' tavern." In the fall after Alice's accident, two independent missionary couples from Oberlin, the Griffens and Mungers, arrived in Oregon Territory. Marcus hired Asa Munger to work on the new house, which was still under construction. His wife helped Narcissa in the house. An ABCFM couple from Hawaii, the Halls, were also at the mission. Mrs. Hall had a spinal disease, and the couple hoped that the change of climate and attention of a doctor would help her ailment. Both Mrs. Hall and Mrs. Munger would have babies at Waiilatpu.

These visitors provided Narcissa with company during a dreadful time. "It seems as if the Lord's hand was in it in sending Mr. and Mrs. Munger here," Narcissa wrote her mother, "and I know not how to feel grateful enough." Mrs. Hall even slept with Narcissa when Marcus was away. Luckily for Narcissa, the newcomers were her kind of people, "interesting and lovely" and "warm-hearted revival Christians." Narcissa had "many precious seasons of prayer and social worship . . . which seems like revival seasons at home that I used to enjoy."

Despite the sympathetic companions and her claim that Alice's death was all for the best, her grieving was stretching beyond the bounds of what the nineteenth century considered acceptable. Although she tried to honor norms by bearing her loss "without murmering thought," she sank into a deep and long depression. Like other women who felt their "occupation . . . gone" when their babies died, Narcissa felt keenly the loss of her maternal role. "I suffer from dejection considerably," she confessed to her father in April 1840. She ruminated about death—her mother's, her child's, her own. "When I have felt the most desponding and cast down I have thought perhaps dear mother was not alive to pray for me any more," she wrote. "I often look up to that place of rest where my dear babe has gone and feel that I shall soon follow her."

Before Alice's death, Narcissa had enjoyed good health. By the fall of 1840, a kidney infection brought her "very low." This was the first of many bouts of sickness that accompanied her depression. She recovered, then had a complete relapse. She did not expect to be able to teach for the rest of the winter and kept to her room. It hurt even to write. "I am very weak and feeble, and much thinking or excitement overcomes me." Although she attributed her breakdown to living in the drafty old house, which she had once found so cozy, she was responding to the loss of both her beloved child and her illusions about missionary work.

While Narcissa had retired from much of the daily round of missionary work by the fall and winter of 1840, she continued to report on the missionary enterprise as a whole. In just four years, the missionary field had changed dramatically. It was becoming clear that Oregon was not always to be a remote mission territory like Siam or India. Americans were learning that overland travel was possible and were becoming interested in the possibility of immigration to Oregon. "A tide of immigration appears to be moving this way rapidly," Narcissa told her mother in 1840. "What a few years will bring forth we know not." The missionaries were in a race with time. White diseases had already had a deadly impact on the Indians. When settlers came, they would bring with them new threats such as alcohol. It seemed almost impossible to work fast enough to save the "hunted, despised and unprotected Indian—from entire extinction."

The Protestant missionary endeavor was facing competion from Roman Catholic missionaries. Many of the Hudson's Bay employees were Catholic, and the company had offered free passage across Canada to two priests, Fathers François Blanchet and Modeste Demers. They arrived in Oregon Territory in 1838. While the priests ministered to present and former members of the Hudson's Bay Company, they also were interested in converting the Indian population. In the summer of 1839 Demers spent about four weeks at Fort Colville, not far from the Walker-Eells mission, and two weeks at Fort Walla Walla. At both sites, he introduced the Indians to some basic Christian ideas and baptized them.

For Catholics, baptism marked the beginning of the Christian life, and it was as appropriate to baptize Indians as it was to baptize newborn infants. For the ABCFM, however, baptism represented a hard-won victory over sin and was usually administered only after a thoroughgoing conversion experience and sustained evidence of a regenerated life. The Whitmans had not found any of the Cayuse ready for baptism. Even Spalding, who worked more effectively with the Nez Percé than the Whitmans did with the Cayuse, or who was less caught up in doctrinaire attitudes, had baptized only eight Indians at Lapwai by 1839.

The Catholics' practice of easy baptism forced the Protestant missionaries to consider disquieting questions. Might the effort to save the Indians from the fires of hell fail—not because the Indians clung to their heathen ways but because they accepted Roman Catholicism and certain damnation? To contemplate the possibility of failure, however, seemed to question God's purpose. Rather than blaming God for sending them on an impossible task, the missionaries had to find other explanations for their slow progress.

Narcissa decided one of the problems was her imperfect command of Nez Percé, and she resolved to learn the language better. Unable to consider the possibility that the Indians might prefer Catholicism to Calvinistic doctrines and standards, Narcissa endowed the Roman Catholic priests with almost magical powers. They had enough "influence to draw all the people away from us. Some they have forbidden to visit us again, and fill all of their minds with distractions about truths we teach . . . say we have been talking to them about their bad hearts long enough, and too long—say we ought to have baptized them a long ago."

Depressed and puzzled that the Lord did not crown their efforts with success, Narcissa heaped criticism on the Cayuse, who were ignoring the good news. Her frustration was one often experienced by Americans who were forced to find reasons for native resistance to American culture. The Indians, she decided, were proud, vain, and frivolous. Not understanding the role that stories played in teaching tribal ethical and behavioral values, she condemned their love of stories, of "something new and marvelous . . . any subject that does not touch their heart. These they will repeat day after day and night after night, as if their salvation depended upon it." They were "supremely selfish" and "displeased the moment you attempt to shake the foundations of their hope."

Cayuse habits grew no more tolerable. When the Cayuse were ill, Narcissa claimed they were "such miserable nurses that they die by their own neglect." She hated their dirt and fleas, the way they made her house filthy and her burden of housework greater. "We must clean after them," she pointed out tellingly, "for we have come to elevate them and not to suffer ourselves to sink down to their standard." What she identified as "the greatest trial" to her feelings as a woman was "to have her cooking and eating room always filled with four or five or more Indians—men—especially at meal time." When the new house was finished, they would be confined to one room. Perhaps there would also be yard fences "to keep the Indians from making a highway of every part of our house and breaking our windows." Venetian blinds would keep out prying eyes.

They were exceedingly "proud, haughty, and insolent"; they stretched her "patience and forbearance." They were never grateful for what the missionaries did for them and were murmuring that the Whitmans should pay for their land.

To Elvira Perkins, with whom it was easier to be candid than with her family at home, Narcissa confessed in January 1840, "I am tired of living at this poor dying rate. To be a missionary in name and to do so little or nothing for the benefit of heathen souls, is heartsickening." For the first time, she expressed some of the conflicts she had been feeling as she hinted at leaving the missionary field. "I sometimes almost wish to give my place to others who can do more for their good." This was no more than a passing thought, to be quickly shunted aside. Yet it reoccurred. In October that same year, Narcissa told her parents that she did not expect to see them again, "unless the Providence of God should make it necessary for us to leave the field." She hastily added, "We had rather die in the battle than to retreat, if the Lord willingly appear for us and remove all that is in the way of His salvation; take up every stumbling block out of our hearts and from this mission."

For the moment, then, there was no retreating. This mission was the last effort the board would make for the poor Indians. At the very time Narcissa was writing, other members of the mission were busily sending the ABCFM tales of contention in Oregon. When the board heard news from the missionaries about their squabbles with one another, they would be even less inclined to pursue a missionary effort that seemed already to be foundering. Narcissa begged for prayers.

CHAPTER 5

I Am Entirely Unfitted for the Work

IN early 1841 Narcissa learned that the Eellses' house at the Tshima-kain mission had burned and that Myra was ailing. The situation at Tshimakain prompted her to reflect that she lived in a "world of trials." Alice's death, her own uncertain health, the continued squab-bling among the Oregon missionaries, and the meager number of converts amply suggested the tribulations of missionary life. Perhaps Narcissa occasionally recalled the last stanza of the missionary hymn she had sung at her own marriage only five years earlier.

> In the deserts let me labor,
> On the mountains let me tell,
> How he died—the blessed Saviour—
> To redeem a world from hell!

If she did, she must have wondered at its misleadingly simple view of missionary work.

In some respects, however, the mission at Waiilatpu had succeeded wonderfully. With the help of hired Indian laborers (mostly from the Walla Walla tribe), Marcus had established a thriving farm. One summer visitor, noting wheat seven feet high and Indian corn of nine feet, estimated a harvest of "about three hundred bushels of wheat, with a quantity of corn and potatoes." The mission garden provided "all the vegetables raised in the United States, and several kinds of melons." The herd of cattle was growing, and the mis-sionaries now dined on beef rather than horsemeat and enjoyed cheese and butter with their meals. A sawmill and several gristmills eased some of the heavy work connected with the farm, and Marcus was having irrigation ditches constructed. Outbuildings such as "Corn Cribs, & Granary. Harness house Smoke & hen houses double back house Cow & Horse pen" gave the mission a bustling and settled look.

Living conditions had also improved. Two "very comfortable"

adobe dwellings now stood on the mission grounds. The exterior of the Whitmans' attractive new house was whitewashed and trimmed with green. Inside, there was a dining room, parlor, private bedroom, and kitchen, which would be furnished with a cooking stove during the winter of 1842. All the rooms had painted floors and slate-colored woodwork and appropriate furniture—settees, rocking chairs, clothes presses, and even a curio case. Pictures hung on the walls, while the family ate off attractive blue and white English china. When she left the mission to stay at Fort Walla Walla in 1842, Narcissa found the accommodations that had seemed so marvelous in 1836 somewhat primitive in comparison with her "good convenient" home.

The mission's material abundance was a tribute to the Whitmans' values and hard work, but the Cayuse were not pleased. Narcissa reported that the Indians feel "we are rich and getting rich by the houses we dwell in and the clothes we wear and hang out to dry after washing from week to week and the grain we consume in our families." Whatever the specific material and spiritual benefits the Cayuse had expected from the missionary presence, they certainly had not anticipated that the missionaries would prosper as the Cayuse looked on. Neither of the Whitmans worried much about the Indians' perspective, however. For one thing, Narcissa reasoned, they were wrong. The wealth did not belong to the Whitmans personally but to the ABCFM. Furthermore, the missionaries believed that their material progress symbolized the superiority of white civilization and its work ethic. Perhaps it would inspire emulation. There was little reason, then, to question its appropriateness.

Life at the mission during the winter of 1841 was unhurried. The alternation of work and leisure that characterized the settled agricultural cycle of Waiilatpu did not correspond to the rhythms of Cayuse life. Only a few Indians camped near the station. There was little missionary work to do. Marcus continued Sabbath services; when the Indians returned for spring planting, Narcissa and Mary Gray did some teaching.

Even though Narcissa was not in good health that winter, she enjoyed the company of the Grays and three independent missionary couples who were living at the mission. The women formed a companionable and compatible group. Narcissa had resolved her differences with Mary Gray and found her a "lovely sister and an excellent associate." Adeline Littlejohn, who came from Prattsburg with all kinds of local news, including a description of sister Harriet's future husband, was a welcome addition to the society at the mission.

Shared female experience created bonds of intimacy and promoted discussion of matters that were important to all of them. What might Myra's illness be? As the women knew, the term covered pregnancy as well as disease. On the basis of "the combined knowledge experiance & observation of all the matron ladies at Waiilatpu," the women concluded Myra was indeed pregnant. They counseled her not to "be anxious about herself [for] it will not be as well for her in the end," and hoped "to hear more about her."

The worst days of isolation had passed. Narcissa still considered Marcus's long absences on medical or mission business a trial. But when she talked about being alone, she often meant alone in her own comfortable house. With the number of people who lived at the mission for weeks or months at a time, she now appreciated quiet time for reading and reflection.

Narcissa still missed the religious life of a settled community like Prattsburg, with a church sanctuary for worship and tolerance of the less dignified practice of allowing women to pray in mixed company. Yet, the size of the group at the Whitman mission allowed a devotional life far closer to that at home than had initially been possible. Narcissa reported a full schedule of religious activities: a weekly Sabbath service with sermon, a prayer meeting held by all the Oregon missions every Tuesday evening, a "regular" prayer meeting on Friday evening, a Bible class, a maternal meeting twice a month, and a monthly prayer concert. Even without a church building in which to worship, the missionaries found "Him present with us."

Yet devotions took on a troubling character as the winter progressed. Asa Munger, would-be missionary to Oregon, began to pray in strange and troubling ways that helped keep Narcissa from concentrating on her devotions. Attempts to talk to him privately were fruitless, for Munger surprisingly "did not receive . . . [admonitions] with that Christian meekness and improvement we expected in him." It soon became shockingly clear that Munger harbored religious delusions. "He claims it as a duty we owe him, as the representative of Christ's church, to obey him in all things," Narcissa revealed. "He is our lawgiver as Moses was to the children of Israel."

No one knew quite what to do with the insane man. In this unsettling situation, Narcissa's sympathy gravitated toward "Poor Sister M." As a woman who relied on her husband for direction but who was often left to manage on her own, Narcissa easily identified with the plight of a wife who had lost her guide and protector.

Asa Munger's behavior grew increasingly bizarre, and it became clear that the couple should leave the station and make arrangements to return to the States. The Mungers departed, but before they could start the long journey across the country, Asa committed suicide. His grisly end (he nailed his hand to a fireplace, apparently expecting that, like Christ, he would rise in three days) shook the missionaries profoundly. The depressing death hardly resembled the ennobling scenes of the triumphant departure toward heaven that the *Missionary Herald* so often described. But perhaps it suited the realities of Oregon missionary life. Narcissa was glad to be "spared such a scene."

Against the unsettling backdrop of a religious commitment gone berserk, Narcissa examined her own heart. In the past, she had been all too ready to find extenuating circumstances for her actions and to see bad temper and anger in those around her rather than in herself. She blamed Henry Spalding's "wicked jealousy," "great pique," and "bitter feeling" for the difficulties between the two families and even believed that he had prejudiced the other missionaries against the Whitmans. Having the Walkers, Eellses, and Smiths crowding her kitchen had understandably made her short tempered. Now depressed, ill, and often gloomy, she did not have the resilience to justify her behavior so easily.

There were immediate and pressing reasons to think about the mission as a whole and her own commitment to its goals. The missionaries disagreed about how the mission should proceed and complained about each other. Marcus struggled with responsibilities at Waiilatpu that he thought excessive and became ill in the winter of 1840–41 from "overdoing . . . & from hard labour." Yet he was annoyed at Henry for erecting a blacksmith shop and establishing a printing press at Lapwai, when they should have been at his own mission station. He was scornful of Henry's ability to master Nez Percé, which the new missionaries had insisted should be the language of instruction. Henry Spalding, for his part, thought that some of the newcomers were too negative about the Indians' possibilities of salvation.

The disagreements and ill will shocked Edwin Hall, who, upon his return to the ABCFM mission in Hawaii, wrote a candid letter to Marcus. "In fact, to look back upon transactions that I *witnessed*, I can hardly believe that they actually took place among missionaries." The Smiths were considering leaving the field, and Cornelius Rogers thought the future of the mission was dark. Complaining letters had already gone off to the board, accusing Henry Spalding of being too independent and even deceitful. Edwin Hall urged the missionaries to work for harmony, even if that meant that some must leave the field. Despite their own prejudices, the Whitmans realized that the missionaries had to have a "right state of feeling" toward one another if the effort was to continue with any promise of success.

The disarray among the mission party might have been less troubling had the missionaries been more successful at converting the Indians. Although Narcissa was hopeful that there might be "an abundant harvest of souls" at Waiilatpu in early 1841, no "melting times" followed. While a modern analysis of the missionaries' failure might focus on cultural differences between the Indian tribes and the Protestant missionaries, organizational problems within the mission, inadequate interpersonal skills, or even character flaws, Narcissa saw the problem in terms of the spiritual corruption of the missionaries themselves.

Narcissa's understanding of the mission's troubles grew naturally out of her religious training. Like many evangelical parents, Narcissa's mother had introduced her to serious devotional books like Philip Doddridge's *The Rise and Progress of Religion in the Soul*. Though it was unlikely that Narcissa recalled the book in any detail, she probably remembered one of Doddridge's main points: the ease with which even the converted could fall away from the living faith. The telltale sign of backsliding, Doddridge warned, was a diminished fervency in prayer. Munger's unorthodox prayers made Narcissa aware that her prayer life was unsatisfactory. Faced with evidence of spiritual decay, Narcissa, as Doddridge advised, set about searching for her secret sin. Only then could the hard work of reformation begin.

Narcissa's self-examination began in early 1841, when she was thinking about the mission's elusive goal. What prevented "an abundant harvest of souls," she decided, was "a right state of feeling— union, faith and prayer among the labourers." If only "each one would go to work about his own heart and leave his neighbors in the hand of God," the great work "would soon be accomplished."

That the progress of the mission depended upon the state of individual hearts was evident. But she was still thinking more about other people's spiritual flaws than her own. The visit of the Methodist missionary Henry Perkins moved her to study herself more closely. She told Elvira Perkins, "Your husband . . . was pleased to show some of us our hearts; at least mine as I never saw it before, and I trust it has been a profitable lesson."

It was with Mary Walker that Narcissa shared the details of her self-examination. Although she was often uncomfortable with Mary in person, perhaps she turned to her because Mary knew of the general troubles of the mission as Elvira Perkins did not. Or perhaps confession to someone who had experienced ill-treatment was easier than confession to one who little suspected one's personal failings. Whatever the reason, Narcissa poured out her discovery of her "awful backslidings" to Mary on March 8. "I think I have not for a long time had so clear view of the state of my heart for a few weeks past," she admitted. "Perhaps never in my whole life have I been led to see so distinctly the hidden iniquity & secret evils of my heart that have grown with my years untill every spark of right feeling . . . has seemed well nigh extinguished." Of all the missionaries, she now regarded herself "to be the most unfit" and "unworthy." She wondered why she had been allowed to come.

Her failure, she believed, lay in her relations with other members of the mission party rather than with the Cayuse. Her "unholy passions" and self-indulgent behavior had grieved the other missionaries, God's own children, and undermined spiritual work. She had been "proud & self confident," hypocritical, and blind to her own faults. It was hardly surprising, she thought, that Spalding had hesitated to join the Oregon mission with her or that other members of the mission party found it difficult to live with the Whitmans.

To twentieth-century observers, it might seem that Narcissa misidentified what had gone wrong and that she was too hard on herself. Her conclusion that she was wholly in the wrong was certainly excessive and doubtless prompted by the feeling of unworthiness that often accompanies depression. Although Narcissa suggested that others were also engaged in the process of self-examination, except for Mary Walker, their journals and letters do not reveal similar feelings of guilt and responsibility.

Narcissa's deep anguish lasted for two or three days. She "could see no . . . evidence of . . . being a Christian." Her "heart was . . .

deceitful & blinded and covered up with sin." She abandoned hope of salvation. Such despair, however, was a necessary stage in the emotional cycle of repentance and reformation and was similar to the feeling anxious Christians encountered just before conversion. The entire spiritual crisis, in fact, resembled a conversion experience and was surely more powerful for Narcissa than her youthful conversion at the age of twelve.

At the end of despair came hope, the realization that salvation lay in an appeal to "the mercy of God," a sense of reconnection. On the other side of the experience, Narcissa begged the Walkers and Eellses to forgive her past behavior. "I see myself now to have been wholly in the wrong—had my heart been right in the sight of God as it should have been, all those difficulties might have been avoided."

Narcissa's remarkable letter troubled Mary and caused her to do some soul-searching. In her diary she wondered about her own responsibility for the mission's problems. "Felt afraid I was more to blame than any body else in the Mission & that altho I might have kept up a better appearance, yet perhaps my motives about every thing had been wrong & in the sight of God I was more sinful than any one. I went about my business but still my mind dwelt on the subject."

Narcissa's confrontation with her moral and personal failings, though it may have been prompted partly by depression, represented a milestone in her spiritual life. As she took responsibility for her errors, she listened more closely to the conscience that her mother had tried to shape. But despite the mortification that came with self-discovery, she could not humble herself before the Spaldings. Although she had openly admitted to Mary Walker that Henry had correctly assessed her character flaws, apparently she did not seek forgiveness from either of the Spaldings. That spring Eliza suffered a miscarriage and was in uncertain health. The only letter that Henry recorded receiving from the Whitmans was a "not very nice letter" from Marcus. During the general meeting that summer, Henry found neither of the Whitmans particularly contrite or conciliatory and was "astonished at self-righteousness manifested by our bro. & sis." Eliza did not attend that meeting, nor the one the following year. Only during the winter of 1843–44 did Narcissa reach a reconciliation with Eliza, at Eliza's initiative after a nearly fatal illness. Narcissa recorded that "Mrs. S. has written me very kindly, showing that her feelings have undergone a change. . . . This is a great consolation to us, and we hope and believe that *they* both feel different toward us."

While Narcissa recognized her tendency to be proud and even arrogant, self-knowledge did not always transform her behavior. That July the Whitmans went to the station at Tshimakain to await Myra Eells's delivery. They stayed with the Eellses, and Mary Walker feared that they "do not feel quite right towards us"; she could not help but notice the attention Myra received and remember the way Narcissa had treated her when she had delivered her first child. "It does seem to me if a little of the care & kindness which she receives had been bestowed on me, I should at least get on much easier." But the two women did have at least one lengthy talk.

In the long run, Narcissa enjoyed more cordial relations with the other missionary women. The rounds of accusation and apology still continued, however, nourished by the evangelical commitment to moral advice and correction and perhaps by the renewed sense of connection that confession encouraged. Mary was often touchy and liable to interpret some of Narcissa's comments as criticisms. And Narcissa still appeared proud to Mary. The next year Mary wondered again how responsible she was for the mission's troubles and whether she had not congratulated herself too often "that I was not like some other Missionaries." Presumably she meant Narcissa. But the women were more conciliatory and flexible than they had been in the early days in Oregon.

Even if Narcissa could not always control her behavior or feelings, her spiritual crisis bore fruit. Prayer and reflection became more central in her life, as her letters suggest. But self-knowledge had a price. The confidence and good spirits that led her to the mission field and that initially sustained her there disappeared. While personal humility might serve the missionary well, the lack of energy and confidence did not. Increasingly, Narcissa talked of the trials and tribulations of missionary life and pictured herself as powerless and pathetic, "a poor weak creature." She needed assistance and pressed her sister Jane to join her at Waiilatpu.

During this difficult year, Narcissa longed for even "one short hour of *conversation, counsel and prayer* with the dear object of my earliest and continued affections, my father and mother." Neither her husband nor her Oregon associates could meet her needs for sympathy and advice. The male missionaries, of course, received regular counsel from the ABCFM, but Narcissa and the other women had no such dependable channels of communication and guidance. Instead, they had to rely on family and friends, when and if they wrote.

Although she never had the energy or perhaps the desire to give her parents all the details of what she now considered her unchristian behavior (perhaps that confession was just too difficult to make), Narcissa sketched a general picture of her state of mind for them. She was finding it "one of my most difficult studies . . . to know my own heart, the motives by which I am actuated from day to day." Now that she knew the qualifications necessary for missionary life, she was astonished that she had been permitted to come. For the first time, she confessed what she must have suspected for some time. "I feel every day . . . that I am entirely unfitted for the work, and have many gloomy, desponding hours."

However unfit she felt for missionary life, Narcissa's dilemma was that she could not openly acknowledge that she might have made a mistake in choosing to become a missionary. Her mother had pointedly questioned her in a letter Narcissa had recently received, "Do you never talk about visiting home for the sake of recruiting your exhausted strength?" Do you "regret the step . . . taken and the sacrifice made for Christ in behalf of the perishing heathen?" While Narcissa sometimes doubted her own motive, "whether it is purely . . . for the glory of God or from some selfish principle," how could she ever admit to a mistaken vocation? At home, Prattsburg neighbors read her letters from the mission field aloud in their monthly concerts, while the *Missionary Herald* informed evangelical Christians of the progress of the Oregon mission. Friends sent barrels of supplies west and prayed for the missionaries' success. Her mother took pride in her Christian commitment. Christ had demanded that she do her duty. Narcissa was boxed in by expectations, support, family and local pride, and faith. So while she could admit weakness, she had to reaffirm her choice. "That I wish myself back again, or that I had not come, I can safely say I have no such feeling; or that I would be in any other field than this, notwithstanding all our perplexities, trials and hardships."

A new note was unconsciously creeping into her letters, however, hinting that she sometimes entertained the thought of another life. After only a few years in the mission field, Narcissa explained that "our lives are . . . spent." The future was uncertain. Neither she nor Marcus knew "how long we shall be permitted to remain" among the Cayuse. Bad health might "require a change of circumstances."

Conditional statements seen in conjunction with her acknowledged difficulty in knowing and analyzing "the motive by which I am actuated day to day" betrayed what she could not admit—doubts about purpose. "If I am not deceived, if I know what my feelings are, it is my prevailing ardent desire to see the salvation of the Lord" among the Cayuse, she affirmed.

Elvira Perkins once asked Mary Walker, "What is the temper of your missionary zeal and courage?" What would Narcissa have answered, had Elvira directed the question at her? Duty and marriage kept her in the field, but she had little energy for the task of conversion. As she told her sister Jane, unless faith and love were "in lively exercise . . . the work becomes burdensome, especially if health fails." The work was "hard, uphill . . . even the best of it."

As Narcissa slowly explored her "evil" heart and flawed character in early 1841, the men of the mission tried to deal with the tensions and differences between them. More self-confident and sure of their positions than a woman like Narcissa, they did not indulge in much soul-searching.

At the general meeting held in July at Waiilatpu, Henry Spalding learned that Asa Smith, Cornelius Rogers, Henry Gray, and Edwin Hall, the Hawaiian missionary, had all complained about Spalding to the board. Marcus had been more restrained in his comments, but he disliked Henry's operations and his independence. It is quite likely he was jealous that Henry's Indians seemed to be making greater spiritual progress than the Cayuse. He still took Narcissa's part in the old quarrel between the two. Yet all the men realized that it was important to resolve their differences if the mission was to continue.

Amazed at the opposition to him, Henry Spalding made the necessary apologies. Marcus informed the board that the meeting "promised . . . harmony." While he was not entirely sanguine about the future, Marcus could say that Spalding "has pledged himself that he will not be so jealous & that he will cooperate with the Mission & most especially with Mrs Whitman & myself." Though the men had reached a resolution of sorts, all were aware that the board would respond to the letters of complaint long before the news of "harmony" reached them. The future of the mission still was in doubt.

Jealousies and misunderstanding, in fact, had not ended. Since Eliza had not been present for the supposed reconciliation, there was reason to wonder how sincere Henry's contrition was. Nor was Henry the only one at fault. Marcus, keenly aware that there were no converts at Waiilatpu, refused to accept Henry's candidates for admission to the church when he visited Lapwai that November. He took the opportunity to detail a long list of complaints against Henry and led him to believe that he would be satisfied only if Henry were out of the mission altogether. Henry sent separate letters of apology to all members of the missionary party in February 1842, but bad feelings lingered. When he refused to come to the general meeting the following summer, the other missionaries insisted on his presence.

The women attended this meeting, apparently to listen rather than to participate. They heard "much to make our ears tingle." As the missionaries made another attempt to resolve their problems, Marcus again called Henry to account. But the tables had turned. Several of the men now accused Marcus of keeping grudges alive. Marcus must have lost his temper, for he threatened to leave the mission unless he could "go on in his own way without being checked." Feelings ran high; Elkanah Walker feared that "all hope [for the mission] was gone."

Reason finally prevailed. Henry and Marcus met separately and reached some agreement. When they called the rest together, Henry again made a "humble" confession. Mary thought "Dr. W. seemed not quite right, but after being called to account for his threats the day before [said] he could not recollect them but said he did not mean so exactly." While no one gave the details of what Spalding confessed or how this encounter differed from previous efforts to resolve tensions, all felt "the difficulty settled." When Eliza heard the news, she was relieved. She admitted, though, she "never could see what real cause there was for so much as appeared to exist."

The board, of course, knew nothing of the reconciliation. The news they had received from the Oregon mission was disturbing enough to call for decisive action. In September 1842 letters written in Boston the previous February arrived at Waiilatpu. Greene minced no words. The disarray of the Oregon mission was "painful & humiliating," especially in light of its initial promise. The dissension was embarrassing to the mission cause, and when the Christian community learned of "the catastrophe," it too would be "grieved and disappointed." The board had decided to close down Waiilatpu and to transfer the Whitmans to the Walkers' and Eellses' station at Tshimakain. The Spaldings were recalled.

Marcus opposed these directives and urgently summoned the other missionaries to Waiilatpu. Despite the lateness of the season, it was decided that Marcus would return to Boston to plead the mission's case with the board. As Narcissa explained to her parents, the interest of the Oregon cause demanded the sacrifice of her husband's absence.

"Could you know all the circumstances in the case," she continued, "you would see more clearly how much our hearts are identified in the salvation of the Indians and the interests of the cause generally in this country." Yet the goal, the salvation of the Indians, that so urgently demanded Marcus's return to the United States, was as elusive as ever in 1842. As visitors to the mission the next year noted, the Waiilatpu missionaries "have not yet, we believe, been productive of much, if any good."

Certainly, Narcissa's own spiritual experience had not resulted in any energetic rededication to missionary work. She undertook various missionary activities: copying sacred materials, learning Nez Percé, reading aloud to a few women or men in her house, some teaching. But as Marcus told the board in 1843, "The school has been more interrupted at our station than at Lapwai where Mrs Spalding has taught a considerable number of people & children to read & write their own language." Narcissa's own description of her activities sounds occasional rather than regular, for she undertook them only "when . . . health permits." "Read a portion of the Scriptures to the women who were in today, and talked awhile with them. Baked bread and crackers today and made two rag dolls."

She made few special efforts to involve native women in spiritual or practical exercises. The female prayer meetings and the maternal meetings at Waiilatpu involved only the white women, with the occasional addition of the Hawaiian serving woman, Hannah. Narcissa knew that training in household skills was a way to introduce native women to Christian domesticity and that Eliza had "succeeded very well in teaching several girls to spin & weave knit & sew some." Some even made patchwork quilts and leggings. But Narcissa found the Cayuse ladies "too proud to be seen usefully employed." Training them seemed pointless. "Those who labour for us are Walla Wallas

principally. One has learned to spin & knit some & others to sew."
The women's progress, she noted, was "very slow."

There are few signs that Narcissa regarded the labor the Indian
women performed as anything more than domestic assistance. And
she believed in the virtue of being a stern mistress rather than a loving teacher. As she advised Mary Gray, who was having troubles
with Hawaiian Hannah, treating servants too well resulted in saucy
and difficult behavior.

The modesty of Narcissa's efforts with the Cayuse could be justified on the grounds of ill health and depressed spirits. She had problems with her eyes, rheumatic pains, stomach and bowel pains, and
headaches. Her many different complaints suggest that Narcissa, like
many nineteenth-century women, used invalidism as a means of es-
caping from some of the difficulties of her situation.

Far from desiring new responsibilities, she wished to be free of
them. "Dear Jane," she wrote in March 1842, "I am sick tonight and
in much pain—have been scarcely able to crawl about all day. The
thought comes into my mind how good to be relieved of care and
to feel the blessing of a sympathizing hand administering to the necessities of a sick and suffering body, and whose presence would
greatly dispel the gloom that creeps over the mind in spite of efforts
to the contrary." If Jane joined her in the mission field, she could
perform some of Narcissa's duties and care for her older sister when
she was unwell.

While she did not often describe her missionary work, Narcissa
did emphasize the obstacles that seemed to interfere with the efforts
to convert the Indians. The greatest impediment, she believed, was
the want of faith and holy hearts among the missionaries. But she
now recognized external factors that had not been obvious to her
when she arrived at Waiilatpu: the Cayuses' wandering habits, the
small size of the mission party, the required manual labor that interfered with spiritual duties. Increasingly, she also blamed the Catholic
missionaries for the disappointing results of the ABCFM missionary
endeavor.

In the eastern United States the decade of the 1840s saw the emergence of nativism directed against Roman Catholicism. Although
the missionaries were thousands of miles away in Oregon, they
shared the distaste for Catholicism. They bitterly observed the way
in which the Roman Catholic missionaries won converts with what
the Protestants saw as wily stratagems and sensuous rituals and how

This Cayuse woman is smoking a buckskin. Despite the work Cayuse women performed, Narcissa considered them lazy and bad housekeepers. National Anthropological Archives, Smithsonian Institution.

they baptized Indians without proof of personal transformation. Because they believed the Catholic approach to conversion deeply flawed, neither Narcissa nor the others could learn anything from the apparent success of the Catholic effort. All they could do was "to stand our ground, if such a thing is possible."

Of course, the Cayuse bore some responsibility for the spiritual wasteland. The tribe's failure to accept the Protestant message over what felt like a very long time increased Narcissa's negativism. Despite an occasional notice of "redeeming qualities," Narcissa continued to see the Cayuse in stark and threatening terms. They were "insolent, proud domineering arrogant and ferocious." Despite the missionaries' warnings, the Cayuse clung stubbornly to their *tewats* and continued their sinful customs of gambling, adultery, and polygamy. Their "drums [and] fifes" and their habits of "painting their faces getting feathers for their hair" were hateful reminders of "old heathenish practices" and ample evidence of recalcitrance, sinfulness, and unconverted hearts. Their dark skin, she thought, aptly symbolized their spiritual state.

Narcissa could find little evidence of real spiritual transformation, even when Indians appeared moved by the Christian message or observed Christian practices. While it was always difficult to evaluate the validity of a religious change, skepticism was particularly necessary with those who did not act like the whites who were judging them. When she read part of the Book of Matthew to one Cayuse, "it seemed to sink deep into his heart; and O may it prove a saviour of life to his soul." But surely the man's having two wives suggested that he was not "walking in the ways of truth & holiness." "He thinks he is a Christian, but we fear to the contrary."

At this puzzling intersection of cultures, Narcissa, like the other missionaries, emphatically repeated the view that damnation awaited Indians who clung to their customary sinful ways. She refused to ease the Indian who had two wives "but urged him to do his duty" and throw off one of his wives. In Prattsburg, these stern techniques might have precipitated guilt and the melting of hearts. Here they often elicited anger. Aware that they had received neither the spiritual or the technological powers or the material goods that had led them to invite the Whitmans to settle among them, the Cayuse increasingly made it clear that they did not want to hear what they called bad talk from the Whitmans.

In the summer of 1841, members of an American exploring expe-

dition headed by Lt. Charles Wilkes visited Waiilatpu and remarked
on the tensions between the Indians and the missionaries. A series
of threatening incidents unfolded in the following months, revealing
Indian dissatisfaction and significant tribal divisions as well as the
Whitmans' inability to understand the sources of conflict.

While the missionaries may not have distinguished between faith
and culture, some of the Cayuse realized that missionaries wanted
changes in both. The Whitmans had defined many traditional customs as sins and as barriers to salvation. The introduction of agriculture and the settled nature of the mission demonstrated that the
whites sought sweeping changes in the tribal way of life.

Some of the Cayuse still hoped to benefit from the missionaries'
presence. They continued to press the Whitmans for white goods or
added agriculture to their yearly routine. By 1843 about fifty Cayuse
were farming in the vicinity of the station. More, perhaps two to
four hundred, came to services at the mission when camped nearby.
But Marcus reported that "all do not now attend our meeting as
formerly; some having adopted the Papal forms."

Marcus's own estimates indicate that some members of the tribe
neither farmed nor attended mission services. This passive resistance
was accompanied by open expression of strong antimissionary sen-
timents only five years after the Whitmans arrived at Waiilatpu. Most
of the troublemakers were young and related to one another. There
is no way of knowing how many Cayuse sympathized with them,
but few stepped forward to defend the missionaries.

There were several fundamental sources of disagreement. One cen-
tered on the status of the mission land. Although the Cayuse had
invited the couple to settle among them, some were now complaining that the Whitmans were using and controlling the land and its
resources and should pay for them. Other tensions grew out of
the missionaries' violation of Indian customs. Not long after the
Whitmans settled at Waiilatpu, it became clear that the Indians ob-
jected to the missionaries' refusal to extend to the Indians the same
freedom of their house as the Indians enjoyed in their own lodges.
In a culture valuing gift-giving, the Whitmans also appeared stingy
when they distributed shirts, food, and blankets only in exchange for
work. In fact, the missionaries' emphasis on work upset the social
order and threatened to reduce men who ought to be lords of the
soil to the position of slaves. Furthermore, farm operations, while
welcome for the food they provided, interfered with the free grazing

Billy O-we-u, a young Cayuse. National Anthropological Archives, Smith-sonian Institution.

of the tribe's horses. Many may have secretly viewed mission agriculture as a violation of mother earth.

Several confrontations may well have been aimed at getting the Whitmans to leave Waiilatpu. The first incident started out innocuously enough. Several Indians turned their horses loose to graze in the mission cornfield, thus suggesting that they rejected the white notions of boundaries and trespassing. Harsh words were soon exchanged as the headman, Tilokaikt, claimed the mission land was his, that the horses were merely eating the soil's growth. What had the missionaries ever paid for the land? he asked. Soon, he struck Marcus, who refused to be provoked. His steadfast refusal to fight was a good example of Christian resignation but appeared cowardly to men who admired bold behavior in menacing situations. Threats of burning the mission mill and another assault on Marcus followed.

An even more troubling incident occurred in early October. Tilokaikt and several others violated the Whitmans' rule against using the kitchen door to enter the house. While Marcus and Gray talked to the men in the dining room, another Indian, Pelaistiwat, also hoping to get in through the kitchen door, stood outside one of the windows waving a hammer at Narcissa. An older Indian, Sakiaph, finally axed down the kitchen door, and a "hord of lawless savages" rushed into the mission house. When the headmen made no attempt to restore order, Gray and Marcus successfully disarmed Pelaistiwat and Sakiaph, who were brandishing the ax and hammer. Pelaistiwat hit Marcus on the mouth, and more weapons were carried into the house. Sakiaph threatened Marcus with a gun and taunted him. Did he not fear death? Marcus responded by describing "the consequence of killing us & sending us in advance of them selves into the presence of God."

The Indians argued angrily that the missionaries should not close their doors to the tribe. Marcus stood firm. As long as the Whitmans were at the mission, the Indians must obey their regulations. The missionaries would order their house as they pleased.

Many showed their displeasure the following day by staying away from the Sabbath service. Others harassed mission animals and broke windows. As the white residents at Waiilatpu were ready to retreat to Fort Walla Walla, the new factor there, Archibald McKinlay, who had replaced Pierre Pambrun, intervened. Alternately threatening and reasoning with tribal leaders, he restored calm. The ringleaders appeared to be contrite and acknowledged their "bad conduct." A few days later, Marcus met with the troublemakers and reviewed the conditions under which the missionaries had come. "We told them plainly that unless they were ready to protect us—& enforce good order we would leave them, that we did not come to fight but to teach them. The former agatators [sic] were very full in their expressions of sorrow."

The Whitmans convinced themselves and argued to the ABCFM board that nothing was inherently wrong between missionaries and Indians. True, the Indians pressed for goods. The tribe had its share of papist troublemakers, whom Joe Gray, "a half breed [Catholic] Iroquois & for a long time a Servent of the H.B. Co.," egged on to demand payment for mission lands. But Marcus concluded, "I do not think we shall again be molested on these points very soon."

Blaming greed, Catholicism, and outside agitators such as Joe Gray blurred the significance and meaning of the escalating tensions and the role the Whitmans played in producing them. Certainly neither Narcissa nor Marcus believed they should make any concessions, especially not on the issue of mission lands. Yet their repeated argument that the Cayuse had invited them to settle at Waiilatpu was beside the point. Times had changed. The demands for payment or, by implication, departure expressed fundamental discontent with the missionary presence.

Others recognized alarming problems at the mission. John Toupin, a French Canadian interpreter at Fort Walla Walla, was well acquainted with the Indian view that emphasized the unfriendly behavior of the Whitmans and the disagreement over the land. He often heard the Cayuse complain that "the Dr and his wife were very severe and hard to them, and often ill-treated them, which occasioned frequent quarrels. For years, the Indians were saying that the Whitmans should pay for their land." The Methodist missionary leader Jason Lee found Marcus "highhanded" and reported that he used "the *lash*" when the Cayuse "deserve[d]" it, while Henry Perkins understood that the Indians considered Narcissa haughty and reserved.

On the day after Marcus met with the ringleaders, Narcissa wrote to her parents, omitting any mention of the recent violence, which lent substance to her view of the Cayuse as dangerously passionate. Eventually, she would call them "outrages," but the events were too fresh and too frightening for her to describe them. Even a full month later when she wrote about the incidents, she distanced herself from the threatening events and the powerful emotions they produced by copying Marcus's account. It was no wonder that she was timid about sleeping alone when Marcus was away on medical or mission business.

Those who heard about affairs at the Whitman mission recognized that the problems were far more serious than the Whitmans admitted in writing at the time. Archibald McDonald, chief factor at Fort Colville, near the mission site of the Walkers and Eellses wrote, "Assuredly I do not feel easy on their account all over the moment I see a letter from that quarter." Henry Brewer at The Dalles Methodist station reported in January 1842 that the Cayuse were at his mission and had come in a "hostile warlike manner." "Dr W's Indians last fall broke into his house," he continued, "pounded the Dr, pulled his ears & as the Dr thought meant to massacre them all but a good Providence prevented."

Not long after Henry Brewer had commented on the seriousness of events at Waiilatpu, the Whitmans precipitated a confrontation that further illuminated the vast cultural gap separating the missionaries from the Cayuse. A Nez Percé Indian had recently died in Canada, and the Cayuse had determined that the local tribe was responsible and must compensate for the death. The Indians were outraged when Marcus told them that the horses and goods they regarded as compensation were stolen goods. He demanded the Indians return the booty.

Although some of the thieves were "great worshipers, or at least feel and profess to be," they did not take Marcus's and Narcissa's reprimands well. "The man who would believe that they could do such great wickedness, and tell them of it and warn them of the consequences, was a bad man and would go to hell," warned one of them angrily.

On the following morning one of the more daring Indians gathered about a dozen of his friends; they pushed their way into the kitchen, with weapons concealed under their blankets. The ringleader repeated that Marcus was bad and "always talking bad to them." As the exchange grew heated, Narcissa saw the weapons, and her fears were excited "greatly." She slipped into another room to call for Packet, their mixed-blood handyman, and for other friendly Indians. Gradually, "the excitement died away."

Narcissa was distraught. Did the Indians want to threaten the Whitmans or to hurt them? Narcissa chose to believe that the Indians had meant only "to frighten us and cause the doctor to take back what he said." Perhaps this was the Cayuses' intention, but there is a good chance that they wanted to frighten the Whitmans enough so that they would either leave the mission station or change their behavior.

Confronted with Indian customs that they could interpret only from a Christian perspective, the Whitmans felt compelled to stand firm. As missionaries, they saw no other choice. Marcus told the Indians "if he did not tell them plainly of their sins the Lord would be displeased with them. . . . It was his duty to tell him that . . . [they] had done wrong."

By the following summer, after several trouble-free months, Narcissa finally acknowledged how close the Indians had come to killing Marcus with the ax. The passage of time had not led Narcissa to new insights on the events of the previous year. Considering her reluctance to think about excessive emotions, her inability to analyze incidents filled with passion was not surprising.

The combination of melancholic episodes during 1841 and 1842 contributed to Narcissa's frequent bouts of gloom. But she was beginning to recover from her depression and was taking steps to rebuild her life. Her options were few. She could not leave the field. Caring for Alice had helped to offset the initial frustrations of marriage and missionary work and had provided her with much gratification. Now Alice was dead, but Narcissa did not conceive again. She must have wondered why all the other mission women were bearing children, and she did not. Perhaps her ill health or Marcus's may have combined with his long absences to prevent conception. Whatever the cause of her infertility, Narcissa determined to have children in whatever way she might. In the fall of 1840 she took into her household the two-year-old mixed-blood daughter of Joe Meek, a former fur trapper. The next year, she adopted another girl, six-year-old Mary Ann Bridger. She found her two "little half-breed girls" "very little more trouble than one." She wrote to a friend that she was "busy with the cares and instructions of my little family, which, by the way increases as my neighbors do, yet in a different way."

By January 1842 she had decided that she did not want to take many more into her family. She disliked the "noise and confusion" caused by two little boys for whom she was temporarily caring. Two months later, however, she added a mixed-blood boy to her brood.

Narcissa learned that the boy's Indian mother "had thrown him away," while his "old and adulterous" grandmother had "no compassion for it." Despite the child's miserable appearance, Narcissa's "feelings were greatly excited for the poor child and [she] felt a great disposition to take him." She named him David Malin, in honor of her Prattsburg friend who had become a minister. By this time, she had determined that she was fulfilling God's purpose for her by adopting children. "The Lord has taken our own dear child away so that we may care for the poor outcasts of the country and suffering children."

Her involvement with the children was a creative solution to the problems of her situation and offered her many satisfactions. They called forth her tender feelings and provided her with company and a noble purpose—training children "for the Lord." The time-consuming nature of her task further legitimated her retreat from laboring with the Indians. While some women missionaries were unhappy when maternal duties took them away from the spiritual work they had come west to do, Narcissa was glad to have her little ones. If she could not convert the Cayuse, she could shape her children.

Like her mother, Narcissa was an enthusiastic evangelical parent. Mixed-blood children offered some special challenges, however. Both Helen and David came in bad physical condition. David was "dirty, covered with body and head lice and starved." Narcissa gave him a thorough washing, oiled and bound his wounds, picked the lice out of his hair, and clothed him. Since Indian parents did not discipline young children, the next challenge involved the long and tedious job of changing habits. In language that she had never felt it necessary to use with her own white child, Narcissa wrote of the need to govern and subdue the children's wills. Helen, even as a two-year-old, was "stubborn and fretful and wanted to cry all the time if she could not have her own way." Narcissa had managed to control her, but "she requires tight reins constantly." Because of their mixed blood, the children were "a double tax upon . . . patience and perseverance."

Missionary motherhood demanded special and "constant watch and care and anxiety." Narcissa was stricter with her mixed-blood children than she had been with Alice and had also resolved some issues that had troubled her during Alice's infancy. Narcissa determined to keep her three young ones away from the contamination of Cayuse. This meant that the children were confined to the house much of the time. Narcissa found herself teaching the children to read and sing and made the girls rag dolls to amuse them when she worked with native women. She also had resolved the language issue. "We confine them altogether to English and do not allow them to speak a word of Nez Percé."

Maternal meetings now became meaningful instead of sad reminders of Alice. Mary Gray and Narcissa made "all the effort our time and means will permit to edify and instruct ourself in our responsible maternal duties." They devoured up-to-date reading material on motherhood such as William Alcott's *Young Wife and Young Mother.*

David soon delighted her in the same kinds of ways that Alice had done. He was "mild and quiet" and learned English quickly. On the second Sabbath that he was with her, he paraded about the house saying, "I must not work, I must not work," and singing the line of a hymn entitled "Lord Teach a Little Child to Pray." In just such a way, little Alice had sung her hymns and pleased her mother's heart.

If motherhood offered one escape from missionary work, there were external events that opened other possibilities. In 1840 Joe Meek and other former trappers completed a wagon trail over the Blue Mountains and then on to the Willamette Valley. The route passed right by the Waiilatpu mission. The next year perhaps one hundred left their homes in the States and headed west.

Attracted by propaganda praising Oregon's climate and agricultural possibilities, more and more white emigrants would decide to come to Oregon in each succeeding year. Although Oregon was still jointly held by Great Britain and the United States, there was growing determination to seize the territory for American citizens. In 1841 Missouri senator Lewis Linn introduced legislation that would provide American settlers with free land in Oregon as well as military protection on the overland journey. Although the proposal never passed, it helped to stimulate westward migration. From the vantage point of Boston, the ABCFM was recognizing the new reality in the West when it suggested that God might be calling the missionaries "in behalf of the future white settlers in Oregon."

Believing that only white men could develop the territory's resources, Marcus was enthusiastic about Oregon's new potential. While no one had ever justified the Oregon mission in terms of the numbers of possible converts, it now appeared that the Indians were too few. "It has been distinctly my feeling," Marcus wrote, "that we are not to measure the sphere of our action & hope of usefulness by the few natives of this country."

Less excited by the vision of economic growth than Marcus was, Narcissa responded to emigration on a more personal level. She found the sight of families passing by the mission in 1841 pleasing and admired the bravery of "such a mother with so many children around her, having come so far—such a dreadful journey." Emigration held out the promise of family society she had enjoyed in Prattsburg as well as the possibility for a more rewarding and successful ministry. In the spring of 1842 Narcissa enthusiastically described to Mary Walker her discussion with a white woman in the throes of conversion. It was "one of the most interesting conversations . . . that I have had since I have been here."

Like her husband, Narcissa realized that the first phase of mission life, "our most quiet time," had passed. Waiilatpu no longer existed just as a mission for the heathen but as a resting spot for weary white travelers. While Narcissa was more tentative than Marcus in envisioning the future, she was beginning to believe, "If we can do good that way, perhaps it is as important as some other things we are doing."

In the fall of 1842, however, the letter from the board raised the question of whether the Whitmans would be allowed to remain at Waiilatpu or whether they would have to join the Walkers and Eells at their more remote northern station among the Spokane Indians. Marcus had determined to return to the East to speak for the entire mission. Leaving in October, he faced a demanding and possibly dangerous journey. It was out of the question for Narcissa to accompany him. She once again swallowed any negative feelings his absences on mission business may have provoked and "cheerfully" consented to remain at home during the year of separation.

Marcus intended not only to go to the ABCFM headquarters in Boston but to visit the Prentisses and his own family in New York State. The fact that he would see and speak to her family made her feel anew the strength of her home connection. Marcus had her letters and would place them himself in their hands. Even more exciting was the possibility that Marcus might escort some of her family back to Oregon Territory. While later settlers would write to relatives of the fertile land or of Oregon's climate, Narcissa relied on the one appeal that she knew would touch her family's conscience. Jane, still

unmarried, was living in Quincy, Illinois, where her younger brother
Edward was studying for the ministry. Narcissa asked Jane, "Are you
going to come and join me in my labours? Do you think you would
be contented to come and spend the remainder of your life on the
mission ground?" She reminded Edward that "there will be work
enough here" by the time he had finished his studies and suggested
to her widowed brother-in-law, Rev. Lyman Judson, that Oregon
country needed "home missionaries for the settlers as well as missionaries for the Indians."

Despite these attempts to lure her family west, Narcissa warned
Jane that she should "count the cost well" before undertaking the
"dreadful" journey that was "becoming more and more dangerous
every year." Her characterization of the trip revealed more about
Narcissa's emotional response to mission life than the reality of coming west. The trip was taxing, to be sure, but it was probably less
hazardous than it had been in 1836, when Narcissa had made it.

Narcissa knew, of course, that she could not expect her entire
family to emigrate. From her parents, she begged for "long letters"
in "their own hand." And from her other brothers and sister, she
requested "their own story on paper themselves." Divulging more
about her marriage than she intended, she explained that "husband
will have so much business on his mind to attend to that he will not
remember half you say to him."

The separation prompted Narcissa to reflect upon her marriage,
particularly during the first few weeks, when she missed Marcus the
most. Over the years, she had written very little about the character
of the relationship. But the original patterns remained. She still
viewed Marcus as the forceful one, a "bundle of thoughts," a coura-
geous leader, above criticism. "Common obstacles never affect him;
he goes ahead when duty calls." She was the lesser partner, susceptible to "Womanish fears," not happy with the independence or responsibilities that Marcus's absence imposed. Her job was not to
lead but to "prove [herself] worthy of . . . [her husband's] confidence
and affection." With Alice dead, Narcissa was emotionally dependent
on Marcus. He was her "greatest and only earthly comfort in this
lonely land."

The early letters were warm. Marcus was "inexpressibly dear," and
Narcissa longed to have him in her "arms again" to enjoy "the sweets
of connubial bliss" and "the happiness it affords." In the first stages
of the separation, when her feelings were keenest, she worried

whether her love was excessive. Alice's death now reminded her of the need to hold earthly affections "more in subserviency." Anxious about the dangers of the trip, she vacillated between "hope and fear" and attempted to put her trust in a merciful Lord.

In the first few weeks after Marcus's departure, Narcissa assured him, "I think of you and feel as if you were in my heart continually." She craved details as she followed him "in imagination & prayer" as he made his way east. As she pictured Marcus visiting family and friends, she appealed to him for reassurance of her place in his affections. "Will it not be too true . . . my husband will wish dear wife was along to make her own visits and give zest to his? I surely have the vanity and the evidence to think so."

While none of Marcus's letters have survived, they were apparently not filled with the information for which Narcissa longed. Narcissa found her husband's letters cheering, but they revealed little of himself. "I wish to hear so much about your own and my other self, and hear so little when you do write."

It was not surprising that Narcissa missed Marcus, even though she attempted to convince herself that his absence was necessary and part of the divine scheme of things. He had, as so often had been the case before, left her in an awkward and uncertain position. The Grays had decided to retire from the service of the ABCFM and were planning to leave the mission soon after Marcus's departure. Narcissa hoped that either the Rogerses or the Littlejohns or both would spend the winter at Waiilatpu. During the summer she was to spend some time visiting and regaining her health. None of these plans were very firm.

Less than a week after Marcus had gone and only two days after the Grays had set off, Narcissa's situation changed dramatically. What happened is in doubt, but Narcissa believed that one of the Cayuse tried to rape her. She explained later that at about midnight one night the sound of someone unlatching her bedroom door awoke her. Befuddled by sleep, she did not at first realize what was happening. When the door opened slightly, she suddenly was sure of the meaning of the faint noises. She leapt out of bed, slammed the door closed, and threw herself against it. "The ruffian pushed and pushed." At first the latch held, but slowly the door inched open. Narcissa believed that only her hysterical screams frightened the assailant away.

Narcissa was in shock and "dreadfully frightened." Finding the dining room door unlocked, she closed it, "lit a candle and went to bed trembling and cold." She could not sleep and finally called the Hawaiian, John, to bring his bed into the kitchen for the rest of the night. She had no illusions about the Indian's intention. What would she have done? she asked herself. She was not sure, but had thought "of the poker" as a way of fending off the "savage."

Narcissa's choppy style and her choice of vocabulary as she described the incident in a letter to Marcus conveyed as much as anything she explicitly said how distraught and fearful she was. She had told no one until the day after the incident. When the news reached Fort Walla Walla, Mr. McKinlay and Henry Gray, who was still there, urged Narcissa to come to the fort. They were "alarmed"; they insisted "upon my removing there immediately"; they were "anxious"; "doubtless it is not safe for me to remain alone any longer"; "our friends are so anxious about me."

There is no way of knowing whether Narcissa's account of the incident was accurate. The Cayuse considered rape a serious offense, and if Narcissa was right, the attempt was an expression of extreme hostility toward her. But always anxious about sleeping alone, she could have dreamed the incident. In any case, if there was someone at her bedroom door, the person was not necessarily an assailant or even a male.

Neither Narcissa nor any of the other whites, however, ever considered the possibility that the incident was anything but an attempted rape. The belief that the white women inspired sexual passion among the Indians was deeply imbedded in white culture. The painter George Catlin had warned the Spaldings that the trip west was dangerous for the women for just this reason. Captivity tales informed many readers what they might expect from Indian men.

The conviction that Indian men wanted white women was not an accurate reflection of Indian sexual tastes or habits but a projection of the middle-class culture's fear of unrestrained sexuality. It may have served this function for Narcissa. More pertinent to her situation, perhaps, was the fact that the incident, real or imagined, gave her a pressing reason to leave the mission. The news certainly would also perturb her absent husband when he realized the perilous situation in which he had left her.

Narcissa's friends convinced her that she must leave Waiilatpu. Later, Narcissa would feel somewhat guilty for having abandoned the mission, especially since Marcus had wished for her to remain there at least until someone came to take charge. She felt compelled to give repeated explanations of her reasons for leaving, her reluctance to do so, and the pressure and advice of friends who forced the decision upon her. But at the time, she hardly hesitated or needed much persuading to leave Waiilatpu.

As Narcissa set out for Fort Walla Walla, she thought, "The Indians did not like . . . [me] leaving very well—seemed to regret the cause." Many, however, must have been relieved to see all the missionaries gone. Not long after her departure, Narcissa learned that the Indians had burned the mill at Waiilatpu. Even at a safe distance from the mission, she was reluctant to analyze the meaning of that event or to discern any larger pattern linking the individual acts of violence together. She was unsure whether the fire "was the work of design or carelessness" and told herself that "the sensible part of the Cayuse feel the loss deeply." Without a mill to grind their grain, the Indians, Narcissa hoped, would learn a valuable lesson and become "a better people." She never thought there might have been some lesson for her as well.

Narcissa's departure ended missionary activity at Waiilatpu for the year of Marcus's absence. Narcissa or others secured the services of a caretaker for the farm. It was months before Narcissa expressed any regret that "we were obliged to submit to see the people scattered and left without a teacher." Obviously, missionary work had not been uppermost in her mind during the crisis. Certainly, Eliza Spalding disapproved of the entire business. She wrote to Mary Walker, "I . . . believe I could not do as she has done even was my health as poor as her's is said to be—I could not, and would not have left under such circumstances, as she has, such a faithful judicious and discreet young man in the situation she has left Mr. Gieger."

Within five days of the assault, Narcissa had moved to Fort Walla Walla. She had left Waiilatpu so sick that she had made the trip lying on a trundle bed in a wagon. Now she was dosing herself on quinine and calomel (highly poisonous if taken in large quantities) and could hardly get out of bed. She was not entirely happy with her situation or very comfortable. "Mr. and Mrs. McKinlay are very kind, but they know not how to make one as easy . . . as Mr. Pambrun used to." When an appealing invitation to spend the winter came from the Methodist missionaries at The Dalles, she recovered enough to accept it. She left David Malin behind with Mrs. McKinlay but took the two girls with her. Mary Walker wrote soon after she arrived at

The Dalles saying that she wished she had enough room for Narcissa. Narcissa thanked her but explained that, in any case, her health would not have permitted her to make the trip. Certainly, The Dalles was far more to her liking than Tshimakain. She was visiting with the Perkinses, Brewers, and Lees, who offered the same happy combination of "social and religious privaleges" she had so enjoyed in Prattsburg.

Narcissa was delighted with the society of the women. She considered the loss of refinement and polish to be one of the trials of missionary life. Now she had excellent company and the opportunity to practice her social graces. Mrs. Lee had "a superior mind" and was "very amiable," as were Mrs. Perkins and Mrs. Brewer. She told Mary Walker, "I am treated with the utmost kindness & attention & could not be so happyly & comfortably situated for the winter as here both for my health & spirits perhaps in the country." There were pleasant events like a New Year's Party and frequent company. The dining tables were "well furnished." Henry Perkins noticed how Narcissa "really seemed to *enjoy*" company, how she "loved society, [and] excitement."

Denominational differences, so important back in Prattsburg, no longer mattered. So much mutual religious sympathy existed that Narcissa thought that the visit would prove to be for her "spiritual good, for truly the society and prayers of such a company of living and growing Christians is very refreshing to me, after having lived so much alone, immerged in care and toil."

On their part, the Methodist missionaries found Narcissa "a very agreeable friend & a good christian." While she was not always up and about, she helped with some domestic duties. In early March, Henry Brewer noted in his daybook that Narcissa was stuffing and dressing a duck for dinner. Elvira Perkins thought Narcissa "an active energetic busy woman when in health, and calculated to exert influence wherever she moves." By the time she left in early April, Elvira felt Narcissa had become "one of ourselves and we miss her society very much."

These views of Narcissa contrast with the way Narcissa pictured herself in letters to her family. While she acknowledged the pleasurable aspects of her visit, her depiction of herself as vulnerable, weak, and alone captured the dependent and needy side of her nature. Never convinced that her family remembered her with the affection she craved, she hoped to capture their sympathy and interest. "My

Dear Harriet . . . I have been thinking all day of writing you, but can scarcely find courage enough; even now, I feel more like taking my bed rather than writing." "Beloved parents," she asked, "what do you think of your lonely child in this lonely world?" "It is very trying to the feelings . . . to be here in this desolate land without my husband. . . . My health is very poor; this increases the trial, because in consequence, I have too many gloomy and depressing hours, and evil forebodings, in which I have not strength of mind to rise above." "My Dear Brother [Jonas] . . . Have you no time to write, or have you forgotten me? I will not think it; not that you do not love me, for this would make me unhappy."

Even if they served a psychic need, her ailments were real enough. Elvira Perkins judged Narcissa's nervous system "much debilitated." Narcissa told Mary Walker she had the "prolapses" (presumably a prolapsed uterus). "Since I have been here it has been difficult for me some of the time to walk & even to move my limbs without groaning." Her eyes were so bad that she usually had to wear spectacles for reading, writing, and sewing. "Sometimes with them I suffer considerable pain." In late March she thought she might be improving in health. But by June she had a tumor in her side that she would have treated in Vancouver. The doctor discovered that her right ovary was enlarged and administered iodine to remove it.

In early April, however, she was well enough to visit Waiilatpu in the company of Dr. Elijah White, the new American Indian agent, and others. The Cayuse and other tribes had been restive and warlike for months. Rumors were afloat that Marcus would return from the East with troops, that the Americans were planning to kill off the tribe. Although Narcissa blamed the Cayuse for the trouble, sure that "if any mischief is going ahead they originate it and carry forward," their anxiety was not surprising. During the winter, Dr. White, feeling responsible for the safety of the missionaries, had persuaded the Nez Percé to adopt a code of laws that would punish crimes against whites such as injuring crops or entering their houses without permission. He had also pressed them to select a high chief to act as tribal representative. Now he wished the Cayuse to do the same.

Despite Indian suspicion and anxieties, White managed to persuade them that the Americans had no hostile intentions toward the tribes. After days of discussion, the Cayuse and the Walla Walla accepted the code and selected a head chief. Narcissa was sure that had

Marcus been home, there would have been no agitation at all. "I
have every evidence to believe that all hearts are fill[ed] with anxiety
to see you back again & none perhaps more so than the one that
pulled your ears. The report of your going home & returning with
men to fight has no weight in the minds of the people generally."

While she was at Waiilatpu, she noted with satisfaction that some
of the Indians had planted their fields. Although few were there on
the Sabbath, she read Scripture to them. "I feel my heart drawn out
more and more with desire for their salvation," she exclaimed. But
with her health, there was little chance that she would remain for the
summer. Instead, she was off to Vancouver to regain her vigor, and
then to the settlements in the Willamette.

Once she was in Vancouver, the warmth she had felt for the Cayuse evaporated, and the image of a "dreary land of heathenish darkness" returned. When she visited with several American families in
the comparatively civilized Willamette Valley, there was little reason
to think of the Indians at all. Surrounded by whites, always finding
"attention and kindness far more than I deserve," she savored the
society and the religious opportunities of the southern settlements.
Free of the "distracting cares of . . . family and the station," she felt
in close communication with God. She was more fulfilled from a
religious point of view than she had been since Prattsburg. A four-
day camp meeting proved to be "a precious season . . . to my soul.
To witness again the anxious tear and hear the deep-felt inquiry,
'What must I do to be saved?' as I once used to, filled me with joy
inexpressible." In sharp contrast to the disappointing yield at Waiilatpu, almost all the "impenitent" whites were converted. Later there
was a protracted meeting. "Having been so long secluded, I was well
prepared to enjoy society," Narcissa reflected, "and I may well say
that some of the moments spent there with Christian friends were
among the happiest of my life."

While Narcissa was enjoying the protracted meeting, news came
that her husband, with a large party of emigrants and his thirteen-
year-old nephew Perrin had arrived in Oregon. His trip to Boston
had brought the desired results. The board, persuaded that the missionaries had mended their differences, revoked their drastic orders.
Spalding and his wife would remain in the field. The Whitmans
would continue at Waiilatpu.

In October the long-awaited reunion occurred, and Narcissa
greeted Marcus with "love and gratitude." "Overwhelming joy" was

not her only emotion, however. She was disappointed that none of her relatives had accepted her pressing invitation to do the Lord's work in the West. And she dreaded returning to missionary life.

Her dismay prompted unusual candor. Writing from Fort Walla Walla to a family with whom she had recently stayed in the Willamette Valley, she confessed that she shrank from the spectacle of Indian life. "What sounds fall upon my ears and what savage sights do I behold every day around me—Never was I more keenly sensible to the self denials of a missionary life—even now while I am writing the drum and the savage yell are sounding in my ears every sound of which is as far as the east from the west from vibrating in unison with my feelings." She was to return to a place of "savage" and "moral darkness." The contrast to the scenes that she had just been enjoying was almost more than she could bear. Waiilatpu loomed ahead, a "dark spot" in her imagination.

Illness, again, proved a way in which to avoid unpleasant realities and to draw Marcus to her side. Narcissa caught cold on her way back to the mission. While her children ran free, as "uncontrollable as so many wild animals," she stayed in her room. For weeks she was mostly in bed, while Marcus cared for her and the household. One ailment followed another. There were two attacks of remittent fever (malaria). Near the end of December, she had an attack of inflammation of the bowels and bloating. She was in "excruciating" pain and spitting bilious fluid. Her life was despaired of. This, she later concluded, was "one of the missionary's greatest trials, to be sick and nigh unto death, and to die away from father, mother, brothers, and sisters, and sympathizing friends."

Narcissa survived this attack but hardly expected health to return. Marcus had discovered "a beating tumor near the umbilicus" that he thought was aneurism of the main aorta. Narcissa wrote Mrs. Brewer, "Never do I expect to continue long on the earth."

By early January, however, Narcissa had somewhat improved. She wrote Mrs. Brewer, "Now I am here, I am happy and love my work and situation. . . . Indeed, I think I never enjoyed the privilege of being a missionary better than this winter." This was the old Narcissa, who rarely admitted doubts. But loving missionary work was perhaps not too difficult at a distance. As Narcissa explained, "I cannot do but little if any more than instruct my family and pray for and sustain the hands of my dear husband in his labours." In fact, it was quite unlikely that she would find the time, even if she had the strength, to devote herself to missionary work. For she had enlarged her family by taking in two more girls. All the children needed her attention if they were to become "quite tame and manageable."

That winter while her children and the children of the emigrants who were wintering at Waiilatpu went to a school run by Mrs. Littlejohn, the Indians had no instruction. With the coming of spring, a Methodist emigrant taught the Indians for a few weeks. Other missionary activities started up again. Marcus reported to the board in early April that Sabbath congregations ranged between two and three hundred. He found "nothing especially different in their attention."

Many of their grievances remained unchanged. The Cayuse still complained that while the missionaries broke Indian land "for nothing," they did not provide the Indians with goods for nothing. But with the arrival of a steady stream of white emigrants, new concerns surfaced. The Cayuse feared correctly that the Americans intended to take over the country. And they saw that the Whitman station was becoming a stopping place where the emigrants bought supplies. The rich missionaries were becoming even richer. The Cayuse forbade Marcus "to break a new field as I desired lest I should make money out of their lands by supplying Emigrants."

The trip east and the return with the large party of emigrants during the summer of 1843 seems to have distracted Marcus from his missionary work, just as Narcissa's visits to comparatively civilized settlements in the Willamette had distanced her. He was fired by the vision of helping to make Oregon "a Christian & enlightened country" and imagining the territory's future. He urged the board to encourage Christian emigration and wondered whether it would be a good idea for the missionaries to take up claims as private citizens in case the United States took over Oregon. The valley would certainly be among the first settled by Americans, and it was important to make sure that emigrants did not claim mission land. As for the Indians, how could they stand in the way of white settlement when they had refused to multiply and replenish the earth? "This [emigration] is only one of the onward movements of the world and it is quite vain for us to wish it to stand still." To Narcissa's parents, he wrote candidly, "It does not concern me so much what is to become of any particular set of Indians, as to give them the offer of salvation. . . . I have no doubt our greatest work is to be to aid the white settlement of this country."

During the summer as Narcissa began to feel better, she wrote to friends and family in New York, urging them "to come and see me and seek a home in Oregon." Nothing would give her greater pleasure than to see Prattsburg people in the West. She even began to think that her parents could make the trip. Of course, she would not expect them to make the fatiguing journey just to see their daughter. They would have to have "a more ennobling object," some "wide door of usefulness." And just such a useful mission existed. If Oregon was to become God's country, to be "seasoned with heavenly influence from above," it must have settlers who were the "salt of the earth"—settlers like Narcissa's family and friends.

CHAPTER 6

As Happy a Family As the World Affords

IN early August 1844 Narcissa sent a short note to her friend Laura Brewer at The Dalles Methodist mission station. Although she devoted much of her chatty letter to discussing the possibility of having visitors at Waiilatpu and to imagining the "social and spiritual" pleasures her Methodist friends were enjoying, Narcissa's thoughts were turning to the by-now-familiar rhythms of fall and the coming emigration. Much as she welcomed the prospective settlers, Narcissa likened their arrival to a siege that demanded a "good stock" of qualities she sometimes did not have: "strength, patience, and every needed grace." The previous fall, the emigrants had bought, begged, or stolen most of the food supplies at Waiilatpu. Although Marcus had made special efforts over the past few months to prepare for the newcomers, no one knew how many emigrants had set out from the States or exactly when they might arrive.

It would be another two months before the emigrants began to come into the mission in force. A late spring had forced them to linger on the Missouri frontier, waiting for the grasses to come up to support their livestock during the long weeks of travel west.

As the horde of 1,500 wound its way over prairies, plains, mountains, and deserts, inevitably some families fell behind. Writing at the end of October to her parents, Narcissa described the grim consequences of the late start and delays en route. "The Blue mountains are covered with snow, and many families, if not half of the party, are back in or beyond the mountains, and what is still worse, destitute of provisions and some of them of clothing. Many are sick, several with children born on the way." Certainly, the missionaries could expect their share of ailing, starving emigrants. "Can any one think we lack employment or have any time to be idle?" she asked. Reverting again to one of her favorite images of heroic isolation, which showed more about her self-conception than reality, she pictured the Whitmans, "one family alone, a way mark, as it were, or center post, about which the multitudes will or must gather this winter."

Among the many people struggling through snow in the Blue Mountains were seven orphaned children. Their story was sad, but not altogether unusual. Their parents, Henry and Naomi Sager, were emigrants from the Midwest who had already moved several times—from Ohio, to Indiana, to eastern Missouri, and finally to western Missouri—before deciding to try their luck in the Far West. Naomi must have wanted to delay this last and most arduous migration, for she was expecting her seventh child in May.

The Sagers had been on the way for just over a week when Naomi gave birth to a daughter. Like other women who experienced childbirth on the overland trail, the new mother had only a few days to rest. Then, still weak from the difficult birth, she and the baby lay in the wagon as it jounced and rattled over the rough terrain. Two months later, nine-year-old Catherine joined her mother and sister, her leg broken when she fell under one of the wheels of the wagon. Within three weeks of Catherine's accident, Henry came down with a severe fever and joined his wife and daughters in the crowded wagon. A few days later he was dead. Naomi worsened, and in early September she died.

Members of the wagon train took the orphans under their wing. Women took turns nursing the baby, while a German doctor drove the family oxen. Although several of the Sager children later wrote about this terrible journey, none of them described the grief and sense of abandonment that they must have felt when both of their parents died. Nor did they express their fear of what the future might hold for such a large family of children, arriving in the West where they had no friends or relatives. On his deathbed, their father had begged several members of the wagon train to see that his family got to the Whitmans' mission. But there was no certainty that the missionaries would be willing or able to care for the children.

News of the pathetic family traveled in advance. Emigrants who stopped at the mission were urging the Whitmans to take the orphans in. Narcissa, never one to act decisively, was uncertain and probably unwilling to make any commitment until she had seen the children. While she would not "see them suffer, if the Lord casts them upon us," her duty was not yet clear. In any case, the emigrants already at the mission made her feel "so thronged and employed that I feel sometimes like being crazy," while "poor husband, if he had a hundred strings tied to him pulling in every direction, could not be any worse off."

At the end of October, six of the children straggled into the mission "in a miserable condition." While adults from the wagon train conferred with the Whitmans, the youngsters waited outside the neat Whitman house with its palisade fence. The boys (John, thirteen years old) and Francis (eleven) were weeping. Catherine (nine), Elizabeth (seven), Matilda (five), and Hannah (three) clung anxiously together.

The children all retained vivid memories of this important day in their lives. Years later, Catherine, Elizabeth, and Matilda remembered Narcissa's striking appearance, her auburn "coppery gold" hair, partly hidden by her gingham sunbonnet, her neat dark calico dress, and plump form. After months of dusty and dirty travel, the girls thought she looked wonderfully civilized and pretty when she greeted them.

The Whitmans made no hasty promises, but the plight of the children moved Narcissa. She ushered them into the house, gathered them around her, and gently asked them questions. Baths and Narcissa's favorite dinner, pork and potatoes, followed. Elizabeth remembered what a crowd there was at the dinner table—the six Sagers, Marcus's nephew Perrin Whitman and the mixed-blood children—David Malin, Helen Meek, and Mary Ann Bridger.

Even before the Sager baby, Henrietta, arrived, Narcissa "expressed her fear lest it should die, saying it was the baby she wanted most of all." Within a few days of the older children's arrival, a "filthy . . . sick emaciated" woman delivered the infant. She was in dreadful shape, at five months no larger than a baby of three weeks. Narcissa judged her to be near death. When Marcus saw Henrietta's state, he was not in favor of taking her. Perhaps he did not want Narcissa to go through another child's death. But Narcissa insisted. "I felt that if I must take any, I wanted her as a charm to bind the rest to me."

The baby proved to be more than a charm to bind the other Sager children to her. In Henrietta, Narcissa found a white infant to replace her own lost daughter, a child more needy and perhaps more worthy of her love and attention than the mixed-blood children she had already adopted, certainly more helpless and malleable than her older brothers and sisters. While Narcissa did not articulate these feelings, Catherine Sager, looking back at those early days at the

mission, recognized that the baby had affected Narcissa more powerfully than had the other Sager youngsters. Narcissa admitted as
much in a letter written in 1846, when she explained, "The little babe
had grown so finely, and won our affections to that degree that we
could not part with it."

Later Narcissa described her doubts and hesitations about taking
the children into her household, while the Sagers also remembered
the Whitmans talking about what they would do with the family.
Despite some differences between their accounts, there was general
agreement that Narcissa was more interested in the little girls than
in the boys. Elizabeth Sager, who was seven at the time, recollected
that Narcissa had announced almost immediately that the girls would
stay but the boys would go through to the Willamette Valley. Narcissa's own experience of troublesome older brothers and loving
relationships between mothers and daughters helps explain her preference for the girls and her decision to send David Malin away during Marcus's trip east but to keep Helen Meek and Mary Ann
Bridger with her.

The real question for Narcissa, then, was what to do with the
boys. Marcus tried to persuade her to change her mind about sending them away. Despite his wife's tendency to cast decisions and actions in terms of duty, Marcus, perhaps realizing how difficult duty
was to identify, appealed to her sense of family. He reminded her
how the dying father had wanted to keep his children together. On
a more practical level, he reassured her that boys could actually be of
some help in the kitchen. Although "it took some time to get his
wife to consent," in the end, Marcus won Narcissa over by relying
on her sense of fair play and wifely affection. "If you are going to
have the girls," he told her, "I must have the boys."

Despite Narcissa's initial hesitations, it is hard to see how she
could have turned the Sagers away. They represented a way to retreat
honorably from the dilemmas of missionary work. Mary Walker
worried that her domestic work impeded her vocation, while Eliza
Spalding mourned her pregnancies, which diminished her opportunities for missionary work. Not so Narcissa. Good luck and determination had allowed her to create a family not so different from the
one in which she had grown up. As she told Mary Walker in a letter
written in June 1846 "That is not you nor me to be unreconciled at
having children placed in our hands let them come what way that
will—on foot or otherwise."

In turning her back on the world, Narcissa was not unlike many women who followed her to the West. Rather than confronting the roughness and promiscuity of mining life or the rambunctiousness of early frontier towns, they channeled their energies into the domestic world. This was an arena that they could better shape and control than the disorderly world beyond their front doors.

Narcissa's perspective on life was not one, however, that enabled her to recognize the coming of the orphans as a stroke of good luck or even to acknowledge just how fortuitous for her their presence was. Her virtual abandonment of mission work demanded a far more powerful justification than luck, good fortune, or individual inclination. She soon convinced herself that she had had no choice in opening her home to the children. Without the Whitmans' offer, she told Jane, stretching the truth considerably, the Sagers would have perished. She highlighted her "feeble" state and the supposed impossibility of "obtaining help." The personal sacrifice was necessary, for, as she informed her family, she was convinced that the hand of God had been at work.

Aware of widespread interest in missionary life and of the semi-public role of missionaries, Narcissa felt compelled to explain her course of action to those outside her circle of family and friends. Narcissa chose *Mother's Magazine* as a sympathetic forum and wrote to the editor in 1846. Her letter explaining her retreat into domesticity soon appeared with an enthusiastic editorial introduction.

Narcissa described for the magazine's female readership both her own doubts and the direct role that "a mysterious Providence" had played in bringing "to our door the family of Henry and Naomi Sager." She emphasized the importance of her choice, her initial reluctance, and the faith that led to her decision. "For a time my mind withdrew from so great a responsibility, until I was led to see the hand of the Lord was in it, and that if He appointed me to the work, He would give grace and strength equal to our day, and enable us to train them all up for his service and glory."

It was not long before this family of white children dominated her letters and her life. References to Helen Meek, David Malin, and Mary Ann Bridger, who had not won her heart in the same way as the Sagers, fell off markedly. Perhaps the color of the mixed-blood children stood in the way of her seeing them as her very own. The Sagers' appearance presented no such problems.

With this resolution of the dilemma that had been plaguing her almost since she had arrived in Oregon Territory eight years earlier, Narcissa gradually regained her health and spirits. In the spring of 1845 Marcus acknowledged that while he never expected Narcissa to be robust, she was so much improved that she could "take charge of the family and . . . perform much important labor." More than a year later, Narcissa was still in "quite good [health] for me." She believed Oregon's "mild and healthy climate," her regime of frequent bathing, and her plain but substantial diet responsible. By the spring of 1847 Narcissa had regained so much energy that she was able to travel 180 miles by horseback to the mission meeting. It was the kind of journey that she had not been able to make for years.

Her increasingly matronly figure (by 1844 her weight had reached 167 pounds) offered material evidence of her renewed appetite for life. While she knew her sisters would laugh at her weight, the bulk symbolized not only her returning vigor but perhaps her maternal power as well. Her mother, Clarissa, was "queenly" in size, and Narcissa may have subconsciously associated weight with her expanded motherly role and influence.

These were the happiest years of Narcissa's life at Waiilatpu. She felt useful and contented. Those who wintered at the mission provided companionship and lightened the burden of farm and household labor. A succession of women and girls helped Narcissa with domestic work and contributed to her good humor.

There were still times when Narcissa felt crabby and short tempered. She claimed that her "fretful and impatient" spells came when she was overworked. Sometimes, however, she was just annoyed when someone disrupted the household order or her priorities as its mistress. During the lean winter of 1844, when the emigrants consumed much of the missionary food supply, the schoolmaster noticed how Narcissa "would sometimes protest that it was not fair that the immigrants should get all the best part while only leavings were available for the family." The next winter was so cold that Marcus brought five sheep into the kitchen to warm them up just at dinner time. Narcissa "was very indignant that he had turned the kitchen into a sheep pen."

But Narcissa was more self-aware than she had been as a new arrival to the West and was making an effort to curb her temper. Should Elkanah bring the Walker children to school, she told Mary Walker in 1846, "he will not . . . find me so cross and ready to scold as when last here—for I do not feel willing to subscribe to the sentiment that women as they grow older become more and more cross and fretful. It may be so but I am unwilling that it should be demonstrated in me."

She was far more hopeful about the future than she had ever been. How lucky that she had not been assigned to missionary work in some remote part of the world. The yearly stream of emigrants pointed to the territory's American destiny that diplomacy finalized in 1846, when Britain officially relinquished its claims on the region. Each white family passing by the mission offered proof to Narcissa that her own relatives might also make the trip west. In the early years of missionary work, her pleas to her family to join her in Oregon had reflected her yearning for them rather than a realistic assessment of the likelihood they might emigrate. Now while Marcus wrote general letters promoting emigration, Narcissa specifically and insistently argued the case of emigration with family and friends. The physical trials of the trip now seemed less troublesome than the spiritual dangers of associating with the inattentive Christians over the course of the months of travel.

Her unmarried sister Jane, who was teaching school, was the most likely candidate for emigration, although Narcissa thought her younger brother Edward might also come west. Narcissa worked out detailed travel arrangements for Jane. Elizabeth Sager remembered as Narcissa cleaned in the fall of 1847 that she told her foster daughter, "Don't you know we are looking for your Aunt Jane to come soon?" And she did not give up the idea that even her parents might make the trip one day.

Meanwhile, there was plenty to do. In the early days after the Sagers' arrival, Narcissa was preoccupied with the children's physical well-being. The baby, Henrietta, was malnourished and ill. Catherine's broken leg had not yet healed. All the children were showing the effects of an inadequate diet during the final arduous weeks of the trip west. As Catherine noted, "It required all the attention of the Doctor and his wife to keep us from overeating ourselves." Now, with the desperate pace of the trip behind them, perhaps for the first time, the children grieved for the sudden loss of their parents. They must have been a sad little group. Years later, Catherine could still remember how lonely she felt during the first days at the mission.

The baby was in the most critical condition and certainly tested Narcissa's mothering skills and commitment. Initially she could not keep any milk down, and Narcissa had to dilute it with water. Gradually a regular schedule and watchful care brought results, although Narcissa confined Henrietta to liquids until she was a year and a half old. By two, she was "strong, healthy, fleshy, heavy, runs any where she is permitted, talks everything nearly, is full of mischief if I am out of the room."

Her married sister Harriet heard many of the small details of Narcissa's care and even a bit of bragging. "I used to think mother was the best hand to take care of babies I ever saw," Narcissa wrote, "but I believe . . . we have improved her plan." The proudest innovation in her sensible child-rearing regime was the introduction of frequent bathing (daily in the summer and at least weekly in the winter). "I should like to have you try them just to see the benefit," she told Harriet. Another innovation was sleeping outdoors during the summer months to take advantage of the "fine, healthy climate." More predictable was Narcissa's determination to prevent her children from indulging in too many "candies, sweetmeats, etc." "Neither do I permit them to eat cakes and pies very often." Medicine was used sparingly—certainly a wise decision, since taking medication could be more dangerous than going without it.

In the early nineteenth century, good health provided the foundation for character formation and intellectual and moral development. As Narcissa quickly discovered, the Sager children lacked essential skills, habits, and attitudes. In fact, the Sagers were just the kind of family that made the Whitmans worry about the future of Oregon. The three oldest children could barely read. The parents had not given their children any religious training, nor had they disciplined the youngsters effectively. Catherine Sager explained that her brothers and sisters had been so long without any kind of restraint that they were all unruly.

One of the first lessons Narcissa had to teach the Sagers was the importance of regular behavior and useful work. Valuing order rather than spontaneity, Narcissa created routines that dominated everyday life. As Matilda recalled, "We had certain things to do at a certain hour." Each child was responsible for a garden plot. The girls helped out with the dishes and housecleaning, while the boys drove the cows to pasture and assisted on the dreaded washday, carrying water and pounding the laundry while the women scrubbed. During the summer, when there was no school, Narcissa re-created a scene from her own girlhood and gathered the girls indoors to sew while someone read aloud. There was little leisure time.

In keeping with the nineteenth-century notions of appropriate parental roles, Narcissa bore the most responsibility for child rearing. Believing that at the heart of child rearing was a struggle for power, she was the strict disciplinarian of the family, the one most concerned with breaking each child's habit of willful stubbornness. Matilda recalled that "when we were told to do a thing, no matter what, we went." Marcus could be more relaxed with the children. To Elizabeth, Marcus was a "genial" parent, "fond of romping with us children, and we did not feel at all in awe of him as we did of Mrs. Whitman."

The Sagers posed a special disciplinary challenge, for they had come in "all at once," rather than by degrees. Narcissa told Laura Brewer nearly a year after the children's arrival, however, that she had not found them too hard to manage and that she did not often have to resort to the rod. "The little one, as all other little children do manifested a stubborn disposition at first which required subduing." The contest for mastery, she confided to her sister Harriet, had taken place before Henrietta was a year old, "but she, of course, had to submit. Since then she has been very obedient. . . . She will obey very well in sight, but loves to get out of sight for the purpose of doing as she pleases." There had been a struggle also with the next-older child. "I have not been able to subdue [her] so completely; but she is much better than when she first came."

Although Matilda called this approach to child rearing "the old Puritan way," Narcissa was influenced by new ideas about child rearing as well as by the example of her own mother. Authority, she believed, had to be grounded in affection and the desire to please rather than the fear of harsh punishments. As Catherine pointed out, "While they held us under strict subjection, every effort was made to render us happy and comfortable and to win our love and confidence." Narcissa often assured the children of her tender feelings for them. Good behavior won warm smiles of approval. Bad behavior, "any deviation from the laid down rules," on the other hand, elicited a quick response—the confiscation of the girls' bead necklaces, or Narcissa's "dreaded . . . accusing finger pointed at us." The Sagers' comments suggested that they feared the rod as well Narcissa's disapproval. "The way we jumped when . . . [her finger] was leveled at us, you would have thought it was a gun and was likely to go off."

When full-fledged punishments were necessary, Narcissa believed in the importance of avoiding passion or anger. She tried to use these occasions to invite reflection and moral growth. She "first set before us our fault; then, the responsibility resting upon her of showing us that it was our own good . . . she had in view."

This approach to child rearing required self-control, patience, and watchfulness. Narcissa felt that she could never relax for a moment. "I must be with them or else they will be doing something they should not, or else not spending their time profitably," she told Laura Brewer. "I could get along some easier if I could bring my mind to have them spend their time in play, but this I cannot." So great were the challenges of motherhood that the burden of caring for the children sometimes weighed Narcissa down. But she felt that the Lord was providing her with both the energy and the will to bear her load as he had never done when she was overwhelmed with the trials of missionary work.

For the older children, schooling was an essential component of an evangelical upbringing. Reading made the Bible accessible, while the routine and content of learning reinforced the character traits that nineteenth-century parents thought desirable. Both Narcissa and Marcus were eager to establish a regular winter school for their own children and other white children at the mission. The Indian school virtually disappeared. But each year the Whitmans recruited a teacher, usually from among the emigrants, and invited Hudson's Bay Company officials and others to send their offspring to the winter session at Waiilatpu. Although Narcissa had always refused to house Indian children, she was now "more than willing" to board "as many as possible" ABCFM mission youngsters in her own home. "We set the table for more than twenty every day three times," she wrote her mother in 1846, "and it is a pleasing sight."

In her desire to root education deep in the soil of the new territory, Narcissa was like other western women who established institutions in their fledgling communities. While she was starting modestly with the mission school, she and Marcus harbored ambitious educational dreams—an academy, maybe even a college, at Waiilatpu. By 1847 Narcissa and Marcus were talking about enlarging the educational community at the mission by building houses for the missionary mothers to occupy during school time. Narcissa was also intent on providing the girls with some of the accomplishments of the academy. One emigrant, Lorinda Bewley, whose good manners impressed Narcissa, was engaged "to teach the girls some fancy work."

The Whitman mission in 1847. Oregon Historical Society, ORHI#637.

The hired schoolmasters spared Narcissa from "the tedious task of starting . . . [the children] all in a, b, c, and ba, be, etc." Narcissa especially appreciated Alanson Hinman, the schoolmaster hired for the mission school in the winter of 1845. She found him "such a good young man," possibly because he was a "good and faithful discipli-narian" who "entirely relieved [her] of the difficult and hard task of breaking . . . [the older Sager children] in to the habits of obedience and order." Her tasks were more pleasant, taking the scholars on botany walks and reading with them. "My labour is comparatively easy," she told Laura Brewer, "and I am now taking new delight every day in teaching."

Increasingly, however, Narcissa appreciated the importance of her supervisory role. An incident in 1846 involving several children living in her household revealed the extent of her responsibilities. While it is not clear what happened, Narcissa's refusal to commit any details to paper and the Walkers' and Eellses' responses suggest that sex probably played some part. Seven-year-old Cyrus Walker learned "one naughty habit of an Indian." Whatever Cyrus learned (perhaps masturbation), he taught the others as well. Narcissa believed the children were not aware of what they were doing. "Poor children all saw from the oldest to the youngest that they did not know of its evil tendency or that it was a sin—no one had told them but every one promised never to do so in the future." Despite the "free and ingenuous" discussion and the promise of reformation, Narcissa vowed to supervise the children more closely after the incident. "I can not rest to have them out of my sight for a moment unless I know where they are," she told Mary Walker, "but prefer to have their work as well as their play all done in my presence."

The Sager girls adapted more easily to life in the Whitman family than did their brothers. Narcissa relied on Catherine as the eldest daughter, in much the same way as her own mother had relied on her in Prattsburg. Catherine became a confidante. "To me she opened all her plans for the pleasure or improvement of the children, and her fears and trouble for them." When Marcus was away, Catherine slept with Narcissa. "She often remarked she could not get along without me." But the older boys, John and Frank, were most used to the easy ways of their parents and, perhaps, most keenly aware of their death. They were restive with Narcissa's discipline and hated the schoolmaster Hinman who apparently beat them.

Although Narcissa hoped to win the boys' love and affection, her efforts resulted in the same kind of resistance to female authority that had occurred in the Prentiss household almost twenty years earlier. Frank found the strict mission life so distasteful and the discipline so strict that he determined to escape from Waiilatpu the spring following the Sagers' arrival. Narcissa tried to stop the boy by telling him "in a mild, firm voice" that he must stay. She motioned John to lock the door, but Frank bolted from the house before his brother had followed Narcissa's instructions. Narcissa "mourned" Frank's departure and said that "it seemed as though someone had died" in the family.

Narcissa's approach to motherhood, overly controlled and cheerless to late-twentieth-century observers, did not appear excessive or cruel to most mission visitors or to the children, with the initial exception of the two oldest boys. The children all commented on the strictness of the household, but they recognized the affection and came to accept Narcissa as mother. John eventually "received her rebukes as meant for his good," while even Frank came home after a few months in the Willamette. Although "it took some time" for Narcissa "to convince him that she laid up nothing against him, and to win his confidence," she eventually succeeded in winning the boy over. The symbol of the reconciliation came when Frank began to call Narcissa "Mother." Years later, Catherine summed up Narcissa as "particularly adapted to the raising of children, having the happy art of combining instruction with pleasure."

Physical, intellectual, and even moral development were not ends in themselves. As time passed, and Narcissa made progress with the children, she worried increasingly about her responsibility to their souls. She confessed to Laura Brewer in December 1846 that she was "tired of living as we have done and distressed to think that the majority in my family and around me are in the Broad road to ruin."

Narcissa often recalled her own upbringing and realized the special obstacles she faced as a missionary mother. The "savage" surroundings, with which she had never been comfortable, tended "to degrade rather than elevate." In Prattsburg, the church and its activities supported and reinforced parental efforts. The Whitmans, however, had to "be the ministers, Sabbath school teachers, parents and all to our children."

With considerable energy, Narcissa set the processes in motion that would lead to conversion. Despite her heathen surroundings, she managed to encourage many of the activities that had influenced her own spiritual development as a young girl. Basic religious instruction within the family proceeded. In addition to family worship in the morning and the evening, all the children memorized a verse of Scripture each day and recited it during evening worship. Narcissa taught the children hymns, and when Andrew Rodgers joined the mission family in 1845, he played his violin as accompaniment. There was a weekly Sabbath school with special homework, Saturday evening Bible study, a special Sabbath service for whites, maternal meetings with children present, and an assortment of special prayer meetings. On Thursday evenings, Narcissa conducted a children's meeting. As she explained to Eliza Spalding, "I simply read talk and pray with them in a simple, familiar way and they appear very much interested in it." Catherine paid tribute to Narcissa's evangelical talents when she described her "habit of collecting the young people around her and holding a prayer meeting with them. At these times she conversed pointedly with each one on the salvation of his soul."

In the fall of 1846 Narcissa contentedly described for her mother the efforts she was making for the children. "Mother will see," she explained, "that my hands and heart are usefully employed, not so much for the Indians directly, as my own family. When my health failed, I was obliged to withhold my efforts for the natives, but the Lord has since filled my hands with other labors, and I have no reason to complain." To a surprising extent, and against formidable odds, Narcissa had been able to re-create at Waiilatpu some of the rhythms of her own early family life.

Eventually, she began to have hopes that the children were making spiritual progress. By the general mission meeting held in May 1845, she had persuaded the five girls and Mary Ann Bridger to be baptized. The next winter she recognized signs of the Holy Spirit at work in the children's seriousness. By April she even thought that the boys might be converted. While the road to conversion was often strewn with unexpected obstacles, she did not lose heart as she so often had with the Cayuse. She continued to exhibit "no small measure of faith and patience, as well as great care and prayerful watchfulness." In late 1846 Catherine and Eliza Spalding gave indications of a change of heart, and Narcissa also saw "evidence to believe that the spirit of the Lord is moving upon the hearts of our neighbors." Before long, she was rewarded with the refreshment of a "little revival" at Waiilatpu.

There were also lighter moments in the Whitman family. When guests were present, Narcissa would line all the children up by height and have them sing to the company. Some evenings she would entertain the children with anecdotes and help the girls make rag dolls and patchwork. On special occasions, there were elaborate picnics; on more ordinary occasions, there might be a walk looking for flowers to press or the treat of a visit to Fort Walla Walla.

Narcissa told her brother-in-law that she loved the baby dearly but that "tender anxiety, so peculiar to mothers, for their own offspring, is not for me to feel toward her, because it is impossible," yet her letters give an enormous sense of domestic contentment and affection. Not long after the Sagers' arrival, she explained how keenly she had felt "a mother's solicitude and interest for them." The children provided her with "so much company in our lonely situation, that we could not think of sending them away." As she told Laura Brewer, four months after the Sagers had joined the family, her "winter in labouring for my family of orphans" had been "very happy." She gave a cozy domestic vignette of the family. There she was seated, pen in hand, "my baby . . . whining and the children . . . busy about me like so many bees," and she their queen. "We have as happy a family as the world affords," she told Harriet. "I do not wish to be in a better situation than this."

Narcissa's evangelical efforts with the mission family, a group that included the emigrant families and those, like the schoolmasters, who were connected with the mission in one way or another, provided additional satisfaction and further justification for her retreat from work with the Indians. The ease with which she worked with these white men and women and the religious success that she enjoyed sharply contrasted with the awkward and frustrating interactions she had had with the Cayuse. In her own culture and setting, she rediscovered persuasive gifts and her ability to move emotions, talents that had been of little use in her Indian missionary work. The confidence she had in Prattsburg must have returned in full measure.

For at least part of the year, there were a good number of women at Waiilatpu. Some were wives and daughters in emigrant families; others stopped at Waiilatpu to do domestic work at the mission. Finally, Narcissa was able to get a proper "female prayer meeting on Wed. P.M." going. She told Laura Brewer, "When we commenced there was only one to pray besides myself and she is a widow lady that is stopping in our family." But the meetings "are interesting to us," and more women became involved. Mary Johnson, "the girl that does my work has experienced religion since she came into our family . . . [and] now takes part." Far from making Narcissa complacent, the success of the female prayer meetings made her eager to extend her efforts to those "in the Broad road to ruin," especially "those about us who speak our language."

Despite her difficulties with the Sager boys, Narcissa felt a special rapport with the young single men who stayed for long periods of time at the mission. Her evangelical work with them highlighted the shift in her missionary focus. Seeing herself in the role of evangelical mother, Narcissa energetically pursued the young men's spiritual welfare. She selected books for them to read, engaged them in intimate and lengthy conversations about their spiritual welfare, and prayed with and for them. None had experienced conversion, but Narcissa was not deterred by their lack of faith or sometimes outright avoidance of her.

Narcissa was able to capitalize both on the mother-son relationship and cultural expectations that mothers properly sought their sons' salvation. She played the maternal role well. "It appeared almost like parting with my mother when I left there," one protégé

wrote. "Mrs. Whitman seem[s] very near to me." Another also testified, weeping, that Narcissa had "been a mother to him, for he
never received such attention before from anyone."

As had been true in Prattsburg, a shared culture, familiar values,
and literacy facilitated Narcissa's evangelical work among whites. But
there were other factors that contributed to Narcissa's effectiveness.
One nineteen-year-old youth was struck by the power and appeal of
Narcissa's personality and person. His comments were reminiscent
of what people in New York State said about her. Her eyes were
"large, soft and liquid," he noted. "She seemed endowed with a peculiar magnetism when you were in your presence, so that you could
not help thinking yourself in the presence of a much higher than the
ordinary run of humanity. I have heard her pray, and she could offer
up the finest petition to the Throne of Grace of any person I have
ever heard in my life."

Narcissa's first success came with the twenty-two-year-old schoolmaster, Alanson Hinman, whom the Sagers detested so heartily. Perhaps without much direct prompting from Narcissa, the "influence
of . . . a Christian family" reminded him of "the prayers and tears
of a pious mother and deceased father." Remorse for his life overwhelmed him, and after bitter tears, Hinman dedicated himself to
Christ. Knowing well the importance of support, Narcissa kept close
to the young man, making him her "associate in instructing and labouring with the children in Sabbath school and otherwise." Hinman formally joined the church before moving to the Willamette
Valley to teach school.

Next, thirty-two-year-old Joseph Finley came to the mission in the
fall of 1845 with an advanced case of tuberculosis. While he was able
to be up and about for the first few weeks of the winter he intended
to spend at the Waiilatpu, by January his health had deteriorated
dramatically. There was no time to lose with the dying man. Convinced that Finley "was work that the Lord put in my hands," Narcissa put him to bed in her own room. As she explained to Jane, her
bedroom was really the only suitable place for an invalid. But there
were other obvious advantages to having him so accessible. "Being
in my family, I was very much with him and read and prayed with
him almost daily towards the close of his life."

As was often the case when sinners began to realize the enormity
of their plight, the outcome was in question. Narcissa felt "deep
anxiety of mind" and "a tender anxious watchfulness for him." In

revealing language, she explained that she was constantly "seeking an opportunity of nourishing and cherishing him as I would a little child." Her labor was not in vain; signs of progress appeared, and the dying Finley united with the little church.

Finley did not exhibit the expected emotional responses to his reception in the church, no "ecstasy, joy, or rejoicing." Rather than criticizing his subdued behavior, Narcissa rationalized it as the result of an incomplete religious upbringing. Because his mother had died early, his tender religious feelings had never been properly nourished; he had never learned how to feel.

Finley's last moments were so "glorious" that Narcissa provided her family with many of the particulars. Nineteenth-century Americans were not squeamish about death and often filled their letters with almost moment-by-moment descriptions of the last hours of loved ones. In Finley's case, Narcissa seems to have orchestrated the ritual drama, and Finley's departure provided the missionaries with what they hoped for. Finley's final words, "Sweet Jesus! sweet Jesus! sweet Jesus!" affected those gathered around his bed "like a ray of glory bursting through him upon our minds." As Narcissa explained, "It completely melted us all." Finley's death testified not only to the validity of the Christian message, so lightly received by the Cayuse, and the certainty of afterlife, but also to the power of evangelical intervention. Narcissa explained, "As for me, I had been asking that the Lord might be glorified in his death, and thus we were left without a doubt that our brother, on whom we had bestowed so much anxious care, had gone to be forever with the Lord; feeling too, that we had been more than amply rewarded for the labor bestowed upon him."

Newton Gilbert, Marcus's former Sunday school student from Rushville, New York, also received Narcissa's attention. His mother was still alive, and her letters had helped pull "back his wayward feet to the Cross." Although Narcissa did not know Mrs. Gilbert, she wrote a long letter describing Newton's spiritual progress, confident that the mother would want all the details.

The vigor with which Narcissa pursued Newton's spiritual welfare suggests that it was not easy to shake off her attentions. She was nothing if not persistent. If Newton had scruples about his worthiness to be saved, Narcissa conversed and prayed with him. When he seemed to want "to avoid all conversation upon religious subjects," she bided her time until he seemed ready. She plied him with reading materials and put a baptism covenant into his hands that he promised to adopt. When he left the mission, she earnestly requested that he would write to inform her "of his situation trials hopes and prospects." If only mothers (and surrogate mothers) realized the power of their influence, Narcissa wrote Mrs. Gilbert. "May we my dear Mrs Gilbert so live and act feel and pray that the blood of the souls of our Children may not be found in our skirts in the great day of accounts."

For this important evangelical work with children and "family" members, Narcissa found a new helpmate in Andrew Rodgers. Rodgers was in his midtwenties when he arrived at the mission with Finley and acted for a time as the schoolmaster. He joined the church with Finley and soon decided to read for the ministry.

While both perceived the relationship as one between mother and son, it came to be far more than that. "We talk, sing, labour, and study together," she wrote Jane in April 1847. Perhaps because she could understand her intimacy with Rodgers only by framing it in familial terms, she explained that now Rodgers seemed more like her older brother Stephen than her son. He had become "the best associate I ever had, Marcus excepted."

In fact, though Narcissa did not say so, Rodgers adopted concerns that her own busy husband did not. He helped with the children's Saturday night Bible class and taught them to sing "admirably." He had a musical voice, loved hymns, and as one of the Sagers put it, was addicted to playing the violin. After years of putting up with Marcus's modest musical talents, Narcissa was delighted. "I can assure you," she told Jane, "it is no small comfort to have some one to sing with who knows how to sing, for it is true, Jane, I love to sing just as well as ever." Music united them in moments of high religious emotion. When Finley died, the two of them sang "in tremulous voices the hymn commencing, 'Ah! Lovely Appearance of Death.'"

Altogether, Rodgers was a tremendous addition to her life. "His Christian society" afforded her "much comfort," especially during Marcus's absences. She had often longed to have a real minister at Waiilatpu who could "draw the mind to heavenly things." Perhaps she found her busy husband's conversation somewhat pragmatic, as did some of the emigrants who traveled west with him in 1843. With Rodgers at the mission, it was almost as if a minister were in residence. He wrote stimulating discourses to be read during the mission Sabbath service and could speak without notes on religious subjects. "Last evening he gave an extemporaneous discourse upon the future punishment of the wicked," she told to Laura Brewer. "It was truly edifying."

At one point, the two agreed to write to one another's friends. Rodgers requested that Narcissa write to his mother. She asked him to write to Jane. He explained to Jane that although he was a complete stranger, he felt as if he knew her well, "having become so much attached to Mrs. Whitman." Because Narcissa had told him that Jane and Edward had some thoughts of coming west, he devoted most of his letter to describing the spiritual trials of the trip, the gambling, the profanation of the Sabbath, the company. A comparison of his letter with Narcissa's suggests that Narcissa may have thought briefly about a match between her sister and her favorite young man. She was familiar enough with arranged marriages at least to consider the possibility. But if such an idea crossed her mind, she never pursued it as her friendship with and dependence on the "dear youth" increased.

The personal satisfactions that Narcissa derived from her work with her children and the small white community gathered around the mission were tempered by occasional problems within the mission. While the missionaries succeeded in avoiding the backbiting and arguments that marred their early years in the field, relations between them still were not trouble-free. Mary Walker confessed in her diary in 1846 that she harbored a "great many evil thoughts towards the members of the Mission as well as towards myself." Letters between Elkanah Walker and Marcus were often testy and suggest that Elkanah resented Marcus's leadership. While, for the most part, Narcissa wrote warm letters to the other women of the mission, often wishing to see them again, negative feelings about her had not entirely disappeared. Complaints against the Whitmans appeared from time to time as Marcus's 1847 letter to Elkanah makes clear. "We are aware that points of grievance exist in your minds towards her as well as towards myself," he wrote.

The difference between the present and the past was, however, that all the missionaries now realized more than ever that animosities and disagreements must not get out of hand. As Marcus had explained to Elkanah a year earlier, "I have little doubt but those of us who are left in the Mission have had trial enough among ourselves and others to be able to bear and forbear with each other and that a mutual and kind explanation will do away with those things which are either real or becoming causes of grief among us."

The new way of dealing with problems was apparent during a clash between Mary Walker and Narcissa at the general mission meeting in 1847. Narcissa came to dine at Mary's house, and the two women continued a conversation begun the previous day. "Mrs. W. seemed not to feel pleasantly. I began to be excited." The next day, however, Marcus stepped in and smoothed things over. "The Dr. received me in so cordial and friendly a fashion," Mary explained, "and seemd so well satisfied with the freedom which I expressed myself that I felt most relieved."

Despite these occasional problems, Narcissa was busy—a point that she stressed especially in her correspondence to her family—and doing useful work. "I desire to do all I can for the benefit of the children and all around me." But the boundaries were clear. She reached out only to the whites at the mission and left work with the Cayuse to others. When Marcus, Rodgers, or Perrin Whitman conducted Sabbath services for the Indians, Narcissa was busy with the children's Sabbath school. The Sager children spoke of visiting Indian lodges occasionally with Marcus but not with Narcissa. The school for the Indians was abandoned, although Rodgers explained to the ABCFM in 1847 that the Indians just were not interested. Attendance in 1845 had dwindled, and Marcus had held a feast to confer with the Indians on the question of school and English instruction. After that, as Rodgers reported, "no particular effort has been made in regard to school instruction, as there seemed very little prospect of doing good."

While Narcissa still referred to the people whose spiritual needs had drawn her west, her comments were infrequent and usually brief. The Cayuse were quiet, friendly, and attached to the Whitmans, she wrote in 1846. The next year she told Jane that prospects had never been more encouraging. To her mother, she painted a picture of the Indians' childlike bafflement and touching dependence on the missionaries as the character of the territory changed. "The poor Indians are amazed at the overwhelming numbers of Americans coming into the country. They seem not to know what to make of it."

Narcissa did not want to think much about the Cayuse and had many reasons for avoiding writing about them. "I would be glad to speak of the Indians, but one sheet is too small," she explained to her mother at the end of a letter in which she had described at great length the character of the white emigration, her happily crowded dinner table, her bathing regime, and the good qualities of her husband. There were ritual expressions of sadness that she now had no time for the Cayuse. "I feel distressed sometimes to think I am making so little personal effort for their benefit, when so much ought to be done," she told Laura Brewer. "But perhaps I could not do more than I am through my family."

Narcissa's comment about working through her family suggests that she believed the assertion so often made in missionary literature that the example of Christian family life would have a positive influence on the heathen. She certainly was convinced that, at the very least, the Indians took "great pleasure . . . to see so many children growing up in their midst." Had Narcissa been more familiar with Cayuse culture, however, she would have been less sure about the lessons they drew from white family life or their pleasure at white children growing up in the Whitman household. Certainly Indians valued children. But the Cayuse could hardly help but notice Narcissa's efforts to protect her adopted children from contact with native life. Like her mixed-blood children, the Sagers were not allowed to learn Nez Percé, nor did they attend the Cayuse Sabbath service. In fact, they had very little freedom to interact with the Indians at all. Narcissa often said that she did not want the children out of her sight unless they were in school.

Although the Indians may have recognized the Whitmans' genuine affection for their children, they must have seen Narcissa, the disciplinarian of the family, as harsh and cruel and regarded her child-rearing regime as odious. The children were confined, controlled, and even beaten occasionally. Indians did not beat their children; obedience to tribal norms was secured by the fear of shame, not punishment.

So wrapped up was Narcissa in the care of her household that she suspected none of these possible impressions of her family life. As she happily explained to Laura Brewer, she was entirely occupied. "I have six girls sewing around me, or rather five—for one is reading, and the same time my baby is asking to go and bathe. . . . Now another comes with her work for me to fix. So it is from morning until evening; I must be with them or else they will be doing something they should not, or else not spending their time profitably."

CHAPTER 7

Their Bones Scattered upon
the Plains

AS Narcissa turned inward to her own household, Marcus eagerly
contemplated the changing situation in Oregon. When the missionaries had arrived at Waiilatpu in 1836, only a handful of other Americans lived in the territory. But as published accounts made the trip
west less mysterious and as economic conditions in the East and
Midwest improved slowly after the panic of 1837, the number of
American emigrants steadily increased. In 1843, the year Marcus returned from the East with the emigration, the overland travelers succeeded in hauling two hundred wagons over the Blue Mountains.
The news of this feat persuaded other families to head for the Far
West, and in 1845 about three thousand people left their homes and
started the overland journey. Their arrival doubled the American
population in Oregon.

Although Great Britain and the United States did not resolve the
issue of sovereignty until 1846, Oregon residents did not wait for the
diplomats to take action. In 1843 settlers in the Willamette Valley
established a provisional government and decided upon a land policy
that made every male over eighteen (as well as widows) eligible for
640 acres of free land. Probably this generous offer further prompted
American emigration.

Marcus enthusiastically supported the new course of events. He
wrote letters promoting emigration and assisted weary and hungry
families when they reached the mission. He had ambitious dreams
for the future and saw few limits on Oregon's prospects. The "mild
equable climate," the fertile soil, and the superior "advantages for
Manufactories and Commerce" all made the territory wonderfully
promising. Could the board encourage a machinist from Lowell and
a general millwright to come west? he asked. Ever aware and fearful
of Roman Catholicism's progress and the mixed moral character
of the emigration, Marcus also called for pious Protestant settlers

(best if from New England), home missionaries, and those who
would establish institutions like schools and colleges. He urged the
ABCFM board to do its part to give Protestantism a firm footing in
the West and to ensure its future.

While most of his epistolary energy went into considerations of
Oregon's future as a place for white settlement, Marcus also provided the board with some assessment of the mission's primary
goals. At best, any evaluation of a decade's work with the Cayuse
was mixed.

All along, most of the positive news had concerned the progress
the Indians were making as farmers. Although the board was fearful
that material progress might come at the expense of spiritual progress, Marcus continued to stress the "vast" gains the Cayuse had
made. He may well have overstated them. His April 1845 report that
some of the Indians were hiring whites to break their land hardly
suggests that they had embraced agricultural ideals. Young Matilda
Sager thought that the entire effort did not add up to very much.
"There was not very much cultivation about anything," she remembered. An emigrant of the mid-1840s, B. F. Nichols, agreed.
The Indians, he remarked, "did not do a great deal of farming
themselves."

Spiritual progress was even harder to discern. Although the Spaldings had managed to convert several Nez Percé and one Cayuse living near their mission, the Whitmans had not converted one of the
Waiilatpu Cayuse. The Christian message had seriously divided the
tribe. Tilokaikt was a candidate for admission to the church, and
many Waiilatpu Indians still continued to attend services. Some
members of the tribe had drifted over into the Roman Catholic
camp, and others preferred traditional ways.

Apparently the Whitmans found it hard to live with this bitter
reality and occasionally exaggerated the spiritual changes that had
taken place among the Cayuse. One 1845 emigrant, Joel Palmer, described spending a day with the Whitmans, who had driven out from
the mission to meet him. They were in an expansive mood and had
many tales to tell of their years at Waiilatpu. In his published journal,
Palmer reported that the Indians "have embraced the Christian religion, and appear devout in their espousal of Christian doctrines."
He concluded that the fruits of the Whitmans' "devotion are now
manifest." His assessment must have been based on what the two

missionaries had told him, for he had no opportunity to observe the Waiilatpu Indians for himself.

Marcus could hardly make similar assertions to the board. Because there were so few signs that the Cayuse would convert to Christianity, Marcus said little about their spiritual condition. During 1846 and 1847 he reported that the Cayuse paid "good attention" to religious instruction and continued to pray in their lodges.

Andrew Rodgers, however, described ABCFM prospects more negatively. The rivalry between the Catholic and Protestant missionaries—each one claiming that what the other taught "would take them to the devil"—could only have produced skepticism and confusion among the Cayuse. But Rodgers did not stress the rivalry so much as the underlying cultural issue: the Cayuse were not attuned to the Protestant message. They loved "names and forms," to which, he believed, the Catholic priests pandered. While the Cayuse were "more or less inclined to receive instruction," they did not care much about "the spirit and power of true religion."

Sensitive to the possibility that the board might think he had neglected the Indians in favor of the emigrants, Marcus did explain in November 1846 that he had so many obligations that there was "little room for the more important spiritual part of our duty." But what was he to do? How was he to reconcile the claims of duty and business? He often wished "to give my whole time to the instruction of the people and resolved to do so more than heretofore, but then a call of sickness [comes] . . . which as a Physician I must regard as superior to any other."

While Marcus justified his choices in this fashion, there were telltale signs that his commitment to the Cayuse had also changed dramatically over the years. As he told his mission brothers in 1845, he did not feel "suited to be left with the entire religious instruction of Indians and whites." But duty kept him in the field. "I do not think I could be induced to come to such a people were it to be done again," he admitted to the board that year, but "it is quite different when the question is of continuance or abandonment." As he explained to Elkanah Walker, leaving the field would expose "the cause of religion to reproach." The entire mission had "to end what we began both in regard to Indians and whites."

At times, the sweeping changes that were overtaking Oregon Territory and the lean spiritual harvest caused all members of the mission to question whether there was any "prospect of permanency or much good." As early as 1844 the ABCFM had harbored doubts whether anything less than the "special intervention of Providence" would save the Indians, although Secretary Greene counseled the missionaries to continue in their work energetically. While Marcus was never able to declare definitively that the missionaries' efforts to bring Christ to the Indians were in vain, the picture he painted of the relations between the missionaries and the Cayuse called into question not only the long-term viability of the entire endeavor but also the survival of the missionaries themselves.

His letters to the board revealed a clear pattern of hostility alternating with periods of amicable relations. Marcus sensed the sequence but lived very much in the present moment. When the Indians seemed to be his affectionate friends, he was hopeful they had changed for good. When they were threatening, he spoke of leaving Waiilatpu but made few substantial efforts to depart.

The instructions from the board did not help him decide upon a definitive course of action. On the one hand, Greene, who was thousands of miles away in Boston, hesitated to give advice because, by the time his letter arrived, all might have changed. On the other hand, he told Marcus that hostility and opposition were nothing new in Indian mission work. "The only way to deal with such people, at these times," he wrote, "is to be fearless, calm, good natured, and ready for every act of love."

The alternating pattern of tolerance and hostility suggests factional struggles and shifts in power and influence among the factions. Some of the Indians, "our friends," "our good Indians," apparently wished the ABCFM missionaries to stay, even if they had little interest in conversion. During peaceable times, these members of the tribe must have kept the peace. Others favored the Roman Catholic missionaries, who were in the process of locating nearby. Still others wanted the Whitmans to leave Waiilatpu. When these gained the upper hand, the atmosphere at the mission grew strained.

The year 1845 was one of "much anxiety" for Marcus. Because some of the Cayuse believed that Marcus possessed spiritual powers, they blamed him and his medicine for events seemingly caused by witchcraft. When one of the headmen fell ill, his son approached Marcus "in a passion," warning him that "it would not be a difficult matter for . . . [him] to be killed." Other death threats revealed deep anger toward the white doctor and the changing world of which he was so prominently a part.

In the spring Marcus discussed his situation with John McLoughlin, who had left the Hudson's Bay Company and now lived in Oregon City. With all his years of experience in dealing with Oregon tribes, McLoughlin agreed with Marcus about the danger facing him and advised him to move to the Willamette.

That fall, Marcus wrote to Cushing Eells and Elkanah Walker, so disturbed by accusations of poison made by Tautai, or Young Chief, that his hand was shaking. Although Marcus had denied administering poison, Young Chief wondered why anyone would expect Marcus to tell the truth. Marcus responded by delivering an ultimatum. The Cayuse must decide by the coming spring whether they wished the missionaries to stay or to leave Waiilatpu.

Cushing Eells thought, probably correctly, that the Indians were trying to force the Whitmans to leave. But Marcus could not bring himself to abandon the mission unless the Indians explicitly requested his departure and took all the responsibility for the decision. Catherine Sager recalled that one day, after trouble with Tomahas at the mill, Marcus had come into the house "exhausted in body and vexed in spirit." He threw "himself on the settee" and said "that if the Indians would only say so, he would gladly leave, for he was tried with them almost beyond endurance." And yet when Tomahas threatened Marcus with a club and told him to leave, Marcus replied that "he could not leave, just because one Indian wanted him to go." "All the Indians" must agree. Thomas McKay recalled Marcus telling him that "he wished all the chiefs to tell him to go away; in order to excuse himself to the Board of Foreign Missions."

By the fall of 1846, however, Marcus concluded that once the status of Oregon as an American territory was clarified, the Indians would "be most quiet." Lulled by their "much kinder disposition," Marcus considered a manual boarding school for the Indians at some point in the future, and even of acquiring The Dalles mission station, which the Methodists were considering abandoning. Soon an eager advocate of The Dalles site, he told the board that it would provide the ABCFM missionaries with access to Indians all along the Columbia River as far as Fort Vancouver.

His interest in acquiring another station in light of the spiritual impasse at Waiilatpu seems surprising. It is as if he had been swept away by the momentary goodwill of the Indians and tempted by the sorts of expansive visions he was entertaining for white society. But perhaps this new scheme seemed more promising and more likely to justify the missionary enterprise in the eyes of the board than what transpired at Waiilatpu. After all, the Perkinses had had some spectacular success in their early days at The Dalles. The competition with Roman Catholic missionary efforts also influenced his thinking. In the end, perhaps it was just human to want to think about a hopeful future rather than a questionable venture at home.

By 1847 events were shifting rapidly. The Spaldings were having serious trouble at Lapwai. Hostile unconverted Nez Percé broke windows of the meetinghouse, tore down fences, and damaged the mill dam. Despite the danger, the Spaldings stayed. While Waiilatpu was calmer than Lapwai, Marcus, like Henry, was unsure about what to do. "I am free to say I would like to be discharged," Marcus revealed, "could I feel as sure I was as wright [sic] in leaving as I was in coming among the Indians. As we live at all times in a most precarious state nor knowing whether to stay or go nor at what time nor how soon. Whether it may be demanded by the Indians or the Board, I think in the course of the ensuing summer I shall locate a claim for land in this lower Country to be ready in case of retirement." Yet only a month and a half later, Marcus was deeply engaged in The Dalles scheme and positive that his trials with his own band was in the past.

Despite Marcus's optimism, any improvement in the missionaries' relations with the Indians was temporary. New sources of difficulty emerged. Early struggles between the Whitmans and the Cayuse had revolved around the relationship between the missionaries and the Indians, particularly involving payment for the mission land or the missionaries' harsh warnings of future damnation for the unconverted. Now increased white immigration reinforced old differences.

Although the Cayuse made some short-term gains from the emigration by selling supplies, trading livestock, hiring men to break land, and occasionally raiding animals and goods from wagon trains, they recognized the long-term dangers of white settlement. Emigrants were destroying the game and fuel upon which the Indians depended, and their stock consumed the grasses needed for the Indian herds. The increasing numbers of white families passing through Cayuse territories every year suggested that the Indians would be soon be outnumbered and displaced.

Indians from eastern tribes, such as the mixed-blood Delaware Tom Hill, warned the Cayuse of the dangers looming ahead. A man "of considerable talent," according to Marcus, Tom Hill had a Nez Percé wife and entrée to both the Nez Percé and the Waiilatpu Indians. He described the negative consequences of white settlement and, perhaps because missionaries sometimes preceded settlers, had especially harsh words about the missionary presence. During 1847 two mixed bloods were living at the mission. One, Joe Lewis, may also have been, like Tom Hill, part Delaware.

Episodes, both small and large, gave weight to the warnings of men like Hill. While Oregon Trail diaries and reminiscences reveal the white perspective on their interactions with the Cayuse, the Indian point of view can easily be imagined.

Young John Minto came west in 1844 and encountered some Cayuse at the Umatilla River. The emigrants were hungry and eager to barter an old shirt for the potatoes one of the Cayuse had in a sack. When the Indian showed off his shirt to two young women, however, they pointed to the worn spots. Angry at the exchange, the Indian decided to retrieve his potatoes. Though the emigrants were famished, they judged that the Indian had "got his dry goods very cheap." "One of our party, keeping his gun in one hand," Minto remembered, grabbed the potatoes and "turned the muzzle of his gun towards the brave. . . . Four of the six of us had guns, and the brave quieted down and went away." Minto's party soon learned that the Indian's behavior "was a common trait of Indian trading," while the Cayuse doubtless learned that the emigrants were willing to pawn off inferior goods and were quick to pull their guns if there were disagreements about the value of the trade.

Jesse Applegate described a scuffle between "we boys" and Indian youths at Fort Walla Walla in 1843. At the heart of the trouble was another exchange, this time nails and scraps of iron in return for a root called *yampa*. Not all the boys had pockets for the *yampa*s, and some fell on the ground. One of the Indians bent down to pick up the root, "when one of our boys attacked him in the rear with his foot, and the young warrior toppled over on his head." A full-fledged battle broke out, with the white boys throwing pebbles and potatoes and the Indians returning fire with arrows and pebbles. Fort Walla Walla's chief trader, McKinlay, broke up the fight. "Our boys began the fight," Applegate recalled, "but it was claimed that the Indians were picking up the yampas that fell to the ground and

selling them to us again." Needless to say, there were no more exchanges of roots; "we noticed that the Indians visiting our camp
were sulky and not talkative."

Secretary Greene warned Marcus of the dangers of becoming
"a man of business," but for the most part, the warnings went un-
heeded. Much of that business about which the board worried
linked Marcus, in the eyes of the Cayuse, to the emigration from the
States. Marcus himself completed a new "shorter & better" wagon
road from the Umatilla to The Dalles for the emigrants. Often both
Whitmans rode out to meet and assist emigrant parties, while occasionally Marcus guided them to safety. In 1845 he and some friendly
Nez Percé prevented hostile Walla Wallas (and perhaps some Cayuse
as well) from attacking a large party of emigrants. According to
Sarah Cummins, Marcus made the right of the travelers and the
might of white government very clear. As he told the Indians, "The
Great Father of the 'Bostons' would send men to defend these travelers, and that shiploads of soldiers and guns would arrive to kill all
the Indians who molested his people on their way to the distant
valley." That night Marcus kept the "sullen" chief captive and insulted him by threatening to have him "shot like a dog" if he moved.
At other times, Marcus recovered stolen property from the Indians,
again using threats of what "the Americans" would do if the goods
were not returned. One young girl later remembered how angrily
one of the Indians had flung a stolen skillet down on the ground. As
her father observed, "They are mad."

During the winter, the mission at Waiilatpu became a white settlement. In 1846, forty-five to fifty emigrants wintered with the Whitmans; the next year seventy did. The Cayuse observed white men
working for Marcus and white children going to school. There was
no school, of course, for the Indian children. In 1846 even the Indian
room was given over to whites for a bunk room. The next year the
Osborn family lived in it. Catherine Sager recollected that "the natives did not like ... [them] being in their room." While many
Cayuse had little interest in assimilation or school, they disliked the
sight of white people replacing them in their own land.

The Cayuse also observed that the Whitmans gave supplies to
needy families at the very same time that they charged the Cayuse
for having their land plowed and their grain milled. Neither Marcus
nor Narcissa considered that their charity to whites bore any relationship to their dealings with the Cayuse. As Marcus reported to

the board, he had long sought to disabuse the Indians from the notion that the missionaries "were under obligation . . . to do these things for them for nothing."

The mood of some of the Indians was turning ugly. During July of 1847, Paul Kane, a Canadian artist, visited the mission. The Cayuse struck him as "vicious and ungovernable." Certainly he found the naked Tomahas, whom he sketched, to be so. After Kane had finished the drawing, Tomahas asked him if he intended to give it to the Americans. As Kane reported, Tomahas "bore a strong antipathy [to Americans,] superstitiously fancying that their possessing it would put it in their power." When he failed to retrieve the drawing from Kane, Tomahas seemed enraged.

The large emigration of 1847, numbering between four and five thousand travelers, encountered harassment from the Oregon tribes during the final weeks of their journey. Any dispassionate observer could recognize the Indians' growing anger at white emigration and settlement. Around the mission, the Cayuse and Walla Walla worried that whites intended to settle on their tribal lands and drive them away. Actually their fears were not entirely groundless. Marcus had hoped for a number of years that he could settle "good families . . . in select spots among the Indians." Although the Cayuse could not know Marcus's dream, his busy intervention on behalf of the whites was proof enough of his basic loyalties.

The arrival of deadly diseases during 1847 lent substance to the Cayuse's fears of extinction and tipped the balance of tribal power in favor of the antimissionary faction. The previous year, a band of Cayuse and Walla Walla warriors had gone to California to avenge the murder of the Walla Walla headman's son. Some of them contracted measles. When the travelers returned to Oregon Territory during the summer of 1847, they reported that more than thirty of their troupe had died. Paul Kane, who witnessed the arrival of the warriors at Fort Walla Walla, was so concerned about what the epidemic might mean for the Whitmans that he went out to the mission to urge them to come into the fort for a few days. Was Marcus too proud to listen to an artist or not imaginative enough to picture the danger? Or was this just another time when he could not give up because of what the world might say? In any case, Marcus refused to leave Waiilatpu. "He had lived so long amongst them, and had done so much for them," Kane said, "that he did not apprehend they would injure him."

To-ma-kus, by Paul Kane, sketched on his visit to the mission. To-ma-kus (or Tomahas) was tried for murder for his part in the massacre and was found guilty. Before he was hanged, he accepted the Roman Catholic faith. The Peabody Museum of Archaeology and Ethnology.

During the summer some Cayuse sickened with dysentery. Then, as the emigrants came into the mission, a new measles epidemic broke out. A recent anthropological study suggests that the epidemic's source was probably the earlier trip made by the Walla Wallas and Cayuse to California. But the Cayuse who succumbed so rapidly to the disease doubtless associated the new onslaught with the emigrants. Marcus's medicine was ineffective, and traditional sweat baths hastened the disease's course. While several white people at the mission also caught the measles, and one six-year-old died, the disparity between the survival of the two races could hardly have been more striking. Perhaps as many as thirty of the Indians living near the mission died during October and November. Catherine Sager remembered seeing "five to six [Indians] buried daily," while young Nathan Kimball, who was living at the mission, recalled the grisly sight of "dead Indians hanging across the fence, the same as you would hang a sack of wheat, waiting for coffins." Other bands living farther away also succumbed to the disease.

For the first years after the Sagers' arrival, Narcissa continued to send contented domestic letters to her friends and family. Her refusal to heed possible danger to herself and her family show her determination to cast the heathen out of her mind and life and to put all her energies into creating a satisfactory substitute for the missionary work in which she had been so disappointed.

Finally even Narcissa became concerned and recognized the serious problems at Waiilatpu during in the summer and fall of 1847. She told one of the women living at the mission that she feared they all would be killed. The Sagers sensed the new atmosphere and overheard hurried conversations between the Whitmans. Elizabeth realized that "serious trouble was feared by them from the Indians. This talk was very guarded on their part, as they did not wish the fears of the children alarmed." Her younger sister Matilda was having nightmares.

Young Eliza Spalding, who had come to Waiilatpu to attend school, was also aware of the rumors of a possible Indian outbreak. She was in a better position to assess the danger because, unlike the children in the Whitman household, she could speak Nez Percé. But familiarity with Nez Percé was not necessary. Joseph Stanfield, a French Canadian, warned Mrs. Wallace, who had expected to winter at the mission with her family, that he had heard Joe Lewis talking. "Don't let your husband stay here. There is going to be trouble. You will be sorry if you stay." The Wallace family packed up and left.

The extent of Narcissa's anxiety and the suspicions of the Cayuse were both suggested by the events following the death of the young Osborn child. Narcissa told the grieving mother that "perhaps God thought it for the best that your little child should be called away; it may calm the Indians to see a white child taken as well as so many natives, for otherwise we may all be compelled to leave within two weeks." Narcissa also took one of the Cayuse in to view the body, hoping "to allay the growing distrust of the red men." If that was her intention, as Nancy Osborn thought, she failed. "The Indian looked long at my sister, then cruelly he laughed to see the paleface dead."

The measles epidemic gave new life to old rumors that Joe Lewis actively encouraged. For years, the Cayuse had accused the doctor of poisoning Indians with his medicines in the same way that he poisoned the wolves that threatened his fields. Not that the Cayuse believed Marcus needed medicine to work harm against them, for they credited him with spiritual powers that they believed he was using malignantly. Now the word about Marcus was reaching other tribes. Many Palouse Indians came to believe that Marcus was a murderer. They heard of "an oldish man who was not healthy and knew he wasn't going to live but two or three years." He "told other Indians that he was going to take Dr. Whitman's medicine to find out if it contained poison." He did so, and died.

Marcus had several warnings of impending trouble. Indians friendly to the Whitmans asked John Settle, a white worker at the mission, to "induce Dr. Whitman to leave." Settle, however, found "Dr. Whitman hardly would listen to him and in fact ridiculed his fear." The Cayuse Stickus bluntly informed Marcus that "the bad Indians" were planning to kill him. While Marcus appeared "much agitated" by the news, he took no immediate action. Eliza Spalding thought that the Whitmans did not believe "feeling was strong enough to cause an uprising." Elizabeth Sager remembered Marcus as a man who overestimated his power and influence and who refused to make a quick decision. "If things do not clear up, I shall have to leave in the spring," he said. To Mr. Kimball, one of the white settlers, Marcus declared, "Yes, the situation looks pretty dark, but I think I shall be able to quell any trouble."

Some of the important men among the Cayuse, however, had de-

termined to take steps to shape the future. Earlier attempts by some
of the Indians to make the missionaries leave had failed, and it was
time for drastic action. Many plateau tribes killed shamans who practiced witchcraft, and the decision to put the missionaries to death
may have appeared appropriate even to those who were not personally hostile to them. According to the Nez Percé Yellow Bull, "the
head-men met in council and made an agreement that the Doctor
should be killed because 200 of the people had died after taking his
medicine." Other evidence suggests that Tomsucky pressed the headman, Tilokaikt, to kill the doctor. Tilokaikt, one of the few candidates, if not the only candidate, for admission to the church, was
initially reluctant. The Cayuse were divided over the plan, but the
young men of the tribe "wished to do it, and they contended so
long" that they persuaded the headman. If one of the residents of
the mission was right, Tilokaikt had a recent cause for hostility; three
of his own children had just died from the measles.

On November 29, a dark, gloomy day, all the children who were
well enough were at school. Narcissa, who had failed to appear at
breakfast and whom Elizabeth had seen crying, was supervising
Elizabeth's and Catherine's baths; Marcus was reading in the sitting
room. When Narcissa went into the kitchen to get some milk for the
children who were still sick with the measles, she found it crowded
with Indians. Their manner was alarming. One tried to follow her
when she came back into the sitting room, but she pushed the door
closed and locked it.

Meanwhile, Marcus had gone into the kitchen to deal with Tomahas, who was asking for medicine. Narcissa and the girls heard
"loud and angry voices in the kitchen and occasionally Father's soft,
mild voice in reply.... Suddenly there was a sharp explosion—a
rifle shot—in the kitchen and we all jumped in fright." Narcissa
shouted, "The Indians will murder us all!" but was in enough control
of herself to help the two Sager girls dress.

In the kitchen, the bullet had hardly been needed. Tomahas had
hit Marcus twice from behind with his tomahawk, while Tilokaikt
slashed Marcus's face. The doctor had only hours to live. His stepson
John Sager, who also had been in the kitchen, lay dying near him.

Mary Ann Bridger, who had been in the kitchen, rushed into the
sitting room with the fearful news. Narcissa moaned, "My husband
is dead and I am left a widow!" With the help of one of the women
who had rushed to the mission house when the shooting began,

Narcissa carried Marcus into the sitting room and tried to stop the bleeding. He whispered to her that there was nothing she could do for him.

Outside, some of the Cayuse had attacked the white men who were dressing a beef in a meadow near the school. One was killed immediately. Before long, the schoolmaster and the operator of the gristmill also lay dead. Many of the terrified whites, including the children who had been in school, tried to hide. There was noise and confusion everywhere. The Cayuse were "painted black and white, yelling and leaping . . . caps of eagle feathers streaming." Not far away, "Indian women [were] singing and dancing." While the whites saw only murder and mayhem, tribal religious rituals were underway.

When Narcissa went to the sash door to see what was happening, someone shot her in the breast or arm. Witnesses disagreed whether Joe Lewis or a full-blooded Cayuse, Frank Iskalome, supposedly a friend of the Whitmans, fired the shot. Narcissa fell back. Rodgers, who was wounded himself, helped her up. Elizabeth Sager remembered that she began to pray, "Lord, save these little ones." As they had throughout her life, her thoughts turned to her mother. Matilda heard her ask God that "dear mother would be given strength to bear the news of her death."

As dusk fell and the Cayuse began to break the windows of the mission, Rodgers and the women and children retreated to the upstairs, where Narcissa sank onto one of the beds. Elizabeth wrote that she "put my arm around her. She said, 'Hold me tight': My hand was covered with blood."

Rodgers was standing at the top of the stairs armed only with an old gun muzzle. The Indians now broke into the house and mutilated the faces of Marcus and John Sager. Women started plundering the pantry while Joe Lewis raided a chest where Narcissa kept her best clothes and started to distribute them. Soon, some of the men started up the stairs. The sight of what they thought was a gun stopped them. Tamsucky urged Rodgers to come down. When the young man finally descended, he found Tamsucky and Joe Lewis. Tamsucky claimed that the house was to be burned and that he wished to save the women.

Having no alternative, the little troupe came down the stairs. Narcissa turned her eyes from the sight of her dying husband and, weak from the loss of blood, lay down on a sofa. Joe Lewis picked up one end of the sofa and Rodgers the other. As they left the house, some of the Indians who were gathered outside started to fire. Rodgers, Francis Sager, and Narcissa were all hit. Narcissa fell into the mud. Eight-year-old Matilda claimed "she saw one of the Indians reach down, catch Mrs. Whitman by the hair, and raise her head and then strike her across the face several times with his leather quirt." Others remembered that the Cayuse also wielded a war club. The children, horrified, fell silent. The next morning, at dawn, they heard the Indians chanting the "Death Song."

The violence had not yet ended, although both the Whitmans were now dead. The Indians smashed windows and doors, destroyed the Whitman's cooking stove, took for themselves the goods they had so long admired, and cast books and papers aside. That day another resident of the mission was intercepted and killed as he attempted to bring water from the river, while one of young men bringing down wood from the mission sawmill in the mountains also was murdered.

Sometime during the day, the Indians herded all those who were still alive into the building used to house visiting emigrants. Three families had succeeded in slipping away during the confusion, but over forty terrified men, women, and children, some still sick, crowded into the house. Several of the children, including Hannah Sager and Helen Meek, would die from the measles. Two more of the men at the mission would also meet their death at the hands of the Indians.

That same evening one of the Roman Catholic missionaries, Father Brouillet, came from the nearby St. Anne mission to visit the Waiilatpu Indian camp. He was horrified to learn what had happened. The frightened captives huddled in the emigrants' house, and the bodies of the dead were still unburied. The situation was "deplorable beyond description." Ironically, the next morning the Roman Catholic priest, whom the Whitmans had so feared, read a Latin funeral service for the couple and the ten others who had been killed. They were buried in a shallow grave that was soon disturbed by wolves.

It would be a month before the forty-seven survivors would be released. During this period, the Indians put some of the women to work sewing and knitting for them. Three of the young men from the tribe took young white women as "brides." One of the young women had already been raped; the man who chose her as his "wife" was a member of the mission church, the sole Cayuse converted by Henry Spalding.

Not all of the Cayuse had been in favor of the drastic actions taken against the missionaries, and as time passed, many began to fear retaliation. Although they did not know it, a small force of American volunteers had been raised and was headed toward Waiilatpu. Before the American troops came up, however, Peter Ogden of the Hudson's Bay Company arrived at Fort Walla Walla. Ogden was not on a punitive expedition, as his entourage of sixteen boatmen made clear. Rather he had come to negotiate with the Cayuse. After meeting with most of the Cayuse headmen, Ogden was able to secure the release of the captives in exchange for a ransom that included fifty blankets and shirts, ten guns, tobacco, and ammunition. On December 29 the captives left Waiilatpu with five wagons filled with baggage and food. After stopping at Fort Walla Walla, where Narcissa's mixed-blood boy David Malin was left behind weeping—none of the white families would take him—they pressed on to Fort Vancouver. For these survivors, the terrible experience was over, although they would never forget the events connected with it.

The Cayuse were not able to escape the consequences of the massacre so easily. The American force of volunteers reached The Dalles at the end of January and engaged in several skirmishes with the Cayuse. They stole Indian cattle and horses and burned down Indian lodges; the Cayuse set what was left of the mission at Waiilatpu on fire. The volunteers did not succeed in capturing those supposedly responsible for the violence, however. But the territory's governor, Joseph Lane, was determined to apprehend the culprits. It would take another two years before some of the tribe, realizing the futility of opposing the Americans, would pursue and turn over five Cayuse, including Tilokaikt, to American justice. They were tried, found guilty, and put to death in less than a month. Before his death, Tilokaikt showed that the teachings of the missionaries had had some influence on his thinking, for he is supposed to have said, "Did not your missionaries tell us that Christ died to save his people? So die we, to save our people."

Although the massacre at Waiilatpu brought to an end the ABCFM missionary effort in Oregon, Protestants promoted the Whitmans as noble martyrs to their faith. A heroic picture of their lives and work developed and even shaped historical treatments written in the twentieth century. If Narcissa had ever dreamed of martyrdom when, as a young girl, she had imagined herself as a missionary, her dream had come true. She had called her vocation a sacrifice, and a sacrifice it had been.

But as is often the case in life, childish dreams lose their luster in adulthood and are no longer compelling or desirable, even in moments of fantasy. Martyrdom came at a time in Narcissa's life when she no longer desired to devote herself to the missionary cause. However earnestly she had wished to be a missionary as she was growing up, however much that desire was motivated by her complex relationship with her mother, she had learned that missionary work was not her work. Caught in a situation from which there was no easy retreat, she had, with determination and grit, created new opportunities for herself. Her ambitions were indeed not exalted. Motherhood and pastoral work in her family circle and community were enough. Had she married a minister at home in New York State, she might have led a useful life much like the kind that she was carving out for herself at the mission station.

Narcissa was the only woman the Cayuse killed. The mutilation of her body suggests the deep anger they felt at this white woman who had failed to be their friend, who had threatened them with hell, who had held herself and her children apart from them. As her friend Henry Perkins wrote after her death, Narcissa had failed to be "familiar—sympathizing—open hearted." Whatever affection she felt for the Cayuse, he suggested, "was manifested under false views of Indian character. Her carriage toward them was always considered *haughty*. It was the common remark among them that Mrs. Whitman was 'very proud.'" Perkins did not believe that Narcissa was aware of the impression she made, but "the natives always spoke of it."

Martyrdom depends on perspective. To many of the Cayuse, of course, the Whitmans were not martyrs but intruders who had threatened their lives and their culture. They had neglected the warnings the Cayuse had given them over the years and deserved their fate. From the vantage point of the twentieth century, the real martyrs would be the Cayuse, who would be punished for their part in the bloody events of 1847 and eventually would experience war, reservation life, and the loss of tribal identity. These would be the unanticipated fruits of the ABCFM missionary endeavors at Waiilatpu.

And we missionized you,
betrayed errors of the gospel,
driving the Cross into your lives
like a sword,
the Good News ringing
a death knell.
—Mass of the Land without Evil*

*This excerpt from a mass by Brazilian bishop Don Pedro Casaldaliga is quoted in Judith Shapiro, "From Tupa to the Land Without Evil: The Christianization of the Tupi-Gurani Cosmology," *American Ethnologist* 9 (February 1987): 134–35.

Sources

IN preparing this biography of Narcissa Whitman, I have relied heavily on
both published and unpublished primary sources. In the late nineteenth
century, many of Narcissa's letters appeared in the *Oregon Pioneer Association Transactions* (1891, 1893). The *Whitman College Quarterly* 1 and 2
(October 1897, March 1898) includes reminiscences from Prentiss family
friends as well as survivors of the massacre. Letters from Marcus Whitman and others connected with the missionary enterprise, edited by
Archer Butler Hulburt and Dorothy Printup Hulbert, can be found in
Marcus Whitman, Crusader (Denver: Stewart Commission of Colorado
College and the Denver Library, 1936, 1938, 1941). While I disagree with
the interpretations of Clifford M. Drury, this chronicler of the ABCFM
Oregon mission was indefatigable in tracking down documentary materials on the Whitmans and their fellow missionaries. Three volumes
entitled *First White Women over the Rockies* focus on the Oregon mission's women (Glendale, Calif.: Arthur H. Clark, 1963–66), while *The
Diaries and Letters of Henry H. Spalding and Asa Bowen Smith Relating
to the Nez Percé Mission* (Glendale: Arthur H. Clark, 1958) concentrate
on the men. Additional materials uncovered by Drury appear in *More
about the Whitmans: Four Hitherto Unpublished Letters of Marcus and
Narcissa Whitman* (Tacoma: Washington State Historical Society, 1979)
and "The Columbia Maternal Association," *Oregon Historical Quarterly*
39 (June 1938). Finally, his two-volume narrative entitled *Marcus and
Narcissa Whitman and the Opening of Old Oregon* (Glendale: Arthur H.
Clark, 1973) contains some primary sources.

Important unpublished sources include various materials on Steuben
County, Prattsburg, and the Prattsburg Congregational Church in the
Department of Manuscripts and University Archives, Cornell University. Housed at Harvard University's Houghton Library are the records
of the American Board of Commissioners for Foreign Missions. This
extensive collection includes letters from candidates seeking missionary
appointments and correspondence to and from the mission field. All
quotations from that collection are by permission of the Houghton
Library and the United Church Board for World Ministries. The Bei-
necke Library at Yale University has a rich collection of letters that shed
light on the personal dynamics of the mission party. The Whitman College Library archives have a range of holdings on the Whitmans, while
the library archives at Washington State University at Pullman are the

repository for many of the Walker papers. The Washington State Historical Society at Tacoma has papers connected with the Methodist mission. The Bancroft Library at the University of California, Berkeley, has a small collection of useful materials. Some materials about the Cayuse are available at the National Archives.

Other valuable original sources include *The Missionary Herald* (available on microfilm at the University of Maryland, College Park), E. W. Dwight, *Memoir of Henry Obookiah* (New York: American Tract Society, n.d.), *Memoirs of Mrs. H. Newell, Wife of Rev. S. Newell* (London: Milner & Sowerby, n.d.), Philip Doddridge, *The Rise and Progress of Religion in the Soul* (New York: American Tract Society, n.d.), C. L. Adams, *Daily Duties Inculcated in a Series of Letters, Addressed to the Wife of a Clergyman* (Boston: Crocker & Brester, 1835), the *Steuben Farmers' Advocate*, the *Bath Plaindealer* (available at Cornell University), and records at the Steuben County Clerk's Office and the Bath County Courthouse in Bath, New York.

My understanding of the issues involved in writing a biography of a woman was enriched by Carolyn G. Heilbrun's *Writing a Woman's Life* (New York: W. W. Norton, 1988) and by Maureen Quilligan's "Rewriting History: The Difference of Feminist Biography," *Yale Review* 77 (Winter 1988).

In each of the following sections, I have tried to point out the works that, in addition to the sources mentioned here, were most helpful in shaping my account. Because I realize some may wish to explore the documentation more carefully than is possible here, I have deposited fully footnoted copies of this manuscript in the Department of Manuscripts and University Archives at Cornell University, the Oregon Historical Society, and the Whitman College Library.

Chapter 1

The background for the account of early New York comes from older works, including W. W. Clayton, *History of Steuben County, New York* (Philadelphia: Lewis, Peck, 1879), Guy H. McMaster, *History of the Settlement of Steuben County, New York* (Bath: R. S. Underhill, 1853), and Harlo Hakes, *Landmarks of Steuben County New York* (Syracuse: D. Mason, 1896). Religious developments are described in James H. Hotchkin, *A History of the Purchase and Settlement of Western New York, and of the Rise, Progress, and Present State of the Presbyterian Church in That Section* (New York: M. W. Dodd, 1848), P. H. Fowler, *Historical Sketch of Presbyterianism within the Bounds of the Synod of Central New York* (Utica: Curtiss & Childs, 1877), and James A. Miller, *The History of the Presbytery of Steuben* (Angelica, N.Y.: Allegany County Republic Press, 1897). More recent works on New York State and on religious developments there include Neill McNall, *An Agricultural History of the Genessee Valley, 1790–1860* (Philadelphia: University of Pennsylvania Press, 1952), S. B. Merritt, *History of the Presbyterian Church, Prattsburg, New York: 1804 to 1954* (Prattsburg: n.p., 1954), Curtis Dean Johnson, *Islands of Holiness: Rural Religion in Courtland County, New York: 1790–1860* (Ithaca: Cornell

University Press, 1989), Glenn C. Altschuler and Jan M. Saltzgaler, *Revivalism, Social Conscience, and Community in the Burned-Over District: The Trial of Rhoda Bennet* (Ithaca: Cornell University Press, 1983), and Franklin Butler Van Valkenburgh, *Grandpapa's Letter to His Children* (n.p.: privately printed, 1978 edition).

For an understanding of the Second Great Awakening and its religious and other dimensions for women, I relied on Mary P. Ryan, *Cradle of the Middle Class: The Family in Oneida County, New York, 1815–1837* (New York: Cambridge University Press, 1981), Carroll Smith-Rosenberg, *Disorderly Conduct: Visions of Gender in Victorian America* (New York: Alfred A. Knopf, 1985), Nancy A. Hewitt, *Women's Activism and Social Change: Rochester, New York, 1822–1872* (Ithaca: Cornell University Press, 1984), Martha Tomhave Blauvelt, "Women and Revivalism," in *Women and Religion in America*, ed. Rosemary Radford Ruether and Rosemary Keller (San Francisco: Harper & Row, 1981), Sandra S. Sizer, *Gospel Hymns and Social Religion: The Rhetoric of Nineteenth-Century Revivalism* (Philadelphia: Temple University Press, 1978), Bertram Wyatt-Brown, "Conscience and Career: Young Abolitionists and Missionaries," in *Anti-Slavery, Religion, and Reform: Essays in Memory of Roger Ansley*, ed. Christine Bolt and Seymour Drescher (Folkestone: William Dawson & Sons, 1980), Leonard I. Sweet, *The Minister's Wife: Her Role in Nineteenth-Century Evangelism* (Philadelphia: Temple University Press, 1983), Anne M. Boylan, "Timid Girls, Venerable Widows, and Dignified Matrons: Life Cycle Patterns among Organized Women in New York and Boston, 1797–1840," *American Quarterly* 38 (Winter 1986), Joanna Bowen Gillespie, "'The Clear and Leadings of Providence': Pious Memoirs and the Problems of Self-Realization for Women in the Early Nineteenth Century," *Journal of the Early Republic* 5 (Summer 1987), Susan Juster, "'In a Different Voice': Male and Female Narratives of Religious Conversion in Post-Revolutionary America," *American Quarterly* 41 (March 1989), and Joan Jacobs Brumberg's fine study, *Mission for Life: The Story of the Family of Adoniram Judson* (New York: Free Press, 1980). Nancy F. Cott's *The Bonds of Womanhood: "Woman's Sphere" in New England, 1780–1835* (New Haven: Yale University Press, 1977) is still helpful for understanding women's lives in the early nineteenth century, as is Philip Greven's *The Protestant Temperament: Patterns of Child-Rearing, Religious Experience, and the Self in Early America* (New York: New American Library, 1979) for understanding child-rearing patterns. A paper delivered by Louise Knauer, "Foot Soldiers in the Kingdom of God: Backgrounds, Motivations, and Expectations of Female Missionaries," at the Berkshire Conference on the History of Women, June 1976, also contributed to my thinking. Although Lori D. Ginzberg's fine study *Women and the Work of Benevolence: Morality, Politics, and Class in the Nineteenth-Century United States* (New Haven: Yale University Press, 1990) was published only in time to help with final revisions, her clear explication of the relationship between religion, benevolence, and class sharpened my thinking.

General works about evangelicalism include Charles I. Foster, *An Errand of*

Mercy: The Evangelical United Front, 1790–1837 (Chapel Hill: University of North Carolina Press, 1960) and George M. Marsden, *The Evangelical Mind and the New School Presbyterian Experience: A Case Study of Thought and Theology in Nineteenth-Century America* (New Haven: Yale University Press, 1970).

Shaping my thinking on the character of family life were Monica Mc-Goldrick and Randy Gerson, *Genograms in Family Assessment* (New York: W. W. Norton, 1985), Edwin H. Friedman, *Generation to Generation: Family Process in Church and Synagogue* (New York: Guilford Press, 1985), Carol Z. Stearns and Peter N. Stearns, *Anger: The Struggle for Emotional Control in America's History* (Chicago: University of Chicago Press, 1986), and their edited volume *Emotions and Social Change: Toward a New Psychohistory* (New York: Holmes & Meier, 1988).

Chapter 2

Background on the missionary movement was drawn from Clifton Jackson Phillips, *Protestant America and the Pagan World: The First Half Century of the American Board of Commissioners for Foreign Missions, 1810–1860* (Cambridge: Harvard University, East Asian Research Center, 1969), William R. Hutchison, *Errand to the World: American Protestant Thought and Foreign Missions* (Chicago: University of Chicago Press, 1987), R. Pierce Beaver, ed., *American Missions in Bicentennial Perspective* (South Pasadena, Calif.: William Carey Library, 1977), and John A. Andrew III, *Rebuilding the Christian Commonwealth: New England Congregationalists and Foreign Missions, 1800–1830* (Lexington: University Press of Kentucky, 1976). Focusing on Indian missions are the following works: William G. McLoughlin, *Cherokees and Missionaries, 1789–1839* (New Haven: Yale University Press, 1984), Robert F. Berkhofer, Jr., *Salvation and the Savage: An Analysis of Protestant Missions and American Indian Response, 1787–1862* (Lexington: University of Kentucky Press, 1965), and Henry Warner Bowden, *American Indians and Christian Missions: Studies in Cultural Conflict* (Chicago: University of Chicago Press, 1981).

Female missionaries are the subject of R. Pierce Beaver's *American Protestant Women in World Mission: A History of the First Feminist Movement in North America* (Grand Rapids, Mich.: William B. Eerdmans, 1980) and *All Love's Excelling* (Grand Rapids: William B. Eerdmans, 1968). Patricia Grimshaw discusses ABCFM women in Hawaii in *Paths of Duty: American Missionary Wives in Nineteenth-Century Hawaii* (Honolulu: University of Hawaii Press, 1989), and her analysis helps to provide a context for understanding Narcissa Whitman's vocation and her experience in the mission field. Page Putnam Miller focuses on Presbyterian women in "The Evolving Role of Women in the Presbyterian Church in the Early Nineteenth Century" (Ph.D. diss., University of Maryland, 1979). Helpful works about later missionary women include Jane Hunter, *The Gospel of Gentility: American Women Missionaries in Turn-of-the-Century China* (New Haven: Yale University Press, 1984), and Patricia R. Hill, *The World Their Household: The American Woman's For-*

eign Mission Movement and Cultural Transformation, 1870–1920 (Ann Arbor: University of Michigan Press, 1985).

For the background of the famous Indian call for missionaries, see Christopher L. Miller, *Prophetic Worlds: Indians and Whites on the Columbia Plateau* (New Brunswick, N.J.: Rutgers University Press, 1985), and Alvin M. Josephy, Jr., *The Nez Percé Indians and the Opening of the Northwest* (New Haven: Yale University Press, 1965).

For insights into courtship and marriage, helpful works include Carl N. Degler, *At Odds: Women and the Family in America from the Revolution to the Present* (New York: Oxford University Press, 1980), Ellen K. Rothman, *Hands and Hearts: A History of Courtship in America* (Cambridge: Harvard University Press, 1987), and Karen Lystra, *Searching the Heart: Women, Men, and Romantic Love in Nineteenth-Century America* (New York: Oxford University Press, 1989). A novel of the period revealing missionary norms is *The Wife for a Missionary* (Cincinnati: Truman & Smith, 1835).

Chapter 3

Helpful in understanding Narcissa's reactions to strange sights and peoples was Gordon W. Allport's classic study *The Nature of Prejudice* (Reading, Mass.: Addison-Wesley, 1954). Phyllis Rose's *Parallel Lives, Five Victorian Marriages* (New York: Alfred A. Knopf, 1984) supplemented other works already cited and helped me recognize some of the issues in the Whitmans' marriage.

Information on the trip west and the Whitmans can be found in W. H. Gray's *A History of Oregon, 1792–1849* (Portland: Harris & Holman, 1870). Deborah Lynn Dawson has written an unpublished Ph.D. dissertation on Eliza Spalding, "'Laboring in My Savior's Vineyard': The Mission of Eliza Hart Spalding," (Bowling Green State University, 1988). James R. Gibson, *Farming the Frontier: The Agricultural Opening of the Oregon Country, 1786–1846* (Seattle: University of Washington Press, 1985), Burt Brown Barker, ed., *The McLoughlin Empire and Its Rulers: Doctor John McLoughlin, Doctor David McLoughlin, Marie Louise (Sister St. Henry)* (Glendale, Calif.: Arthur H. Clark, 1959), Thomas E. Jessett, ed., *Reports and Letters of Herbert Beaver, 1836–1838* (Portland: Champoeg Press, 1959), and Sylvia Van Kirk, *Many Tender Ties: Women in Fur Trade Society, 1670–1870* (Norman: University of Oklahoma Press, 1980), help provide a picture of life in Oregon at the time of the mission party's arrival.

Chapter 4

In order to understand Indian society and culture, I read a variety of studies not only on the Cayuse but on the Nez Percé and other Columbia basin tribes. The most helpful works not already mentioned were the following studies of the Nez Percé tribe: David Agee Horr, comp., *American Ethnohistory: Indians of the Northwest, Nez Percé Indians* (New York: Garland Publishing, 1974), Francis Haines, *The Nez Percés: Tribesmen of the Columbia Plateau* (Norman: University of Oklahoma Press, 1975),

Herbert Joseph Spinden, "The Nez Percé Indians," *Memoirs of the American Anthropological Association* 2 (November 1908), Allen P. Slickpoo, Sr.'s, acerbic *Noon Nee-Me-Poo (We, the Nez Percés)* (n.p.: Nez Percé Tribe of Idaho, 1973), and Deward E. Walker, *Conflict and Schism in Nez Percé Acculturation: A Study of Religion and Politics* (Pullman: Washington State University Press, 1968). Robert H. Ruby and John A. Brown have written a study entitled *The Cayuse Indians: Imperial Tribesmen of Old Oregon* (Norman: University of Oklahoma Press, 1972) as well as a more comprehensive work, *Indians of the Pacific Northwest: A History* (Norman: University of Oklahoma Press, 1981). Two other comprehensive works are invaluable: Robert J. Suphan's *Oregon Indians II: Ethnological Report on the Wasco and Tenino Indians; Ethnological Report on the Umatilla, Walla Walla, and Cayuse Indians* (New York: Garland Publishing, 1974) and *Oregon Indians: Culture, History and Current Affairs: An Atlas and Introduction* (Portland: Oregon Historical Society, 1987), by Jeff Zucker, Kay Hummel, and Bob Hogfoss. Although I disagree with many of his conclusions, James Fraser Cocks III's unpublished dissertation, "The Selfish Savage: Protestant Missionaries and Nez Percé and Cayuse Indians, 1835–1847" (University of Michigan, 1975), is still helpful. Clifford E. Trafzer and Richard D. Scheurman have a suggestive study, *Renegade Tribe: The Palouse Indians and the Invasion of the Inland Pacific Northwest* (Pullman: Washington State University Press, 1986). The character of Indian culture is vividly conveyed by two works by Jarold Ramsey: his edited book *Coyote Was Going There: Indian Literature of the Oregon Country* (Seattle: University of Washington Press, 1977) and his excellent interpretative study *Reading the Fire: Essays in the Traditional Indian Literatures of the Far West* (Lincoln: University of Nebraska Press, 1983). Also insightful is Karl Kroeber's edited study *Traditional Literatures of the American Indian* (Lincoln: University of Nebraska Press, 1981).

General works dealing with Native American religion include Walter Holden Capps, ed., *Seeing with a Native Eye: Essays in Native American Religion* (New York: Harper & Row, 1976), Ake Hultkrantz, *Belief and Worship in Native North America* (Syracuse: Syracuse University Press, 1981), and Robert S. Michaelsen, "Red Man's Religion/White Man's Religious History," *Journal of the American Academy of Religion* 51 (December 1983).

Anthropologist Jean L. Briggs suggests some of the emotional difficulties felt in a strange culture in *Never in Anger: Portrait of an Eskimo Family* (Cambridge: Harvard University Press, 1972). Michael C. Coleman studies the responses of Presbyterian missionaries in *Presbyterian Missionary Attitudes toward American Indians, 1837–1893* (Jackson: University Press of Mississippi, 1985).

The material progress and status of the mission appears in Thomas J. Farnham's *Travels in the Great Western Prairies*, which appears in vols. 28 and 29 of Reuben Gold Thwaites's edited series *Early Western Travels, 1748–1846* (Cleveland: Arthur H. Clark, 1904–7).

For understanding Narcissa's response to Alice's accidental death, I profited from *Bitter, Bitter Tears: Nineteenth-Century Diarists and Twentieth-Century Grief Theories* (Minneapolis: University of Minnesota Press, 1983), by Paul C. Rosenblatt; "'A Very Peculiar Sorrow': Attitudes toward Infant Death in the Urban Northwest, 1800–1860," *American Quarterly* 39 (Winter 1987), by Sylvia D. Hoffert; and Nancy Schrom Dye and Daniel Blake Smith, "Mother Love and Infant Death, 1750–1920," *Journal of American History* 73 (September 1986). More general works that were suggestive included Barbara Snell Dohrenwend and Bruce P. Dohrenwend, eds., *Stressful Life Events and Their Contexts* (New Brunswick, N.J.: Rutgers University Press, 1984), and John Bowlby, *The Making and Breaking of Affectional Bonds* (London: Tavistock Publications, 1979).

Chapter 5

To put the Oregon mission into perspective, I read various studies of other mission efforts. Most helpful were T. O. Beidelman, *Colonial Evangelism: A Socio-Historical Study of an East African Mission at the Grassroots* (Bloomington: Indiana University Press, 1982), and the following articles in *American Ethnologist* 14 (February 1987): "From Tupa to the Land without Evil: The Christianization of the Tupi-Gurani Cosmology," by Judith Shapiro; "Ancestors and Protestants: Religious Coexistence in the Social Field of a Zambian Community," by George C. Bond; and "Constituting the Church: Catholic Missionaries on the Sepik Frontier," by Mary Taylor Huber. Also of assistance were two unpublished Ph.D. dissertations: Sandra Elaine Wagner's "Sojourners among Strangers: The First Two Companies of Missionaries to the Sandwich Islands" (University of Hawaii, 1986) and George L. Thomas's "Catholics and the Missions of the Pacific Northwest: 1826–1853" (University of Washington, 1986.) Still other comparative material included Robert J. Loewenberg, *Equality on the Oregon Frontier: Jason Lee and the Methodist Mission, 1834–43* (Seattle: University of Washington Press, 1976), Pierre Jean DeSmet, *Letters and Sketches: With a Narrative of a Year's Residence among the Indian Tribes of the Rocky Mountains*, vol. 27 of Reuben Gold Thwaites's edited series *Early Western Travels, 1748–1846* (Cleveland: Arthur H. Clark, 1904–7), and Clyde A. Milner II and Floyd A. O'Neil, eds., *Churchmen and the Western Indians, 1820–1920* (Norman: University of Oklahoma Press, 1985).

In understanding Narcissa's emotional state, I found helpful George W. Brown and Tirril Harris, *Social Origins of Depression: A Study of Psychiatric Disorder in Women* (New York: Free Press, 1978). My analysis of the supposed rape benefited from David T. Haberly's article "Women and Indians: *The Last of the Mohicans* and the Captivity Tradition," *American Quarterly* 28 (Fall 1976).

Chapter 6

Various reminiscences provided a vivid picture of this last phase of Narcissa's life. Recollections of the surviving Sager children include Catherine, Elizabeth, and Matilda Sager, *The Whitman Massacre of 1847* (Fairfield,

Wash.: Ye Galleon Press, 1981), Fred Lockley, *Conversations with Pioneer Women* (Eugene, Oreg.: Rainy Day Press, 1981), Matilda J. Sager Delaney, *A Survivor's Recollections of the Whitman Massacre* (Seattle: Shorey Bookstore, 1966). Other primary sources are James R. Robertson, "Reminiscences of Alanson Hinman," *Oregon Historical Quarterly* 2 (September 1901), and Fred Lockley, *Voices of the Oregon Territory* (Eugene: Rainy Day Press, 1981).

Peter Gregg Slater provides an analysis of ideas on child rearing in *Children in the New England Mind in Death and in Life* (Hamden, Conn.: Archon Books, 1977).

Chapter 7

Firsthand accounts that reveal the atmosphere at Waiilatpu include Joel Palmer, *Journal of Travels over the Rocky Mountains* (Ann Arbor, Mich.: University Microfilms, 1966), J. W. Nesmith, "Annual Address," *Oregon Pioneer Association Transactions* (1880), J. B. A. Brouillet, *Authentic Account of the Murder of Dr. Whitman and Other Missionaries, by the Cayuse Indians of Oregon in 1847* (Portland: S. J. McCormick, 1869), Sarah J. Cummins, *Autobiography and Reminiscences* (Fairfield, Wash.: Ye Galleon Press, 1987), John Minto, "Reminiscences of Experiences on the Oregon Trail in 1844—II," *Oregon Historical Quarterly* 2 (September 1901), Jesse A. Applegate, *A Day with the Cow Column in 1843* (Chicago: Caxton Club, 1934), Samuel L. Campbell, *Autobiography of Samuel L. Campbell, 1924-1902: Frontiersman and Oregon Pioneer* (n.p.: privately printed, 1986), Russell Harper, ed., *Paul Kane's Frontier, Including Wanderings of an Artist among the Indians of North America by Paul Kane* (Austin: University of Texas Press, 1971), Eliza Spalding Warren, *Memoirs of the West: The Spaldings* (Portland: Marsh Printing, 1916). Specifically on the massacre are accounts in the *Whitman College Quarterly* 1 and 2 (January 1897, December 1898). Also in print is Mary Saunders's *The Whitman Massacre* (Oakland, Calif.: privately printed, 1916). Thomas E. Jessett has written *The Indian Side of the Whitman Massacre* (Fairfield: Ye Galleon Press, 1973), while Robert Thomas Boyd deals with the role of disease in his 1985 Ph.D. dissertation for the University of Washington, "The Introduction of Infectious Diseases among the Indians of the Pacific Northwest, 1774–1874."

Index

ABCFM (American Board of Commissioners of Foreign Missions): 30, 35–41, 42; Clarissa Prentiss and, 20; and women, 30, 36–37; formation of, 35; matchmaking by, 53; and Lapwai, 131–32; and Waiilatpu, 131–32; and Oregon missions, 149, 160–61, 172, 173, 180, 220, 221; M. Whitman and, 206, 212–13; and American Indians, 208; *see also* Greene, David; *Missionary Herald;* Parker, Samuel
Adultery, among Cayuse: 164
Africa, ABCFM in: 36
Agriculture, Cayuse and: 124, 165–67, 206
Alcohol, as white man's gift to Indians: 147; *see also* drinking
Alcott, William: 172
Allis, Emeline: 62, 72, 73
Allis, Samuel: 62, 73
American Board of Commissioners for Foreign Missions: *see* ABCFM
American Fur Company: 41, 58
Amity, N.Y.: 34; S. Parker in, 41–42, 44, 46–47; M. Whitman in, 53–55
Andrew, Charles: 5
Angelica, N.Y.: 34, 56, 58–59
Anglicanism, N. Whitman on: 97
"Anxious seat": 31–32
Applegate, Jesse: 211
Asia, ABCFM in: 35
Auburn, N.Y.: 25

Auburn Academy: 20, 25
Auburn Theological Seminary: 25
Bannock Indians: 80
Baptism: 147–48, 162
Bath, N.Y.: 4, 33
Bears, of Prattsburg: 5–8
Beaver, as cash crop: 38
Beaver, Herbert: 94–96, 97, 98
Beecher, Lyman: 27, 64–65, 71
Bewley, Lorinda: 193
Bird (clergyman): 108
Blacks, of Prattsburg: 24
Blanchet, François: 147
Blue Mountains: 87, 88; as wagon-train challenge, 184–85
Boise River: 87
Boyle (evangelist): 32
Brewer, Henry: 169, 178
Brewer, Laura: 178, 181, 184, 192, 193, 194, 196, 197, 198, 202, 204
Bridger, Mary Ann: 170, 186, 187, 188, 197; and Waiilatpu massacre, 217
Bridgeses (Prattsburg family): 41
Britain: *see* Great Britain
Brouillet (Catholic missionary): 219
Buell, Calvin: 8–9
Buffalo: 77–78, 79; Cayuse and, 124
Buffalo chips, as fuel: 64, 77
Bull, Aaron: 8
Bullard, Artemas: 71
Campo (Waiilatpu convert): 127
Casaldaliga, Don Pedro: 222n.

231

Osborn, Nancy: 216
Osborns (Waiilatpu boarders): 212
Otoe Indian Agency: 76
Oxen, of Waillatpu: 133
Packet (Waiilatpu handyman): 169
Palestine, ABCFM in: 36
Palmer, Emeline: see Allis, Emeline
Palmer, Joel: 206
Palouse Indians: 216
Pambrun, Catherine: 100, 101–104,
    106, 110, 120
Pambrun, Pierre: 89, 95, 100–101, 104,
    167, 177
Parker, Mary: 108
Parker, Mrs. Samuel: 61
Parker, Samuel: 39–42, 47, 51, 52, 61,
    80, 93, 98; in Amity, 41–42, 44,
    46–47; M. Whitman and, 47,
    52–53, 55–58; as matchmaker, 52–53;
    as N. Whitman sponsor, 55; at Fort
    Vancouver, 94, 96
Parsons, Warham: 5
Pawnee: missionary activity among,
    54–55, 62; N. Whitman among, 82,
    91
Pelaistiwat (Waiilatpu Cayuse): 167
Perkins, Elvira: 108, 118, 119, 135, 141,
    145, 149, 155, 159, 178, 179; and In-
    dian women, 120; successes of, 210
Perkins, Henry: 108, 145, 155, 168, 178;
    successes of, 210; judgment of
    N. Whitman by, 221
Phelps, Lucy: 23
Pittsburgh, Pa.: 62–63
Platte River: 77
Polygamy, among Cayuse: 164
Porter, Robert: 5, 8, 9, 24
Powell, Oliver S.: 54–55, 56
Pratt, Cornelia: 25
Pratt, Ira: 8
Pratt, Joel: 4–5, 8

Pratt, William: 19
Prattsburg, N.Y.: 3, 4–34, 196; lay di-
    versions of, 21; poverty in, 22; sin
    in, 23; population of, 24; S. Parker
    in, 41
Prattsburg Laboring Society: 21
Prattsburg Religious Society: 12
Presdestination: 12
Prentiss, Clarissa (mother): 3–4, 5–8,
    9, 12–17, 25–26, 33, 64, 189; reli-
    gious fervor of, 12–17, 18, 20, 29, 42
Prentiss, Clarissa (sister): 15, 135
Prentiss, Edward (brother): 15, 18, 20,
    26, 33, 64, 77, 174, 190, 202; voca-
    tion of, 17, 131
Prentiss, Harriet (sister): 15, 34, 64,
    77, 152, 179, 191, 198
Prentiss, Harvey Pratt (brother): 5, 15,
    17, 26; marriage of, 30
Prentiss, Jane Abigail (sister): 15, 23,
    63, 68, 69, 128, 140, 157, 159, 188, 199,
    201; as missionary timber, 17–18,
    142, 162, 173–74; as teacher, 33,
    190; and N. Whitman journal, 130;
    A. Rodgers and, 202
Prentiss, Jane Holbrook (sister-in-
    law): 29, 30
Prentiss, Jonas Galusha (brother): 15,
    17, 23, 26, 34, 179; rebelliousness of,
    27–29; reform of, 29; marriage of,
    56
Prentiss, Mary Ann (sister): 15, 17, 65,
    69, 130; marriage of, 17; engage-
    ment of, 30
Prentiss, Narcissa: see Whitman, Nar-
    cissa Prentiss
Prentiss, Stephen (brother): 4, 5, 15,
    17, 26, 201; desertion of, 29, 69;
    family of, 29, 30
Prentiss, Stephen (father): 3–12, 22,
    24, 33; religiosity of, 13–14, 23–24,

CPSIA information can be obtained at www.ICGtesting.com
Printed in the USA
LVOW042240130512

281553LV00002B/1/P